Vision upon Vision

George Guiver is Superior of the Community of the Resurrection in Mirfield, Yorkshire.

He is the author of *Company of Voices: Daily Prayer and the People of God*, also published by Canterbury Press.

Vision upon Vision

*Processes of Change and Renewal in
Christian Worship*

George Guiver

CANTERBURY
PRESS
Norwich

© George Guiver CR 2009

First published in 2009 by the Canterbury Press Norwich
Editorial office
13–17 Long Lane,
London, EC1A 9PN, UK

Canterbury Press is an imprint of Hymns Ancient and Modern Ltd
(a registered charity)
St Mary's Works, St Mary's Plain,
Norwich, NR3 3BH, UK
www.scm-canterburypress.co.uk

British Library Cataloguing in Publication data

A catalogue record for this book is available
from the British Library

978-1-85311-992-7

Printed and bound in Great Britain by
CPI Antony Rowe Chippenham SN14 6LH

Contents

Acknowledgements

Five chapters of this book started off in life as lectures at the College of the Resurrection. The others are the result of an engrossing journey into some elemental aspects of worship and human societies. I am indebted to many, not least the German Liturgical Institute in Trier, many invaluable contacts through *Societas Liturgica*, Ian Burton (especially for pressing me to look at liturgy and drama), Ben Gordon-Taylor, my brothers John Gribben and Peter Allan in the Community of the Resurrection, and many others. I hope this may be a worthy synthesis of so much received.

List of Illustrations

Reference to plates

Illustrations in the text

Part One

HOW WE BECAME THIS KIND OF WORSHIPPER

I

Introduction

Christian worship will always tend to reflect its time and today is no exception. In the wake of the Enlightenment and the age of Romanticism which followed it, there has now followed the age of Shopping. Even the financial collapse of 2008 is responded to in terms of our ability to shop. In the Church, personal preferences on worship abound, from traditionalists turning the altar back to the wall, to progressives seeking life in a spree of creativity. There is plenty of argument on how we should worship, which is a sign of life: but what is the quality of the argument? The variety in worship around is healthy, but our approach is neither wide nor deep enough: often there is insufficient nuance in the weighing of issues, and a failure to use all our faculties in the weighing of them. How does liturgy need to change? How may such change be helped along? What is it that changes, what is constant? How far do analysis, description and planning fail us? The questions go on, and they bid us, it would seem, to admit to much that we do not and cannot understand, much we overlook, and much that cannot be engaged with by the means we usually employ. This book explores the interesting and fruitful path to be discovered by looking at such issues more closely. It also explores some parts of our human nature that can be left out of the process: shopping for God has to be transformed into a relating which is real, with a God who is disconcertingly *other* and not to be shopped for.

If our preferences in worship are often on the crude side, how can we be helped to move beyond our too-clear horizons? History rightly plays a large part in our thinking about worship, for Christianity is nothing if not a historical religion. Under the umbrella of history come a range of considerations to do with culture and tradition. If history were our only reference-point, life would be fairly straightforward, but unfortunately it isn't. There is also that very awkward thing, daily life in the here and now as we know it. Under that umbrella come a range of considerations about what it is to be a human being (or, in defiance of our individualistic age, we should rather say 'human beings'). This becomes more complicated when we reflect that daily life as it was lived, say, in the fourth century or the ninth, is an important consideration in looking at the history. On the other hand we cannot hope to say anything about life on the street today without history being part of its fabric. Reflecting that tension, many chapters in this book fall into pairs, a predominantly historical chapter being followed by a 'what-it-is-to-be-a-human-being' chapter.

The part played by history

History can tell us how we came to be as we are. In this book we take an unusual route through worship's history up to the present day, all the time seeking to relate it to human life in general. In the process some things become clear. The last three centuries have seen a revolution in the Church's relationship to its liturgy as historical study of texts, monuments and traditions has dispelled mists of unawareness: there is a growing mass of information on worship's details and a new sense of the sweep of its evolution. The continuing progress of research brings us then to ask more searching questions, for we have to be extremely careful about the ways we consult history. In order to understand why, we turn to the most recent insights, tellingly represented in the writings of Paul Bradshaw.[1]

Paucity of data

An earlier generation of scholars thought it was possible to trace worship back to a single apostolic root, in the belief that underlying our inherited liturgies were structures that transcended later differences. So Gregory Dix identified his 'shape' of the eucharistic liturgy, a fourfold form of taking, thanking, breaking and distributing.[2] Scholars have now begun to show that we were able to hold up such tidy schemes only because we passed over forms of liturgy that failed to fit them. Dix's 'shape' is subverted by early forms of eucharist where blessing the cup preceded blessing the bread, and where no unitary eucharistic prayer is to be found, but rather a mosaic of smaller prayers and actions that were only later sorted and fused.

Perhaps more disconcerting than the evidence now available is the amount not available. Ninety-nine per cent of possible information on how Christians worshipped in the first three centuries has disappeared for ever, either by wholesale destruction of documents and monuments, or because most of the content of worship was transmitted orally, and most of its practice by memory and habit; this leaves us with the slenderest

4

base for claiming knowledge of how the earliest Christians worshipped. Either we have to see minute surviving fragments such as the eucharistic prayer in the *Apostolic Tradition* (formerly attributed to Hippolytus)[3] as too random a survival to give certain guidance, or we need to consider the possibility that their random survival was divinely inspired: not an easy matter to assess.

Bradshaw paints a picture of diversity from the beginning: just as the four Gospels show different emphases and theologies, so the forms of worship passed on by apostles would have reflected their particular emphases and approaches. Tendencies to change and development were heightened in a world of limited communications where groups could live in considerable isolation. The upshot was a cornucopia of differing practice. According to Robert Taft, at a certain point there came the need to sort and unify a great variety of forms of worship, and 'what one finds in extant rites today is not a synthesis of all that went before, but rather the result of a selective evolution: survival of the fittest – of the fittest, not necessarily of the best'.[4]

For Bradshaw the fourth-century tidying-up operation stemmed from improved communication and Christians' new public freedom; but it also met new needs generated by large church buildings now going up in towns and cities of the empire, needing worship that was more formal and organized. A consequence of the change was a transition from oral to written liturgy, and the gradual disappearance of improvisation. Constant struggles against heresy also made local churches anxious to be seen as worshipping in the main stream.

What we do with the data

While there is much we can say about how Christians worshipped in the first two or three centuries, it is only a small part of the picture, and we are left with an uncomfortable awareness of how little we know, and how little justification we have for making categorical assertions on principles. If the early history leaves us with little clear guidance and large areas of uncertainty, where else do we look for guidance? What we have tended to do is to take as our guide the earliest period of which we do have clear information, supplemented wherever possible by added information from even earlier times. The earliest period to provide us with adequate information is the fourth century, and so it is no surprise that recent reforms have drawn heavily on that century for guidance, while also referring to information from earlier times wherever it is adequately available.

5

By the middle of the twentieth century there was growing pressure for change in worship. Historical study had made it clear that part of the problem was an obscuring of original structures by later accretions. A good parable of this can be found in Italy, where in the seventeenth and eighteenth centuries many ancient churches were transformed into baroque extravaganzas through application of plaster and decoration over the ancient structure. It became common from the end of the nineteenth century to strip a church of such accretions and reveal once again its original medieval form. In a similar way liturgical scholars have stripped away accretions and distortions in the eucharist to restore something like its shape at a primitive stage.

It is not always as simple as that, however: sometimes it seems more sensible to work in the opposite direction, as Christian worship sometimes throws up new developments that are truly inspired. The high altar in the basilica of St Ambrose in Milan stands under an ancient canopy. Not long ago restorers removed its fourteenth-century blue ceiling studded with gold stars on the ground that it was not authentic. It was replaced with bare, unadorned plaster on the reckoning that as we do not know what was originally there, we simply fill the gap with a blank. Some have protested at this slavery to the 'myth of the original stratum'. We do not need to look far to find a liturgical parallel. One of the most powerful moments of the liturgical year is the stripping of the altars on Maundy Thursday. Its origin is in mundane spring-cleaning of the church for Easter. Some inspired person somewhere, possibly in Spain, recognized its potential for the liturgical drama. It would be ludicrous to suggest that in the interests of restoring purity this powerful moment in the liturgy should return to being spring-cleaning. Secondary developments like this can sometimes manifest such authenticity and power that restoration to the original state would lead to loss. We need criteria to be able to discern between one and the other, a hot topic where there are longings for restoration of lost practices.

The part played by modern perceptions

In addition to the Holy Spirit's inspiration through history, ancient and intermediate, there will be some present-day attitudes and practices that seem clearly inspired by the Holy Spirit. Contemporary reforms have been firmly selective, for instance: many elements of baptismal liturgy have been lovingly restored according to fourth-century practice, but only by picking and choosing what to restore. The ancient practice of baptizing in private in a darkened baptistery building is spurned in favour of a public setting in the midst of the assembly; and while fourth-century candidates for baptism were excluded from attendance at the eucharist, we encourage it. Whereas some developments in the past may therefore be judged to have been inspired, there is a strong and even irresistible tendency to regard our contemporary standpoint as inspired too – we seek the roots, certainly, but only those that accord with our present view of things. In the ancient hidden baptisms and the contemporary public ones we can see sociological, cultural and pastoral influences coming to bear, and that needs to be recognized.

Otherness

These considerations bring us to another aspect of Christian worship not so congenial today (or we are unsure what to do with it): even from a secular point of view, the human situation is one of 'sitting under' the givens of an amazing cosmos. Our standpoint cannot be sovereign – we are faced with the unavoidable challenge of what is *other*, what will never change for us. In our relating with God this otherness is a given of the gospel: God can be elusive, uncapturable, presenting us with the unexpected and the unimagined. If you have travelled even a little in different parts of the world you will have discovered areas of human life that took you by surprise in ways for which you could not have been prepared by anything you might have read. My knowledge of church history, for instance, and of contemporary Roman Catholicism, and even reading *Don Camillo*, did little to prepare me for the host of surprising impressions that flooded about me on a two-year stint in Italy with little contact with English people. Who could have prepared me for the different moral key that is breathed in that very different land, and the many instances of attitude and behaviour that left me staring at the wonderful diversity of things? Or take a different example: monastic life can have a very different character in different countries. For those who sometimes visit religious communities, what could prepare them for the shock of surprise when moving from a French to a German monastery, with many presuppositions being questioned at every turn? In many areas of study and not least that of Christian liturgy, not enough is done to acknowledge this truth about human life. A textbook's portrayal of Christian life and worship in fourth-century Syria, for example, may describe the case accurately and in detail, giving the reader a vivid impression, and yet the resulting portrait would do little to prepare them for the lived reality, were they able to take a time machine and be plunged into the puzzling maelstrom of impressions that had been so simply outlined in their reading. As God is *other*, so also is the past irretrievably *other*. Victor Turner gives a good illustration of this from anthropological studies. He suggests that those who study another culture need to find ways of enacting in the form of drama situations within such a culture that are typical, if they are to begin to get under the skin of what they are studying:

> Alienated students spend many tedious hours in library carrels struggling with accounts of alien lives and even more alien anthropological theories about the ordering of those lives. Whereas anthropology should be about, in D. H. Lawrence's phrase, 'man alive' and 'woman alive', this living quality frequently fails to emerge from our pedagogic, perhaps, to cite Lawrence again, because our 'analysis presupposes a corpse'.[5]

All those pure, dead buildings in liturgy books like this one make you feel you are examining something dead and mechanical, rather than a living reality. The church in Plate 2 for instance speaks of sober functionality – we would not immediately associate it with amusement. If we were able to travel through time, however, coming from our very different culture we would find in the worship offered there things to please us and things we disliked, and certainly things that would cause a wry smile.

Another way to help us see the point would be reading a description of our way of life by a writer outside our culture. I have seen things in overseas newspapers and magazines that left me realizing the author has no way of knowing what it means to live in Yorkshire, let us say. (Any person who does not live in Yorkshire will have to substitute for it their own locality to savour the point.) Study of the history of Christian worship needs to find ways of taking seriously this hole that cannot be filled. Even if all we can do is say of any worshipping situation, 'here is a hole – don't forget it', that would help remind us to be modest in our pronouncements about worship in other ages. Not only does this apply to history – it is equally true of our attempt to gain a picture of traditions other than our own today: how far is it possible for a British Roman Catholic or Evangelical to gain a true sense of what it is like to worship as a Russian Orthodox, or a member of an African independent church? There are cases where we can make helpful assertions about culture, mindset and so on, but we need as well to recognize the limitations to our ability to get 'under the skin' of the real people who are or were framed by them. The past is other, God is other, other Christian traditions are other, and we do well not to delude ourselves that we have an accurate picture of them on which to base our assessments.

The shape of the book

One key theme of this book will be the phenomenon of liturgical amnesia: Christians quickly forget their history – through the last 2,000 years significant aspects of worship have had a tendency to disappear from view. We will explore these issues by treading a little-followed path through liturgical history, mapped out by milestones of liturgical change, some of them deserving more attention than they tend to receive. The path starts in familiar territory for some readers, the worship of the first Christians and the transformations that came with the accession of Constantine to the imperial throne in the fourth century. Leaping to the eye of the beholder at this point is the affinity between liturgy and drama, a topic which then has a chapter of its own. Continual change and development came to another turning-point in the eight to ninth centuries in both East and West, and we focus on the consolidation of that process in the West under the Emperor Charlemagne. The Christian epoch that in Western Europe we term the Middle Ages, deep in our psyche and in some ways so distorting for Christian worship, had its main characteristics already set in his time, and was a long spinning-out of that single tune. Here another theme leaps out – culture – and we turn aside at this point to explore what that reveals.

The next turn in the tale is unexpected: an investigation into a consequence of baptism that turns up issues for worship today to do with the complexity referred to earlier. There are significant things to be learned from looking into the history of use of the font, both in what was done with it and, as we see in the following chapter, in what is going on in us as we do these things. We then look briefly at the Reformation period, which has received abundant attention elsewhere, while consequences of it remain at issue in the whole of the rest of the book.

By this point we will be beginning to gain a sense that worship never stands still, either at the level of grand events and changes, or at the more elusive level of local and period character: like waves on the beaches of time, the irrepressibility of life's sources ensures that liturgy continues to change. This brings us to the next point of focus, the Enlightenment and the reformed liturgies it produced, especially in Roman Catholic France and Germany, unnerving to us because so much in that process seems very familiar to us in our own time. In the steps of the Enlightenment follows the convulsion in Europe's entrails that produced Romanticism, the Oxford Movement and many nineteenth-century parallels across the Channel. We will never be able to relive that urgent awakening in its first freshness, and yet it sets the scene for much that still exercises us today. Indeed, while the Enlightenment was the great target of these nineteenth-century reformers' wrath, both of them turn out to be terrible twins, joining hands in holding a mirror up to our face.

Through the rolling-forward of time vision has been piled upon vision, building the most complex of creations, each age laying down its mixture of true perceptions and mistaken judgements: and so in conclusion we come to today, which needs a whole section of six chapters to itself. Here we see emerging in all its problematic complexity the question around which we circle throughout the book: how may we find true worship, the worship God has in store for us?

2

From House to Hall

Beginnings

The early Christians are frustrating people to study: they have passed on hardly any records of how they lived and worshipped, leaving us with a maddening lack of information. Like anyone seeking their roots through a family tree, we want to know about Christianity's beginnings, but the first Christians show not the slightest interest in telling us, leaving us largely in the dark. The frustration grows as we become aware how different they were from us. Their ways were not our ways, their presuppositions not ours, and we have precious little to help us feel our way into their minds and experience: this great gap probably never will be filled. Intelligent guesswork can help us a little, though we cannot be certain of much. We can be sure Jesus' immediate disciples had Jewish habits: when they came together for community prayer they will have carried assumptions and practices with them derived from familiarity with family prayer, synagogue and temple. The Jewish character of Christian worship is immediately obvious to any Jew exposed to it. If, however, we try to identify anything in contemporary worship that goes back to first-century Judaism we encounter another problem: we know next to nothing of how first-century Jews worshipped, though we do know that worship varied from place to place. It is furthermore difficult to see how far this Jewish worship will have shaped the liturgy of a radical group whose worship looked to the example of its radical founder.

What were our earliest forms of worship? The New Testament makes reference to singing and speaking in tongues, and to other items of worship's content, for instance in Colossians 3.16: 'Let the word of Christ dwell in you richly in all wisdom; teaching and admonishing one another in psalms and hymns and spiritual songs, singing with grace in your hearts to the Lord', but there is little information on the shape services had or how they proceeded. What little there is – Paul's midnight sermon at Troas (Acts 20.7), his eucharistic guidelines in 1 Corinthians 11, or the theory that the story of the Road to Emmaus gives the outline shape of the eucharist (Luke 24.13–32: liturgy of the word v. 27; liturgy of the eucharist v. 30) – is minutely examined in many writings on the subject without any great certainty emerging. The nearest we come to a picture of early Christian worship would be in a document like the *Didache*, in its chapters 9 and 10.[1]

Although our picture of the beginnings of Christian worship is as vague as that, it is reasonable to suppose that in its first days and weeks the apostolic community in Jerusalem had a common way of worshipping; but what about all the little groups of disciples that had arisen in other places in the course of Jesus' ministry, happily praying away on their own?[2] What worship were they used to by the time of Pentecost? Were they all doing just what they wanted, or were there guidelines? Were there lines of communication with the central group, or were they scooped up only once the Church got going? Soon the message was taken further afield, and then we ask, was there a standard form of worship set down that people were required or encouraged to follow? Evidence is conflicting. With relentless clarity Paul Bradshaw has seen the surviving evidence to indicate variety from the start. Worship differed from one location to another, and was only gradually brought to order from the beginning of the fourth century in a process where some forms disappeared completely.[3] The eucharistic prayer, for instance, seems only to attain a relatively standard form by the fourth century, a form hitherto competing with others, some of which so totally fell out of use that surviving traces, like dinosaur bones, look alien to our eyes.

For Bradshaw, the early Christians freely invented their worship in a spree of creativity. Here we need to make a distinction: all the evidence points to Bradshaw's variety, but how do we interpret it? There is a question here which, so far as I am aware, no one has yet investigated much. When apostles went out from Jerusalem to found new Christian communities through much of the then known world, were they, and those to whom they brought the faith, folk who would pursue that sort of creativity? Premodern cultures, certainly urban ones, operate fairly universally on tramlines. Groups of hunter-gatherers can tend to looser frameworks to life, but we don't hear much about them in the early records. Christianity was an urban phenomenon, riding on the back of developed civilization. (Interestingly, modern industrialized society is more akin to that of hunter-gatherers: a life with low group cohesion, and lived under dominance of larger, impersonal realities such as world economic structures[4] – this sea-change is part of a new challenge for Christianity.) Developed cultures normally evolve gradually: there are occasional bursts of creativity, but in the normal run folk follow established patterns and look for authorities to respect. This would certainly be true of the urban milieux in which the Church made its main impact. The first Christians were no post-Enlightenment free spirits: it is more likely that they reflected the relation between authority, tradition and creativity prevailing in the ancient world, and in this way they will fail to fit our own assumed frames of reference. Then there is that anxiety to be 'correct' that can preoccupy new converts. Would not the first Christians have felt some urge to practise the new faith according to accepted practice, to learn 'what you are supposed to do'? This is illustrated in the disciples asking Jesus how to pray – he responds by giving them the clearly marked pathway of the Lord's Prayer.[5] There is a need for research in this area, drawing particularly on insights of social anthropology and cultural studies. If at the earliest stages of the Christian faith evidence suggests that worship varied from place to place, then this evidence needs to be understood in the light of the freedoms people were culturally capable of.

How then do we explain the variety? Here we need to take account of a perennial human trait – inconsistency and lack of a scientific outlook. Both then and now, people can think they are observing the norm while unawares creating their own version of it: in ancient Christian communities 'doing what you are supposed to do' was in the hands of people who lacked a mentality for exactitude, not greatly aware of the potential difference between what we think is required and what we are in fact doing. We will know that even today from our own experience. Much of the variety and development will have come in sideways, unnoticed by people all the while trying to do 'what you are supposed to do'. In a culture of improvisation texts and practice will vary somewhat, even within one local congregation Sunday by Sunday. Changes come about unawares – there are plenty of examples in liturgical history of local liturgies that have changed constantly, but at each stage it was believed the performance of the rite was faithful to apostolic practice, a handing-on of unchanging tradition. In the conditions of the time, variation naturally sprang up – we should expect this, and not be surprised. It was not that people believed in group-to-group difference in principle, but that proper coordination had to await adequate systems to be in place: the wait took three centuries.

The filling of a house

The first Christians were in a unique position that was never to be known by Christians again. Like the newly married couple moving into their new house, they had a basic supply of new furniture, an immaculate, unscuffed house, and a few personal possessions from their individual past lives. The new religion was like that. Over the years the house fills up, bits and pieces accumulate in every corner as it becomes a real home and the paintwork gets knocked. The worship of the first Christians would necessarily be simple, but over the years a mass of details falls one by one into place. This was like learning a new language: the first forming of sentences is unsubtle, inadequate, and only over the years do the riches of linguistic sophistication build up. For the very first Christians resources for worship were basic and necessarily untested, not yet subjected to laws of natural selection. They would have been short on that depth of richness needed for living a religious faith through the years, and it is not surprising that for a time there was heavy reliance on the Old Testament. All was carried by the first fervour, like a huge launcher-rocket taking a small craft out to space and then falling away. One of the strange characteristics of a great tradition is a combination of congenial and uncongenial, pleasant and unpleasant, obvious and not so obvious, the mouth-watering and the acidic. Real traditions are odd things. That could only come with time, and therefore in assessing early Christian worship we need to remember that the practices of those who lack a tradition need to be interpreted very carefully if they are to be helpful to us who are inheritors of a complex and rich, even over-rich, tradition. Here lies a dilemma that has caused many to fall out: how do we discern between valid and invalid developments of the tradition? There are for instance good reasons for and against continued use of the title 'the Reverend' for clergy – but we would never introduce it now had we not inherited it: why is it so firmly entrenched? Much work needs yet to be done on criteria for clearing out the cupboards of the tradition whenever the household of God needs a spring-clean.

The first Christian communities

As the gospel spread across the Roman world communities were founded in many places. We have a vague picture of the early Christians holding worship in each others' houses, a picture that has been helpfully filled out by James Burtchaell. He has shown that these early communities were organized in a similar way to synagogues of the time (and other kinds of association, religious and secular, in Rome and in society at large):

The synagogue assembly was, in theory, omnicompetent for its own ordinary affairs. In fact, it was answerable to higher authority, Jewish and Roman, and it exercised a governance through its own officers that could be more titular than supervisory. The activities they would typically have undertaken would include scripture reading and inquiry, prayer, election of officers, and disciplinary proceedings. The services rendered by the synagogue might have included collection and remittance of taxes and levies, social welfare for the dependent and indigent, hospitality to travellers, Hebrew school, custody of documents and valuables, and water provision for ritual and possibly domestic purposes. Their gatherings would have been in members' homes or in the open or at an all-purpose meeting house. In brief, the instrumentality for virtually all communal aspects of life beyond the family – religious, civic, economic and educational – was found in their local synagogues. For most Jews it was perhaps the only organization to which they would ever belong.[6]

Burtchaell gives evidence for a plausible continuity in community organization from the Hellenistic Jewish synagogue to the early Christian Church:

As regards the programme and undertakings of the two social units, there are multiple similarities. The *synagôgê* and the *ekklêsia* both typically met in plenary sessions for prayer, to read and expound and discuss the scriptures, to share in ritual meals, to deliberate community policy, to enforce discipline, to choose and inaugurate officers. Both maintained a welfare fund to support widows and orphans and other indigents among their memberships. Both accepted the obligation to provide shelter and hospitality to members of sister communities on their journeys. Both arranged for burial of their dead, and maintained cemeteries.

There are also clear similarities in the structures of community offices. The presiding officer, the college of elders and the assistant appear to carry over from synagogue to church. As in a Jewish context, so in a Christian: the authority to initiate and formulate policy on behalf of the community resides in a group, and that group is served by a presiding officer who appears to be stable in that position. He disposes of the services of one or more assistants whose duties can extend to the limits of the community's programme, but he is especially occupied with provisioning those whose welfare depends upon community funds.

Each community exists in a network that comprises all others. There are no lawfully autocephalous communities, except for the mother community in Jerusalem. A local community was bound by adhesions in many directions, through correspondence, embassies, hospitality and disaster relief.[7]

These Christian worshipping communities seem to have been united by mutual bonds, strengthened in times of persecution when members suffered or lost their lives in painful and tragic circumstances. Although they had similarities with other groups, Christian communities were unique in being open to all: pagan brotherhoods and clubs contained people from particular backgrounds, and Jews gathered on the basis of race, even though there may be gentile adherents: only Christians were universal. There is a strong ethical dimension to them, eloquent in their care for one another and particularly for the needy. Reading between the lines of the New Testament we can see that life in primitive Christian communities was often colourful with plenty of knockabout. Its wide diversity of characters included the uncultured poor: communities would need firm hands at the reins, and there is every reason to expect they would reflect the marked vertical structures of contemporary society. Strong characters from all economic and social levels needed keeping in hand. Democracy is a fruit of Christianity, but we have taken a long time to get there. While not all Burtchaell's theories on continuity of ministry from the synagogue to the church are immune from criticism, he has to be correct in supposing these local church communities will have needed strong authorized leadership and strong structures for life and worship. It is impossible to conceive it could be otherwise. We should beware of imagining an empathetic informality of relationships that has only become possible in modern times: consultative leadership styles of the modern world are a new phenomenon, and for those of us for whom that is normal the strong exercise of personal authority exercised today by Christian leaders in places other than Europe can appear shocking. To be sure, St Benedict in the sixth century emphasizes consultation in his *Rule for Monks*: his advice to the Abbot is, 'always consult, and you will never regret your decisions' (Rule of St Benedict 3.13); but that goes together with a strong view of the Abbot's authority and his position in a pyramidal structure typical of the ancient world, and away from which we have only just begun to move. It is difficult also to see how such authoritative leadership would not carry with it the positioning of such persons in a framework, a texture of special kinds of relationship. In an all-too-human way this could easily degenerate into patterns of 'status', but where the gospel life was healthy it will have been part of the key concept of 'role', to which we will give more attention shortly.

Part and parcel of such pyramidal configuring of corporate bodies was patronage: without dependence on patrons, J. Michael White observes, it would have been virtually impossible for a local Christian community to have its own church building. Congregations might sometimes even have been made up of patrons and their households and slaves.[8]

The basis of Jewish worship is ethnic, the relationship of a biological people to their God. This fell away in Christianity, to be replaced by a radical development for the ancient world as a whole, the valuing of each human being as an individual. This was rudimentary in comparison with our modern understanding of the individual, but enough to be revolutionary: many individuals gained a new awareness of being no longer merged in an undifferentiated and downtrodden mass, but honoured as prophets, priests and kings through their baptism – 'once no people but now God's people' (1 Peter 2.10); once like sparrows, two a penny, but now loved by God, who knew every hair of their head. There is a new language about valuing each person's gifts. Two poles of this breakthrough are essential to each other: we are now one people in a corporate identity full of positive life, and are also of the greatest worth individually, equal in God's sight.

The New Testament references to worship bear this out – its characteristic spirit breathes an air of family. The individual dimension is evident in the encouraging of people's gifts to flourish, the corporate in a care that these gifts work harmoniously together, led by the Spirit. The individual valuation derives from the corporate – it is through new life found in the Body of Christ that we discover our individual worth. We would expect the worship in people's houses to be very participatory with shared-out responsibilities, and so it was. This sense of participatory family is part of Christianity's genes, a natural consequence of Jesus' vigorous message, and a genetic characteristic that would play a key part in the next development.

What can we claim to know?

Having looked at the context, if we now return to asking how the first Christians worshipped, we must admit with Bradshaw that, however we interpret the little available evidence, the truth of the matter is that there is next to no information, and any hypothesis can only be just that. Bradshaw is not saying there is nothing to say, but he is insisting that a variety of hypotheses is possible, all of comparable status. The hypothesis I would like now to offer is one of those.

How it might have been

It seems from reading contemporary texts (such as the *Didache*),[9] tracing the few but important constant threads through the centuries, and bearing in mind the likely mindset of a premodern society, that as the apostles went out they took with them guidelines. They may have reached some degree of verbal, even written, formulation, but the guidelines must largely have consisted of an oral and practical handing on of skills and conventions from the worship they were used to back at base with the core group. While the origins of the eucharistic prayer are obscure, for instance, its constant affinity through the centuries to the tradition of Jewish blessing/thanksgiving formulae right through from the earliest stages is remarkable, especially as it was handed on through times when familiarity with Jewish prayer-forms and their underlying theology had been forgotten. If we compare perhaps our earliest text, that in chapters 9 and 10 of the *Didache*, with the Roman Canon, we find an identical formula of blessing/thanking God for his good gifts, associated with the forms of prayer known as *berakah* and *hodayah*. How was that form so faithfully adhered to? One hypothesis to join the queue of the others would be that the apostles were familiar with Jesus' way of praying, particularly the form it took at the Last Supper, and when training worship leaders of new convert communities they will have told them to give thanks over the bread and wine to the best of their ability, and to do it 'like this'. They would stay long enough to give touches to the tiller until presiders had learned the drift needing to be followed in their formalized improvisations. Improvised prayer needs structures, and premodern people, like ourselves to a lesser degree, rely on patterns and conventions for personal expression. Different apostles also pass on different emphases, largely unawares, while local peculiarities become more pronounced with the drifts and shifts of time.

Finally a stage is reached where many people become too aware of the differences from place to place. There has always been a desire to 'do it properly', but changes creep in as it goes along. From the fourth century there is a tidying-up operation and establishment of a consensus in broad terms: here laws of natural selection come into play. Some ways of praying over bread and wine disappear and there emerges into the first daylight of our archaeology a family of closely related forms. One outstanding fact would make this inevitable: the church emerged from marginal obscurity to become the religion of the empire. Its worship moved from private dwellings and small adapted buildings to the large churches going up even before the time of Constantine, spaces where small-group intimacy was no longer possible. There is less need for hypothesis now as information becomes more abundant.

Evolution of buildings

While the earliest Christians worshipped in each other's houses, there are obvious reasons why that could not last. Apart from difficulties posed by growth in numbers, dual-purpose worship spaces bring inconvenient chores which people tire of, and so the need grows to find somewhere of the community's own. Justin Martyr (mid-second century) operated from rented premises over a swimming baths. He taught there, his local Christian community worshipped there, and they probably hired the baths for baptisms.[10] The house church at Dura Europos shows a further stage of development. Christians in this Syrian frontier town at some point in the early third century bought a corner property and converted it, providing a worship space, baptistery and meeting rooms.

The Christian place of worship evolved gradually, in a similar way to that in which local synagogue communities and even worshippers of Mithras moved from a domestic base through various stages of adapted buildings to a final stage of hall-like worship spaces built for purpose. It used to be thought that purpose-built churches only began in the fourth century, but J. Michael White and others have shown that Christians started to build churches much earlier: large church buildings already existed in some places in the third century. In Britain the church became a significant presence in towns, its places of worship probably a familiar sight.[11] As far as we can see such early church buildings tended to be plain rectangular halls with moveable furniture.

The basilica

If the first church buildings were simple rectangular spaces, St John Lateran in Rome, dedicated in 324, was built on a new plan, based on that of the secular building known as the basilica: a long hall with aisles on either side, each divided from the main space by a row of columns. At the far end was a semicircular area known as the apse.[12] St John Lateran set a fashion quickly imitated everywhere.[13] While the East later moved away from this plan, in the West it remained basic until modern times, triumphantly so in medieval cathedrals.

As Constantine got into his stride one major difference between Christianity and paganism became very apparent: pagan temples and the temple in Jerusalem had small interiors, large enough to house a few clergy, the worshippers gathering outside. In Christianity everyone had to be inside, and the effect of this was immediately apparent in so many churches put up in Constantine's time: huge interior spaces designed to welcome everyone in. Many of the people in their first congregations must never have had the experience before of being in such a large building. This demonstrates the naturally missionary character of Christianity – there has to be room for all, a building open to all. It is also public, not sectarian. For a period in Rome between the late third century and the end of the fourth some basilicas had an open west end with no doors, the church merging with the space before it.[14] To be sure, there were moments when non-believers were excluded from worship, but they were the exceptions that proved the rule. This new kind of religious building embodied a fundamental theological truth: the restrictions of human relationships outside, in the family and the city, were secondary to free relationships within the new family brought to birth through baptism. However much in succeeding centuries congregations might be divided according to class and rank, the fundamental, equal dignity of all the baptized could not be completely lost from sight. Baptism and the eucharist ushered in a new way of being human persons, relating with God and with one another in a *communion* which ordinary human life could never enable.[15]

The transition from house to hall to basilica had an inevitable effect on worship's character. The intimacy and informality of house meetings became more difficult to sustain in the larger setting, but a genetic characteristic of that early worship enabled the change to be a positive one: there emerged a new and brilliant solution to the problem of how to retain the authentic Christian spirit when multiplying converts brought a new problem of scale. From earliest times Christian worship seems to have been characterized by the allotting of *roles*. This was now a striking characteristic of the basilicas.

Roles

In the New Testament we hear of a diversity of roles: of apostles/bishops/presbyters and deacons, of prophets, speakers in tongues and interpreters, singers, widows and more. The synagogue had a range of officers with roles in worship, and this seems to have passed over into Christianity. Then with the emergence of the public church the worshippers' roles now moved into another gear: a corporate sense of family had somehow to be maintained in the larger setting, and it was done, consciously or unconsciously, through developing a principle of *roles* by which the gathered assembly was articulated; they were many, and could include the best part of the following:

- bishops
- priests
- deacons
- deaconesses
- canonical widows
- subdeacons
- readers
- charismatics
- virgins (men and women)
- ascetics
- acolytes
- porters
- cantors
- choir children
- 'women presbyters'/elderly women
- charismatics (variously providing healing, knowledge and tongues)
- exorcists
- catechumens
- baptism candidates (*competentes*)
- the faithful:
     men
     women
     children
     orphans
     penitents
     energumens (the 'demon-possessed')
- interpreters (in Jerusalem and probably other places)[16]

Some roles were like shooting stars that rose, had their day, declined, disappeared, or transmogrified into something else. The scope of roles varied from place to place and one period to another. What is clear is that the assembly was sorted in an extraordinarily diverse manner. Some of the best descriptions of this ordering of the faithful at prayer come from the East. The *Testamentum Domini* is a Syrian document of the fourth or fifth centuries, but containing much earlier material including reference to prophets in the liturgy, something extremely primitive. Among all the roles mentioned, some stand with the bishop within the curtain in front of the altar: the priests, deacons, canonical widows, subdeacons, deaconesses, readers and charismatics. Important also were virgins, both men and women, who had a place at the front of the congregation.[17] Another document, the *Apostolic Constitutions*, compiled in Antioch in the fourth century, but, as with all these documents, including much older material, mentions exorcists, baptism candidates (*competentes*), penitents, energumens (the demon-possessed), porters, cantors, ascetics and orphans.[18] In Rome and elsewhere in the West most of these roles were likewise to be found. Some of them had an indeterminate status: anyone could perform exorcisms for instance, but special recognition was given to those with gifts for it, while the acolyte's role was probably unique to Rome, originating there in the mid-third century.[19]

These and other sources paint a picture of worship where the bishop presided at the far end of the building surrounded by a semicircle of priests and deacons, while other deacons, subdeacons, deaconesses and porters kept watch by the doors on who came and went, and helped keep order in a congregation itself articulated in separate groups of men, women, children, catechumens, penitents and so on. There were strong risks that these various roles could come to be seen in terms of rank and status, and there were warnings against that. The *Apostolic Constitutions* is careful to insist that 'the bishop must not exalt himself over deacons and priests, nor priests in regard to the people, for the Church is made up of all of these'.[20]

As the small local Christian groups developed into large assemblies, and particularly after the Peace of the Church under Constantine, it became impossible for all present to have an active role, if ever it had been, and there emerged a dynamic of representation: roles carried out 'on stage' by the few, who were representative of all. The bishop presided, assisted by presbyters, the deacons fulfilling a role of service; a cantor and choir led the singing in an energetic ping-pong with lusty refrains from the congregation; lectors read lessons, doorkeepers took care of those entering and leaving; acolytes carried candles not only to illuminate texts but also showing where the action was in the midst of a large crowd (like the tourist guide waving a bright umbrella); exorcists had their role in healing and baptism; lamplighters busied themselves at the evening services; and so it went on. Here was a drama in which there was no audience – all were actors, together with God. The church was an arena, and on its boards the liturgy took its course as a sacred *action*. There is a sense here of common *ownership* – the main roles are *representative* – sufficiently numerous to bridge by gradations the gap between leaders and led, and thereby engendering a sense of the worship as *ours*. This can be sensed in good worship in a parish church today, where a few roles create a sense of all having a role.

Churches soon came to be laid out to reflect this articulation in roles. The typical Christian basilica of the fourth and fifth centuries had a range of focus points in relation to the place of the laity, the nave (see Plate 1). An *ambo* or raised tribune was placed somewhere centrally in the nave, and a holy table for the eucharist stood in the nave just before the triumphal arch that marked out the semicircular apse, or in some places further forward or further back from that position. Over the table or altar rose a canopy or ciborium on four columns, drawing attention to the table and marking out its special character. Before and around it would be low walls or *cancelli* (hence the English word chancel) to ensure a clear space for choir and clergy to carry out their duties. Behind the holy table was a seat for the bishop in the centre of the apse, and on either side of him a seat following the curve of the wall for assistant bishops and presbyters. While this was the typical layout, variations were many, so that among the surviving buildings and remains hardly any two plans look alike, something that should not surprise anyone familiar with the variety in church interiors that is just as normal today.

In our examination of roles we begin with the majority, in English called the *congregation*, the general company of the baptized. While usually segregated into men, women and children, plus other categories such as catechumens and penitents, the congregation was not ordered in rows of fixed seats but had an open space where they could freely move around. The nave was more akin to the marketplace than the theatre. By our standards, people were unruly: they were noisy in church, not least for the reason that personal prayer was always done aloud. The capacity to pray silently is an art we have learned over more recent centuries, and while an expectation that people ought to be quiet in church has been with us a long time, so has clerical frustration at the inability of people to keep it. Because the congregation would be given to standing with their hands aloft and praying aloud, one of the tasks of the deacon was periodically to call for silence. In the medieval liturgy of Milan at major services 'a deacon by the side of the altar gives the order: *parcite fabulis* (stop talking); the two custodians loudly repeat: *Silentium habete* [be quiet]; then [when the deacon has announced the reading] . . . the custodians make their *silentium habete* resound'.[21] People could need a lot of telling! In North Africa Augustine warned his mother not to be drawn into the general conversation that could mar the worship. This reminds us to beware of clean, tidy pictures of worship in the ancient world, whether in a basilica or in the earlier house church. People's behaviour will have varied in quality, as would the degree of their commitment, and both clergy and laity will have believed and acted in ways strange to us. In the New Testament itself we mentally edit out behaviour foreign to us, such as a belief apparently accepted by all parties that something significant could happen if the shadow of an apostle fell on you (Acts 5.15). In contemporary Romania mothers can lay their babies on the ground in the path of an entrance procession for the clergy deftly to step over – the same beneficent shadow. At another place in Acts we are told that 'God did extraordinary miracles by the hands of Paul, so that when kerchiefs or aprons were carried away from his body to the sick, diseases left them and the evil spirits came out of them' (Acts 19.11f). Stranger things than that are likely to have been part of the regular worship of Christians. We ought to expect that some aspects of their worship would seem weird to us. So with their bearing in worship – they are unlikely to have been as polite and as quiet as mice as we would like to think.

The *cancelli* (barriers) were placed around the altar to help protect clergy from jostling by a milling congregation. They also marked out the holy space, as the altar came to be seen to represent Christ's presence. Eusebius (fourth century) says of the new church at Tyre built by Paulinus its bishop, that 'he placed at its head a seat to honour the presidents, and on either side of it other benches in strict order. In the centre he added the place of the altar, the Holy of Holies. To make this inaccessible to the congregation he surrounded it with wooden rails . . .'[22] Here is another intriguing question: while the overall shape of the basilica quickly became established, the detail of its furnishing shows endless variety, and theories on this abound. While in some places the congregation gathered in the central nave, in others they seem to have been excluded from it by a low screen between the pillars, having to stand in the side aisles. Some authors believe congregations were regularly confined to the side aisles, but not all agree.[23] In many basilicas it would clearly be impossible, given the width of the nave and narrowness of the aisles. The sides could just as well be for catechumens. The *Testamentum Domini* speaks of people being in the side aisles, men on one side, women on the other.[24] Germanus (eighth century) refers to the area outside the rails [of the Holy of Holies] as the place of the laity.[25] Jaime Lara says,

Some Greek buildings had a low balustrade and curtains separating the nave proper from the side aisles. It is believed by some that the catechumens were allowed to remain in the aisles during the Eucharistic meal but were not permitted to see what was happening because the curtains were drawn closed. In many a medieval cathedral or monastic church, the narthex or *galilee*, was the place for the penitents and *energumens*; they were not permitted to enter further. In Spain they were kept outside under a covered porch on the north and south sides of the church.[26]

In Hagia Sophia in Constantinople practice was complex, but it is clear the people milled around in the nave during the liturgy.[27] In some churches with an apse at both ends a walled *solea* or walkway runs between the holy table and the west end, confining the central path and clearly implying that the people came up to the walls of the *solea*, which would have been a processional way for the clergy; it is equally possible it was used for distributing communion, or making a clear (safe!) division between men on one side and women on the other. If *cancelli* were to mark out the holy place, walled soleas seem nonetheless to have a practical purpose rather than indicating a path as holy. Some Spanish examples have walls projecting into the middle section of the nave in a square-bracket shape. Others again have a wall running along the front of a square altar area. Then there is the type of enclosed 'pen' found in San Clemente and other basilicas in Rome and many other places (Plate 1).

Frequently in North Africa and elsewhere the altar was placed well down in the nave, sometimes almost halfway down it – this would help to explain Augustine's comment that the congregation could see everything happening on the altar. Jaime Lara observes that,

> with the altar moved forward three or four bays into the nave, the congregation stood on three or possibly four sides. They were in the most literal sense of the word the *circumstantes* spoken of in the Roman Canon, who surrounded the activity at the altar. In Spanish buildings with double apses and the *solea* passageway connecting the apses, the congregation was divided in two down the middle and squeezed in between the ritual activity.[28]

At Sabratha in Libya (Plate 2) there was a low wall between seven of the ten pairs of pillars. Here the central placement of the altar would imply very close association with the congregation even if in the eastern part of the church they were in the aisles.[29]

Despite this variety the universality of the form is striking. Basilicas were even mass-produced – parts were made in abundance on the Greek island of Proconnessos and exported all over the Mediterranean: many an ancient church in Italy has fittings of Proconnesian marble. A shipwreck has been discovered off the coast of Sicily at Marzameni near Syracuse, containing the principal elements of a basilica. Had the weather been better, it might have become a venerable monument visited by tourists today.[30]

In much modern writing on the church building the basilica has tended to be absolutized: there were other forms, especially the circle. Constantine built a number of circular churches, and this shape crops up after him – the old eleventh-century cathedral at Brescia in northern Italy is a vast plain drum: we have little idea of the choreography of the liturgy in these circular buildings, or how the congregation may have disposed itself. By its nature a round building suggests a congregation gathered round, rather than in longitudinal formation. While the basilica layout came to dominate, in the fourth century when it first became general, it was not the only form the church building took.

Choir and readers

A significant item of furniture was the *ambo*, whose name is perhaps derived from the Greek for 'hilltop', aptly describing this raised platform often flanked by two staircases. It was placed in the nave often slightly to one side, and gave visibility and audibility to singers and readers. It was not originally used for preaching, which was done by the bishop seated in his place in the apse, although preachers tended to move to the ambo or a second pulpit for better audibility as time passed: we hear of John Chrysostom transferring to the ambo because of the difficulty of speaking from the apse in a large and full church. Augustine too in larger churches stood forward of his throne in order to be heard. Ambos multiplied in some places, becoming two or three; in this way the ancestor of the pulpit came into being.

From on or under the ambo the singers led the psalmody, the staple material of liturgical music. They sang the verses of each psalm, after each of which the congregation would repeat a well-known refrain (which in medieval chant became the *antiphon*). It is not difficult to imagine the congregation crowding round – this would create difficulties of access, and soon we see appearing in some places a walled pathway linking the ambo with the altar area. Then the ambo began to move towards the altar and become part of the *cancelli*. In some places the ambo was huge, big enough not only to accommodate a choir, but also, as in Hagia Sophia in Constantinople, to provide the venue for the emperor's anointing, a practice that survived in the specially built ambos of French and English coronations until the threshold of the modern era.

The apse

We might think that the semicircle at the far end of the building where the bishop and other clergy sat was intended as the primary goal of everyone's attention, situated as it was in a position later filled by eye-catching decorations above an altar; but in the early basilica the altar, usually in the nave, was the central and primary symbol of Christ. The clergy behind appear as Christ's servants. All are gathered around Christ. If there had been spotlights in those days, the main light would have been trained on the holy table, not the bishop. In the second half of the eucharist the bishop came forward to the table to sing the thanksgiving over the bread and wine. In front of it the holy gifts were distributed, and from it at the end of the eucharist all were sent back out to their daily life.

Shifting focus

At worship in the ancient basilicas there was a shifting focus; the entrance of the bishop and his opening greeting firmly drew attention to the building's focal point, but this was straightaway diverted to the ambo for the readings, then back to the apse for the sermon. From where were the intercessions led? By a deacon in the nave? The altar then became the focus for the rest of the rite. Did people move about to come nearest to the focus at present in play? That is what they can be seen doing in a modern Orthodox service, adding to the sense of worship as a drama in which all are actors.

Hidden meanings

Modern attitudes to church buildings are strongly functional, and we have tended to assume a similar functional attitude in Christians of the fourth century. While we may judge the basilica to be eminently practical, we find in the few surviving writings about the church building in early authors an interest in it as symbol. It is spoken of as a city and as Jerusalem, something that continues into the Middle Ages. Every element in the building will have come to receive a symbolic interpretation, just as the scriptures were confidently interpreted in terms of typology (such as Abel murdered by Cain, and Isaac almost sacrificed by his father, are types of Christ). We find in Methodius, writing before AD 311, such a symbolic interpretation of the people who make the church up:

the [Old Testament] Tabernacle [in the wilderness] was a symbol of the Church, and the Church is a symbol of the heavens . . . The brazen altar is therefore to be compared with the place in the community of holy widows. They are indeed a living altar of God, and to it we should bring calves and tithes and freewill offerings.[31]

Such a mentality that could interpret the Old Testament place of worship in this way would also be quick to invest the contemporary church building with symbolic interpretations. If the place of worship was seen as a symbol of heaven, the details of its layout and furnishing will have been given colourful and perhaps strange forms of significance of which we now have no record. We know that the altar came to be seen as embodying Christ's presence, and later on in southern Italy we have reference to the ambo as the sepulchre and the (permanent) paschal candlestick as the pillar of fire in the wilderness. For Eusebius (early fourth century) the four corners of the outer courtyard remind him of the four Gospels, the twelve columns around the tomb of Christ in Jerusalem were the twelve apostles.[32] The *Testamentum Domini* in the fourth to fifth century tells us the three entrances to the church are the Trinity, and the 21 cubits' length of the baptistery is the number of the prophets, while the width of 12 cubits represents the apostles. For St Ambrose in Milan the ciborium over the altar is the 'second Tent', and the ambo the Ark of the Covenant – 'above it in heaven stands God the Word'.[33]

In the days of the fourth-century basilica, the impression is that such interpretations were modest, but from that simple beginning they expanded and grew in popularity. If in the twenty-first century we want to see fourth-century worship as giving us good basic principles for today, we need to be aware of dimensions of understanding that go beyond our more rational approach, and to beware of oversimple, rational pictures of people's view of the basilica. There was a mystique about basilicas. A striking characteristic of some patristic writing is the love their authors had for them. Ambrose, Prudentius, Eusebius, Paulinus of Nola and others wrote poetry about basilicas, some of it intended to adorn their walls. Decoration was a major element, and various of the Fathers comment on decorative schemes they or others had devised, and their accompanying interpretation and texts. Multiplication of basilicas was a sign of the emotional bond people had with them. Paulinus loved putting them up, even sometimes building a second basilica alongside one already existing.[34] Double basilicas sprang up, two parallel connecting churches as in Trier, Aquileia, Grado and elsewhere.[35] For Margaret Miles there was tremendous excitement at the triumph of the Church and at its universality, welcoming all through its doors whoever they were.

> As the churches were built, flooded with light and filled with beautiful and precious tapestries, vessels, sculptures, and decorations, the numbers of worshippers increased geometrically . . . From the emperor Constantine to the humblest Christian, highlighting the triumph of Christianity with monumental architecture and exuberant furnishings and decoration seems to have been a unanimous desire.[36]

The effect this new building, the basilica, had on people's imagination can be seen in an ancient chandelier found in Algeria, now in a museum in St Petersburg. It is in the form of a basilica, complete with a small throne in the apse for the bishop (Plate 3). If you make a lamp in the form of a religious object, then that religious object has some special significance for you. Basilicas were understood in an incarnational way as God's house, but with a marked difference from the way ancient temples had been regarded. Augustine, commenting on the fact that both building and people are called 'church', likens the building to the cup, the assembly to the wine, the building to the body, the people to the soul.[37] Eusebius, overcome with excitement at the completion of the new cathedral in Tyre, elides into one image the manifold roles of the people in the human temple and the roles of the architectural features of the physical building.

> The function of his metaphor is to demonstrate the inclusiveness of the church. It is inclusive, Eusebius says, both in the sense that *whole* human beings are engaged in the building and support of the church and in the sense that *all* human beings are needed and useful: 'From end to end of the building [God] reveals in all its abundance and rich variety the clear light of the truth in everyone, and everywhere, and from every source [God] has found room for the living, securely-laid, and unshakable stones for human souls. In this way [God] is constructing out of them all a great and kingly house, glowing and full of light within and without, in that not only their heart and mind, but their body too, has been gloriously enriched with the many-blossomed ornament of chastity and temperance.'[38]

Improvisation

The words of worship in at least the first two centuries seem to have taken the form of an oral tradition: little existed in the way of written texts apart from psalms, hymns and passages of scripture. Prayers were improvised, including the great eucharistic prayer. Again we are faced with the question of freedom versus prescription. The hypothesis of an original apostolic liturgy disseminated and exactly reproduced among the first churches has been shown to be false. The question does, however, need refining: while for various reasons it would be mistaken to imagine a single apostolic liturgy in modern terms of fixed texts and practices, it would be equally unlikely to think nothing was disseminated. The task is to find the degree to which liturgical practice was prescribed. The most likely hypothesis is that some guidance was given to young churches. We have already suggested that a picture of unbridled creative freedom at the local level is almost inconceivable in the cultural context. More likely is an expectation of a certain way of doing things. While further light on this could be shed by anthropological and cultural studies at the general level, much is also waiting to be done through work on the texts and other data that have come down to us.

An example of such work is an initial study by Achim Budde on techniques used in improvising eucharistic prayers in the early Church.[39] Budde compares them with jazz improvisations by Charlie Parker which relied on three tools: style, a harmonic scheme, and set *licks* or melodic phrases. Budde compares three eucharistic prayers of different provenance; Nestorius (Syria), James (Palestine) and Basil (in its Egyptian version). The similar wording of the post-Sanctus account of salvation history found in all three cannot be explained either as reflecting a common fund of widely distributed formulas, nor in terms of redactions of an earlier original text. They can only be explained as resulting from conventions employed in improvisation. Budde identifies identical thought sequences, verbal agreements and differing phrases which yet share the same underlying structure. Returning to Charlie Parker, he then points out the evidence for the same three tools for improvisation:

1. *Style*: a biblical style of narration aimed at praising God;
2. *Structural scheme*: commemoration of saving events through a chain of particular aspects represented by key words;
3. '*Licks*': phrases and variants of phrases arising out of practising this use of key words, these then becoming established as models.[40]

Budde's findings raise two questions needing more serious attention: (1) if such a tightly ordered approach applied to improvisation of the eucharistic prayer, then it would seem natural to suppose the rest of the eucharistic liturgy to have been subject to similar conventions; (2) taken together with what we may presuppose of premodern cultures from an anthropological point of view, Budde's thesis strengthens the argument for more serious consideration to be given to the probability that early Christians felt it important to have authoritative guidance on what they were 'supposed' to do. It is hardly possible to imagine that there was nothing at all of the sort in the apostolic message.

Golden age?

The liturgy of the early Christian basilica has been so influential on liturgical developments over the last 50 years as to earn for itself the status of a paradigm. For some it has been seen to hold up the shining example of a golden age of Christian worship. More recent voices have questioned this, seeing it to mark a falling-away from primitive simplicity. With the basilica liturgy came clericalism, a sacralizing of the worship space, watered-down commitment among laity, and other ills that contrast sharply with the informality and intimacy of primitive worship where the church was the people, not the building. This is probably too simple, for although the seeds of clericalism are there, that danger would be unavoidable once an organization like Christianity grew beyond a certain size, and does not detract from the fact that in itself the early basilica liturgy was neutral in this respect. What is to be questioned is an assumption that what preceded the basilica was any better.

Ordinary experience of life should discourage us from idolizing particular periods. At any point in Christian history, beginning with the disciples themselves as they accompanied Jesus, the Church's life has been imperfect and its worship just as imperfect: there is plenty of evidence for that in the New Testament. We have no good reason to suppose that Christian congregations were any better behaved in the first, second or third centuries than they were to be in the fourth. Nor have we any good reason to think that principles on which primitive house worship operated were any more satisfactory than those of the basilica. Human beings are universally guaranteed to produce good and bad in their life, and to make pigs' ears of the beauty of truth, a law from which no generation is exempt. If the smaller worshipping groups of earlier years were more intimate, they most probably were often in need of having their horizons widened. There is more to be said for the wider horizons of the basilica any day than the narrow world of small groups worshipping in front rooms and converted bungalows. If some aspects of the basilica developed into poor embodiments of the gospel faith, there will have been corresponding poor embodiments in the worship of previous generations. All are corrupt, none are perfect; there are no golden ages. There will have been few Christian communities in the first three centuries where elders did not sometimes have sleepless nights over conflict, bloody-mindedness or subversion of their authority, or where they themselves abused their position, or congregations fomented warped opinions about one another.

The main reason we find ourselves turning to the basilica for a model and principles is because it represents the first age in the history of the church furnishing adequate information about how Christians worshipped. Should a large fund of detailed information about worship in the second or third century become available, we would naturally turn to it for insights and may find ourselves relying less on the period of the basilica. But so far there is none, and the basilica therefore represents the earliest model available to us; for all its faults it is important in being closer to the original first life and inspiration of the Church than any other form of worship we know. That privileges it for two reasons: it brings us as close as we can get to the first flush of life of the Church, but we also need to identify waymarkers throughout Christian history in order to stay in touch with the Christian worship's narrative, and this is the first one visible. If it represents, as I have suggested, the first opportunity early Christianity had to do some necessary sorting, then that gives us another reason to look to it. Last and not least, it marks a point where the Body of Christ was at last able to develop a strong consciousness of its interlocking nature on the international scene. The development of large, public places of worship opened up a new aspect of what it was to be the Church as a public, supranational organism.

Liturgical drama

The liturgy of the Christian basilicas was an *action* in which all took part – all had their roles. The bishop presided from his throne in the apse with the presbyters ranged on either side on the *synthronon*. Deacons, acolytes, singers, porters and all the rest carried out a diversity of interlocking roles in an act of worship understood to be offered by the whole people of God. The Liturgical Movement which began in the early twentieth century, but with roots going back to the eighteenth, strove to restore this theological vision of worship. Comparison has been made with Wagner's invention of the 'Music-drama', a total work of art (*Gesamtkunstwerk*) in which music, literature, theatre and art come together in a unity. If Wagner's music-dramas were that, then the liturgy is more. With Wagner the performers perform, the audience watches and listens and can clap at the end. In the liturgy this is not so, for all are performers: the drama is enacted by every person present; it is not outside them – they are in it as its constituent materials. Ancient Greek theatre was probably religious in its origins, all its participants co-actors with the gods. So it is in the liturgy – not performers on one hand and audience on the other. There is no audience: all are co-actors with God in the liturgical action, all transfigured by it. One early figure in the Liturgical Movement shows his enthusiasm for this in a beautiful passage:

> One imagines the stately basilica with its glistening mosaics, one sees the bishop at the altar surrounded by his priests and deacons and lesser clerics in order of rank and splendid vesture, one hears the chant of the choir and of the whole assembly, and one understands why in the writings of the post-constantinian period the thought so frequently recurs that the basilica, the church-edifice here on earth, prefigures the eternal court of heaven. In the fifth and sixth centuries the liturgy had reached the term of its development as a complete art-synthesis (*Gesamtkunst-werk*).
>
> ... Hence, as the idea of transfiguration is the art-principle of the liturgy, so is the liturgy itself the principle of the Christian art of life. The liturgy produces that divine life which assimilates us to the eternal Logos, the archetype of all art.41

The early liturgy is a profoundly rich source for insight into the nature of Christian worship, and we shall be distilling some of those riches throughout this book – but one aspect that now especially calls for our attention is the thought that liturgy might be drama.

3

Drama

I can take any empty space and call it a bare stage. A man walks across this empty space whilst someone else is watching him, and this is all that is needed for an act of theatre to be engaged. (Peter Brook)[1]

What is drama? At its simplest the word is used of a story performed by actors, bringing feelings, situations and characters to a particular focus and strength in a context of suspension of disbelief. The word is therefore used also as a metaphor for real-life events where feelings and relations are heightened, often with an electric sense of uncertainty and risk; so if you were present at the meeting of Roosevelt, Churchill and Stalin at Yalta you would feel the drama of the moment. Both senses are applicable to liturgy and its outworking in daily life.

Like and unlike

Some parallels between theatre and liturgy are obvious: in both there is usually a multiplicity of roles, and an 'audience' or general mass of people who are in relationship with the roles. There is a stage or arena as the focus of attention for all present, where individuals enact their roles. While improvisation has always had a place in both, generally there are set words known by heart or recited from a written text. In both a narrative is enacted – in theatre a story, in liturgy a series of actions directly related to the story though not always following its sequence. Both liturgy and drama are ritual performance, and both make use of the arts: visual effects, music, poetry, movement and dance. Both concern themselves with what it is to be human: joy and sorrow, life and death.

Already we can see a great deal to explore in this affinity. It will help, however, at this point to outline as well some of the differences. A Sunday service is not intended as relaxation: the congregation are expected to make an effort with something that is rarely an easy ride, for the 'quality' is situated elsewhere. In the theatre we expect to find it in standards of performance and the overall effect on us: in church, however much we may expect the performance to be of the best, the best is useless without that other quality that comes from elsewhere. Worship can achieve its aims even if done badly, for its aims are not centred on itself, but the people and their relationships with each other and God. In liturgy it is hoped that all present will relate to each other, while this is not expected in the theatre, even though an audience may cohere in certain ways. Committed Christians will still go to church if the music is bad and enunciation poor, the setting drab and the effects less than inspiring. Theatre has to hold an audience's attention – liturgy looks for harder work from the participants, who cannot always expect to feel they have 'got something out of it'. None of it depends ultimately on anyone's ability to perform. In a play the storyline is all, in church we know it already – it is constantly repeated and we don't expect always to be gripped by the unfolding of the plot; in classic drama such as Shakespeare the plot can be well known, but the performance relies on the vivid unfolding of the story in a way that liturgy can not. While theatre relies on surprise and the unexpected, these may indeed be present in worship, but can't be expected often, unless each week there is, say, a brilliant preacher or outstanding musicians. In a play the actors are seeking, by their own talents, to be someone they are not, while in worship it is essential they be themselves, even if all are seeking a conversion that enables them to become what they are not yet. While in the theatre all attention is on the play for the play, in worship the action is in reference to something beyond itself – the leading actor is always the same person, always acknowledged but always invisible, and while known within the action, this leading actor is always beyond it too. The worshippers look beyond the play to a horizon outside the 'theatre' of the church (this is also often true of the theatre, but the distant horizon is not the constant, universal focus of the person of God). There is too in worship a sense of the Church united through time and space, carried along by grace while at the same time always struggling to realize its corporate nature.

A play usually differs from liturgy in having an author, a director, producer and named leading actors. In the case of the liturgy this is not at all normal. Indeed anonymity of provenance for most of its parts is important for Christian worship as I hope to show. Furthermore, the whole lifespan of a dramatic performance is in the theatre, while each act of worship belongs with other elements in the Christian enterprise that lie beyond its walls, such as leading a moral life and care for the needy.

The gifts of drama

It is when we try to identify the differences between church and theatre, however, that we begin to realize how close they are. One writer who has sought to explore this affinity is Hans Urs von Balthasar. For him theatre mirrors to us our selves and our lives in a concentrated and focused form. It interprets back to us, enabling us to remember who we are, as our existence is set before us in a clarifying form.[2] In doing this it throws a ray of light on life, often in ways difficult to put into words. The sense of meaningfulness that comes upon us in experiencing a play can be at a level that is less than obvious. A play can open up a new horizon which reminds us that we are larger than we thought we were, so providing a release from feeling enclosed in our world. Daily round and common task can clip and shrink us. Theatre and the other arts put us back in touch with the greater truth about ourselves and the wider (vaster) horizons we tend to forget. In this sense drama is not only a mirror showing us ourselves, or giving clearer insight into our own world, but also a door into a greater world beyond us. For Peter Brook the theatre offers conditions that enable us to perceive the invisible. It assumes horizons beyond the audience's horizon. Christian worship similarly reveals to us the larger environment that is the real context of our lives: it opens up to us the 'other world'.

Because of their particularity, societies can put limits on that process. Many say for instance that the genre of tragedy is not possible for our society, because, as Schopenhauer put it, 'middle-class people lack the necessary height from which to fall'.[3] This is true not only because of prosperity, but also because of our practical, analytical approaches to what it is to be human, exemplified in setting psychology for instance in a higher place in the quest for human understanding than it ought to have. True tragedy is not negative, but a revelation of the depth of the cosmos: so it was in ancient Greek theatre. True tragedy is a positive thing; von Balthasar calls it 'Tragedy under grace'. Our society is often only capable of 'graceless tragedy'.[4] The sophisticated, managerial way our free and open society is run also makes it incapable of real satire: it tends to create not character, but blandness. Rowan Williams suggests that this may have a good deal to do with 'the erosion . . . of the sense of being located in a significant universe, a folk tradition, a religious metaphysic . . .'[5] This throws some light on the difficulties modern people have with worship. In 1964 the German liturgist Romano Guardini asked in a famous open letter whether modern human beings were any longer capable of worship, a question that has haunted German liturgical thinking ever since.[6]

Part of our task is not to bewail lost capacities for tuning in to the depths of the cosmos, but to discover where the platforms for that are now to be found in contemporary culture. Von Balthasar shows interest in 'the modern myths of Melville (such as in *Moby Dick*), Conrad and T. Wolfe, where the most uncanny and unique interconnections suddenly become visible through very ordinary foreground realism, restoring to the heroes that "height" of which psychology had robbed them'. [7] Great theatre takes people up to a height from which to see into the depths of the tragedy of the cosmos without being daunted. The metaphor of height applies not only in giving us a profounder appreciation of suffering, but also in itself as a raising-up of the person. One function of the liturgy is to take the reality of daily life as we experience it, but to turn it into a launch-pad from which we will be enabled to rise above daily life and bring to it a counter-critique. The droves of ordinary people treated as rubbish in the ancient world were told in the apostolic message that once they were no people but now they were God's people. As the crowds of the poor, the orphans and the widows found themselves part of the praying church in the fabulous basilicas put up under Constantine we can imagine them hardly being able to believe their luck. I think also of experiences I have had of worshipping in village churches in Romania in the time of the Ceauşescu dictatorship. The entire congregation, after a week struggling to survive in a cynical and oppressive world working like ciphers on the collective farm, would often be dressed in their folk costume, bright with the colours of the rainbow, arrayed as kings and queens. The drama of the liturgy is there to enable us to realize humanity's true grandeur.

For von Balthasar there is a relation between the drama in the theatre and the drama of life: the theatre throws light on the drama of the world, bringing it into particular kinds of focus. The world itself is an unending drama in which we all are actors. God treads its stage, and there is an organic connection between God's action and the world's drama.[8] Life is God's play and our own life a play within the play. The whole of life is a drama, and the theatre is a stylized and concentrated reflection of it. The stage makes the drama of existence explicit so that we may view it.[9] Christians are brought to realize that in this drama of life they are co-actors with God. Although von Balthasar surprisingly makes little mention of the liturgy (the Jesuits, to which he belonged, are well known for lack of interest in it), there are clear possibilities for fruitful reflection here on the relation between the drama of worship and that of life, and we must make clear that it is the whole of life. You cannot find life without allowing a proper place to vulgarity. Our examples from tragedy need reference to humour. Tragedy stands cheek-by-jowl with comedy as

Shakespeare repeatedly shows. The searing moments of King Lear alternate repeatedly with the jester's burlesque. Mozart looks into dark depths of things only to switch to bubbling gaiety. Life's awesome darknesses keep company with laughter, and they do it naturally in the humour, for instance, that often accompanies a funeral. Tragedy's essential playmates are burlesque and the vulgar. Liturgy that touches the sources of life will have the vulgar as part of its fabric. Thereby lies a whole subject that would need a book of its own. Few topics need more nuanced discussion than that of the vulgar and the popular. Suffice to say that if all of life, from the exalted to the earthy, is not represented on the stage or at the altar, that is a sure recipe for mediocrity.[10]

Romano Guardini's famous question, 'are modern human beings any longer capable of worship?' has rebounded through the years in Germany in a way it never has in English-speaking countries,[11] but von Balthasar himself, whether consciously or not we do not know, asks the same question about the theatre – are we witnessing the death of real drama? The theatre 'lives on as a traditional and (more and more obviously) commercial organ of public entertainment: it lacks an ultimate raison d'être . . . the audience is no longer a society with a particular mental and spiritual horizon . . . but an amorphous mass gathered together to watch something or other'.[12] Many societies have never known 'elevated drama', and there is no reason why it should inevitably survive among us, but we need to ask the question. Real drama for him comes out of the public shared life of a society and is played out before that society. The social framework that was found in ancient Greece or sixteenth-century England has disappeared, and such drama is impossible without it. Not all would agree with such a bleak assessment, but it throws into relief the important role of the audience.

The audience

We have said in the previous chapter that the liturgy is a drama in which there is no audience, for all present are co-actors with God. A major difference from the theatre is worship's corporate nature, only found in the world of theatre where a play is staged by and within a close community. The liturgical audience speaks and sings, moves bodily, brings up gifts, eats and drinks, engages with its neighbour, and provides family members for the front roles. There is also one way in which all present have a function similar to the actor's – they are growing up into a role that has not been fully theirs. The actor seeks to inhabit a character, Christians seek to grow up into Christ. That involves preparedness to be an under-study – seeing the need for 'sitting under' another.

While this is true, there is also a clear distinction between designated persons who move and speak in the liturgical arena and the body of the faithful, something akin to the relationships between actors and their audience. The congregation are not an audience as found in the theatre, and yet there are similarities. Good worship needs competent and engaged ministers and an engaged congregation. A critical element in any worship is the relation between ministers and people. Where one side fails, the skein woven between them droops. Incompetent clergy can make worship an ordeal. Gifted and saintly ones can be paralysed by a flabby and uncommitted congregation. Peter Brook makes a distinction between living and dead theatre: theatre is living when there is a communion between actors and audience. The quality of the acting depends heavily on the relationship struck up between actors and audience. In the theatre we, the audience, project ourselves onto an ultimate plane that gives meaning and thus we are giving ourselves. The 'actors' for their part need communion with the 'audience' if they are to give their very best. Brook tells this story:

> When the Royal Shakespeare Company's production of King Lear toured through Europe the production was steadily improving and the best performances lay between Budapest and Moscow. It was fascinating to see how an audience composed largely of people with little knowledge of English could so influence a cast – these audiences brought with them three things: a love for the play itself, real hunger for a contact with foreigners and, above all, an experience of life in Europe in the last years that enabled them to come directly to the play's painful themes. The quality of the attention that this audience brought expressed itself in silence and concentration: a feeling in the house that affected the actors as though a brilliant light were turned on their work. As a result, the most obscure passages were illuminated; they were played with a complexity of meaning and a fine use of the English language that few of the audience could literally follow, but which all could sense.[13]

Von Balthasar gives further examples of actors' dependence on communication with the audience; one of them says, 'I communicate directly with the audience; I feel very clearly whether they are with me or against me.' The actor's sensitivity seems to him to have something to do with the solemnity of what is going on.[14]

So we can say that the audience is a participator in the drama, making a contribution that is unique, and without which the drama cannot be fulfilled. The fulfilment of the drama needs the fullest engagement of the whole self, both of actors and of audience. One thing that will fire up an audience is an actor gripped by what he or she is doing. The actor in turn will be stirred by excitement aroused in the audience. Brook tells of another occasion when:

> During a talk to a group at a university I once tried to illustrate how an audience affects actors by the quality of its attention. I asked for a volunteer. A man came forward, and I gave him a sheet of paper on which was typed a speech from Peter Weiss's play about Auschwitz, *The Investigation*. As the volunteer took the paper and read it over to himself the audience tittered in the way an audience always does when it sees one of its kind on the way to making a fool of himself. But the volunteer was too struck and too appalled by what he was reading to react with the sheepish grins that are also customary. Something of his seriousness and concentration reached the audience and it fell silent. Then at my request he began to read out loud. The very first words were loaded with their own ghastly sense and the reader's response to them. Immediately the audience understood. It became one with him, with the speech – the lecture room and the volunteer who had come on to the platform vanished from sight – the naked evidence from Auschwitz was so powerful that it took over completely. Not only did the reader continue to speak in a shocked attentive silence, but his reading, technically speaking, was perfect – it had neither grace nor lack of grace, skill nor lack of skill – it was perfect because he had no attention to spare for self-consciousness, for wondering whether he was using the right intonation. He knew the audience wanted to hear, and he wanted to let them hear: the images found their own level and guided his voice unconsciously to the appropriate volume and pitch.[15]

The actor enables the audience to engage, but the audience enables (or disables) the actor. There is something here for churches. Worship may be perceived as dull or mediocre because apathetic worshippers are failing to inspire clergy, the clergy failing to inspire the congregation, and all are caught in a downward spiral. It is not enough, however, simply to try harder. Dead worship need not be dull: it can be crammed with human zeal, like a stage of bad actors trying ever so hard, or an enthusiastic orchestra of unmusical people. Such worship, very common in our churches, is mediocre not through lack of effort or energy but because it has failed to tap into the well of life.

Gifts of liturgy

If we can say that the theatre and the church have an affinity that also includes strong differences, how does the Church's drama work this out in practice?

The early church building has similarities to the theatre, and uses some of its terminology, such as 'ambo' and 'chancel'. It is an arena set out for an action. Roles in this action are so stylized compared to the theatre that one wonders whether the Christian liturgy is akin to a very primitive stage of theatre's development. While the assertion that ancient drama grew out of religious rites is more surmise than proven fact, one can see why it might be thought.

As the people gathered in big local basilica churches in the Christendom of the time of Constantine and after, the drama of the marketplace came in with them. The town square, its bustle and badinage, spilled into the House of the Church, not only on Sundays but every day of the week. Deacons had to call for quiet, a difficult thing to achieve in a world where people could only pray aloud, each in their own way, with arms raised up expressively.

As the choir strikes up and the first of the actors come in, the drama of life begins to be placed in a different climate, an opening-up to the holy. It is difficult for us to imagine the potency of this experience, for our aesthetic and corporate experience is much more compartmentalized. Worship at this time and for centuries to come was to provide people with their concerts, poetry, storytelling, drama and art gallery. The church came, in tandem with the marketplace, to hold the centre ground of people's lives, so that as the liturgical drama gets under way its enacting of a corporate reality is elemental for people. The two arenas overlap, for liturgy rapidly took to the streets in public processions to and from the church, in Rome in one way, in Constantinople or Milan in another, a liturgy with stopping-places and observances through the city's thoroughfares, in places every Sunday of the year.[16] This could still be found in modern times in Lutheran areas of Romania as neighbourhoods with their designated leaders converged each Sunday in procession on the place of worship. Roles in the liturgy which in earlier times will have been the backbone of scattered Christian communities intermittently suffering persecution gradually became part of the civic imagination, with all the pitfalls that could imply, not least in bishops often coming to be identified with mag-istrates or rulers. The coming alongside of *ecclesia* and *polis*, however, is to be expected in any outworking of the incarnation, setting before the Body of Christ a sharp test of its capacity to discern a wise course. In various times and places the Church has seen itself as needing to stay unspotted from the world, uncompromised, clearly distinct. While that is attractive for its straightforwardness, more demanding but incarnational is a preparedness to live with a messy picture where the church throws itself into involvement with the *polis* aware of the vigilance needed to ensure inevitable compromises and arrangements do not lead it too far astray. The aspect of that which concerns us here is the fact that in many places, and increasingly in most places, the perception of the liturgy by its participants will not have been bounded by the church building and all it stood for. They were participating in what at some levels of their consciousness was a public drama of the city, even though a strongly other-worldly piety and theology meant that the distinctiveness and holi-ness of the liturgy were clear.

The drama of holy places, holy things

While the early Christian basilica was a practical arena, it differed from the modern theatre in also being a holy place housing holy things. In this way it offers conditions that make possible the perception of the invisible. It is often assumed that the first Christians abandoned such notions, but on various grounds this is hardly credible. Homer is credited with saying that you may drive human nature out with a pitchfork, but it will always return through the back door. Origen in the early third century says that Christians have no altars, but also that 'there is a place of prayer which has charm as well as usefulness, the spot where believers come together in one place, and, it may be, angelic powers also stand by the gatherings of believers, and the power of the Lord and Saviour himself, and holy spirits as well . . . we must not despise the prayers that are made there'; and he speaks of 'the superiority of the place where the saints meet when they assemble devoutly together in church'.[17] A very early example of such a sense of holy places and things comes from Pompeii and Herculaneum, where various crosses have been discovered, apparently confounding the general impression that the cross was not used as a Christian sign till much later. In Herculaneum one wall in a small upstairs room bears a distinctive oblong area of plaster in which a cross had been embedded, being of the same design as one found in a baker's shop in Pompeii down the road, with tapered arms and stem and a short top member. It looks as though two lamps had been hung either side of it (Plate 4). The cross had been wrenched from the wall to which it was nailed, with a tool that damaged some of the plaster in the process. Below it stands a wooden cupboard looking for all the world like a kneeling desk, and this had been shoved to one side. Someone in the terrifying clamour and darkness of the volcanic eruption, even though they had no time to lose, seems to have rushed upstairs to the room and, giving a frenzied push to the cupboard to get it out of the way, violently prised from the wall the life-giving sign to escape out into the night with it as a revered protection.[18] We may see in this very early reverence for a Christian symbolic object a too simple translation of pagan devotion to household gods by early Christians: bodies have been found in the volcanic deposit of the same eruption clutching household gods hastily snatched from their niches. But this is what we would expect in Christianity's early development – much had yet to be refined, but there was no way that Christianity was going to blot out, or would want to blot out, the natural human instinct for symbolic holy things and places. In fact I would have done just the same in those circumstances myself, particularly if I was aware that I and my children were likely to die once we got outside. Who knows if this family had not crossed the Bay of Naples 18 years before to hear Paul preaching at Puteoli, a town where Paul had found a Christian community already existing?

Ironic symbols

If the early Christians retained a sense of holy places and holy things, there is a key difference: holy places and things for pagans were *categoric*, essential in relating with the gods; in pharisaic Judaism the need to perform the right actions was likewise essential to being righteous in God's sight. Such a categoric view of things, places and actions is replaced in Christianity by a view of them as inevitable but capable of being dispensed with: they are in essence *ironic* – with some key exceptions, they are second-level realities. The exceptions are the people of God and the sacraments, especially baptism and eucharist. So when we light a candle in prayer or sprinkle holy water or consecrate a church building or pray in front of an icon, we are aware at some deep level that this is no utterly serious binding action but holy play. All that is necessary for our salvation has already been done. Holy places, things and actions stand not on a foundation of human anxiety, but on our confidence in something else beyond them. The irony of a Christian attitude to holy things is akin to the suspension of disbelief that is a part of drama. It is well illustrated by the Good Friday liturgy, which enters imaginatively into the solemnity of Christ's death on the cross, all the time knowing, as no Christian can forget, that Christ is risen.

On this question of holy places and things it is important to recognize our presuppositions for what they are. Colin Buchanan has speculated on

> what John the Evangelist, Stephen, or Paul, or the writer to the Hebrews or Peter would have said if asked to write a discourse on Christian use of space. I think in each case they would have said something like 'we have no temples (bar being ourselves the dwelling-place of God): we need to meet weekly so a place which is accessible and will accommodate us will be very helpful; but under persecution we will meet as we can, not necessarily always in the same place, often in people's homes; and if we employ art or symbol it will have to be such as can be left behind or can travel with us; in any one place we have no continuing city.' If this is right, then no New Testament theology of physical space separated or circumscribed for worship is possible – we are either discussing what is *convenient* (as, for instance, we might be discussing the size of print in a Bible used for reading in the assembly), or we have strayed into Old Testament thought-forms.[19]

We can agree with Buchanan on that sense of ultimately sitting light to all symbols, but his picture of convenience rather than expressive power is culturally impossible to imagine in ordinary people of the ancient Mediterranean world. It is a modern fantasy. We have to beware of imposing post-Renaissance mindsets and paradigms on people who pre-date them. Even we today would say 'we have no temples', but only in the sense that a pagan understanding of the holy place has been replaced not by nothing, but by something else of a different order but comparable significance – we have churches, and a rich treasury of further symbols.

Beyond liturgical geography

Relating corporately to God works itself out in two ways that are always in tension, with a God both in the midst and beyond. The bishop in his seat at the end with clergy either side of him facing the people embody that knowledge of God that comes from people facing each other in a corporate act. In a church such as that in Plate 2 many of the congregation would also be facing each other. This seems to be fundamental, primary. But at different moments other elements in the building take their turn to work as focus, especially the ambo and the altar. It was natural to gather round the ambo to sing refrains and hear the readings, facing the leading voices. It was natural for all to face the altar for the intercessions that followed, whether in eucharist or office, for the holy table of the basilicas rapidly came to be seen as a presence of Christ. The powerful reverence for martyrs' tombs was attached to the Holy Table, seen increasingly as Christ's tomb and eventually called in the West (but not in the East) an altar (that term for Easterners refers to the whole sanctuary area). So it became a potent geographical focus. There was one moment, however, when this focus on geographical focal points was eclipsed, and that was in the celebration of the eucharist, when the sacramental presence of Christ in the bread and wine drew all attention to itself. The table-become-altar, as an 'ironic' holy object that had evolved through inspired human creative imagination, passed at that point in the liturgy from being a geographical focus to being handmaid to the sacramental presence.

Orientation in prayer

On the question of orientation in prayer, there is not much evidence on which direction the leader of the intercessions in the basilica faced, but we know that the intercessor faced the tomb in the morning and evening offices in the Anastasis in fourth-century Jerusalem, and the deacon in the Byzantine liturgy faces east today in any litany. This has also been common in Anglican practice, the intercessor standing halfway down the nave facing the altar. There is much to be said for all, clergy and people, facing together towards the symbolic crux of the building when praying together.

At a certain point basilicas began to be built where the apse at the end faced an easterly direction, something that became normal practice from then on. Quite early a practice spread westwards from Syria of the celebrant standing before the altar to celebrate the eucharist with his back to the people – facing east. There is little problem with this in itself – it can be particularly appropriate in a small and intimate setting – but it ran the risk of creating a confusion: when someone leads intercession facing with the people towards the altar, a geographical point in the building can be described as a 'sacramental', reinforcing our address to the creator and instilling in us a sense of what it means to conceive of transcendence; in the eucharist proper, however, the transcendent point is actualized in the midst, and *sacramental* (facing east in prayer) is replaced by *sacrament*. Geographical orientation is overwhelmed by the coming of the Lord in the midst. To aim this offering at a geographical focus (the east, or the unpeopled beyond) is to confuse one liturgical mode with another. Once the gifts are on the altar and the eucharistic prayer is under way there is no 'geographical' focus any more beyond the location of the gifts: no other focal point of a spatial kind can help us. Eastward-facing celebration can in some places be appropriate, but there has to be care in the interpretation put upon it.

The question has become a matter of controversy in recent years, with some calling for a return to the east-facing position for the eucharist, on the grounds that (a) east is the traditional direction for Christian prayer, (b) offering the Mysteries in that direction best expresses the community's offering of its prayer to the Eternal Father, (c) the eucharist has nearly always been celebrated in this way and (d) that in this position the priest stands with the people, leading them to God.

Without digressing far into this matter, it is enough to respond here that (a) while the geographical east came to be established as the direction for orienting churches, it did not survive long as the direction for Christian prayer in general – there has never been a requirement for instance that clergy face east when reciting the divine office; in the church building, but not outside, it has been a natural practice to face the *altar* (normally oriented for that purpose) for many of the prayers; (b) offering prayers in that direction does indeed help instil into us what it means to speak of transcendence, and it is a good way of giving expression to our looking outwards to the Father; but that is subverted by the eucharistic presence – we cannot aim at a geographical beyond when the heavenly is in the midst. Any symbols here, such as candles or works of art, are working with the grain insofar as they enable Christ in the midst and his eternal offering to the Father to be just that; facing 'east' may be appropriate in some settings – in itself it does not distort, so long as our focus is not the 'beyond' but the Mystery on the altar – otherwise, rather than working with the grain of the Mystery it becomes a striving for effect; (c) it is not difficult to find artistic depictions of the eucharist from the first thousand and more years that show the celebrant facing the people over the altar, as in Plate 5, which gives examples up to the fourteenth century; in addition we can often see people going round to face the celebrant, as in the famous illumination of the 'Mass of St Giles'; (d) celebration 'facing the people', despite the disadvantages it can sometimes present, has to be the archetypal way of celebrating the Supper of the Lord: the community's own roles come to the fore as the presider leads the *mimesis* of the Last Supper, the single figure at the centre playing the role of Christ in dialogue with the people.

The instinct for emphasizing transcendence is sound in a world strong on human-centredness and weak on a sense of God's holiness; in certain actions, when the ministers face the altar together with the people it can be appropriate and powerful; but we should resist urges to gratifying swings of a pendulum that should really find balanced if rather complex repose.

Clergy and secular models

It has become clear from what used to be called the 'mission field' that a century or two can be needed for the gospel to go more than skin deep in a newly evangelized population, so that old, categorical attitudes to holy things can still be found among Christians side-by-side with the new irony. In more recent history newly evangelized peoples have taken time to leave behind their old gods. Syncretism in South America is a familiar but far from unique example. Some say it will take another 200 years for Christianity to be more than skin deep on much of the African continent. This seems to have been the case with the congregations of early Christian basilicas. Women were discouraged from going to the popular night-vigils, where congregations were not to be relied on for best behaviour. Nearly all of them recent converts, the faith of worshippers was often thin, still mixed up with pagan formation. Many were barely Christian at all: bishops had to tackle rowdy groups of troublemakers disturbing the service, people were poor at paying attention, either busy uttering prayers aloud, chatting or doing business. There will have been for many clergy and more committed Christians a frustration at the strong sense of smudging with paganism, civic life and popular culture. The monks who fled the cities for the empty countryside and desert left tearing their hair out at the rumbustuous worship they left behind.

As for the clergy, the first thing striking any person experiencing the transition under Constantine would be Christianity's passage from a position of marginality to one of power and influence. Bishops were now favoured, had beautiful cathedrals built for them, and began a long involvement in civil and legal administration. They became important civic figures, increasingly conscious of their dignity and power. They took to wearing courtly robes associated with magistrates and rulers, and accompanying gestures of deference crept in: bows, kisses and the carrying of lights before them. Their throne in the apse flanked by seats for subsidiary bishops and presbyters might perhaps have recalled for people the audience-halls of aristocrats and emperors, who would also sit in a far apse to receive in grandeur their visitors and suitors. Such an apsed audience-hall is still there to be seen in Trier in Germany, a miraculous survival from the fourth century. A difference from Christian churches, however, would be the absence of columns or side aisles so that no one might be shielded from the emperor's sight. In the Christian basilica the bishop on his seat was further obscured from view by the altar and its tall canopy. His position was smudged by interrupting features of this kind which no emperor would have tolerated. So there are ways in which the basilica was almost a send-up of earthly notions of authority. The Eastern document the *Didascalia Apostolorum*[20] tells the bishop he should have a seat in the apse among the clergy, and is to show no special deference to important visitors, but if a poor or very old person arrives and there is no seat, he should give them his throne, even if he has to sit on the floor. A point came where in some places the clergy bench in the apse had to be raised to a great height, as in Torcello Cathedral near Venice, in order for them to see and be seen. Bishops began to feel so out of it that they started to move to a seat at one side in the body of the church.

Clergy slowly began to become a class apart, however, and within two or three centuries we begin to see the stratification that was to characterize feudal society. This tangling with the unedifying in human life may be regretted but cannot be avoided unless the Church is to keep its nose fastidiously clean from real life. In any age of Christian history there will be plenty to deplore. Even the monastic tradition at its wisest suggests that reality is to be found by engaging with this tangle, not running from it. St Benedict in his Rule shows that the quest to live according to ideals cannot be pursued without messy, less-than-ideal facts of reality as part of the recipe. Christian worship will probably always look so unedifying to some that they will want to seek perfection elsewhere, but the continual struggle with sin and imperfection in worship is an unavoidable condition for the process of gradual conversion. In perfect worship that avoided all risky associations such conversion would be sterilized. Where worship is really happening there will be human mess, and this needs to be remembered in our repeated quests for improved worship. There is a Christian propensity to live out of the dominant culture rather than that of the gospel, but the reverse temptation is also common. Much more difficult is the way in between.

Liturgy and ethics

What then, in the fourth century, was the relation between worship and the moral life? Sermons of the time often give a picture of authoritarian bishops chastising wayward congregations. Not all sermons were like that, and not all worshippers will have been the target of such admonitions, but clearly we should not expect all or even many of the faithful present at the basilica liturgy to have discovered true spiritual life and the ethical formation of the person that goes with it.

Our ethical awareness is closely connected with the inner life of the spirit, and that inner life was different from what we expect today. People could not easily internalize: mental arithmetic had not yet made an appearance, even with the most educated, and nor had silent reading. Just as a reader had to read their text aloud, so did the pray-er need to pray aloud. The deepest life of the spirit could still be lived in such a context, as many writings of the Fathers show, but it was by a different route from the one taken as normal today. As praying aloud was fundamental to the practice of prayer, so were other external expressions. For many people participation in the daily services of the basilica simply *was* their prayer. There was little else, apart from the small vocal exercises, perhaps many, perhaps few, that marked the life of a family during the day. The spiritual life for most people was objective and extrovert, and found strong visual expression in the basilica building. The holy table was the main focus, a tangible presence of Christ. It came always to stand beneath a ciborium or roof sustained by four or sometimes more columns. Curtains were hung between the columns, open in service-time, but otherwise they may have been closed. The Presence was at least by implication behind a veil, and in those very religious times this arrangement must have helped engender a powerful awareness of the Divine mystery. There was no problem about the reality of God – everyone knew God was there.

Strong too was the perversity of human nature – while people were fervently, even obsessively religious, there are the frequent exhortations to more reverent behaviour in church. The difference from the twenty-first century would be that this went together with a powerfully strong sense of the presence of God.

In such an extrovert context it is easy to see that people may not always have reflected enough on what they were doing – surface routine could in that way be accompanied by a fervour misplaced or ill-formed. Then one casualty is likely to be the demanding ethical conversion of the self towards which the gospel nudges us. It has always been so in church life, the insufficient and mediocre cheek-by-jowl with exemplary living.

In the fourth century on the other hand the message was preached, standards were expected, and the ethical requirements of the gospel were visible each Sunday in a gathering-in of gifts for poor and needy; the sharing of the kiss of peace was a weekly demonstration of reverence and love due to one another; and the repeated dialogues between the liturgical participants were a civilized conversation expressive of the life Jesus had shared with his disciples. The liturgy was able to draw into that conversation those who were open to it, much as good theatre will have an effect on those in the audience who are open to something others may simply miss. Wherever this happens, liturgy not only prepares us for heaven, not only forms exemplary individuals: it also contributes to building the life of civic society.

The basilica and the building of civic society

In the fourth century we seem to see precisely this at work: the Body of Christ in the basilica, the Christian *civitas*, celebrating its gifts. How far Christian worship through its history has contributed to building civic life would be an interesting area for research, but in the ancient and late antique world it clearly had the capacity to do so. At the further end of a 2000 year course, voices wishing to defend the special place of Christianity in the life of Europe have pointed to its unique role in fostering democracy, the arts and a caring society – in fact the modern 'free' world, which is now turning to its detriment from these Christian moorings. There is more to be said on this question, and we shall return to it in the final chapter. A good place to seek out this contribution in early Christianity is the post-baptismal catecheses that have come down to us from various fourth-century Fathers. Of the sense of belonging in relationships of trust rooted in God's love, Cyril of Jerusalem says:

> Then the Deacon cries aloud, 'Receive one another; and let us kiss one another.' Do not think that this kiss is of the same character as those given in public by common friends. It is not like that: this kiss blends souls one with another, and courts complete forgiveness for them. The kiss is therefore the sign that our souls are mingled together, and that we banish all memory of wrongs. For this reason Christ said, If you are offering your gift at the altar and there remember that your brother has something against you, leave your gift there on the altar and go your way; first be reconciled with your brother, and then come and offer your gift.[21]

If the Christian drama inculcates in us the call to love our neighbour by dramatic enactments such as the kiss of peace, then there may be a hope that by recovering its dramatic aspects the liturgy may be a force for renewal that will not only strengthen our faith and trust in God but also nurture social gifts and an ability to see the full ethical implications of the gospel in the public arena.

God

Something follows from this which, among all the things we could say about the early basilica liturgy, may be the most important of all: in celebrating the eucharist in this rather than other ways people learned something about the truth of God in himself. John Zizioulas tells how early theologians such as Origen and Justin struggled to find concepts from the Greek thought-world with which to talk about the nature of God. Their approach was in terms of abstract ideas about the cosmos and the Logos. Those who finally cracked it, however, were not professors but bishops struggling with pastoral problems, bishops like Ignatius, Irenaeus and Athanasius, who, as they wrestled with this question of the nature of God, came to the view that God's 'substance' was not to be defined by abstract Greek concepts, but in terms of communion – persons in relationship. Ignatius speaks of the eucharist as 'medicine of immortality', but 'a careful study of Ignatius' thought as a whole . . . reveals that the eucharist for him is not ["medicine of immortality"] by virtue of possessing in its "nature" a potential for life . . . The eucharist for Ignatius is above all a *communion* expressed by the assembly of the community around the bishop. The "immortality" of the eucharist is to be sought in this communion – and not in the "nature" of the eucharist as such.'[22] If Zizioulas is right, it was the powerful experience of celebrating the eucharist with the people of God in the basilica that revealed the nature of God himself to Athanasius, Ignatius and the others. They saw that God was not to be defined first in abstract terms, but by what happens in the basilica as the eucharist is celebrated by the gathered believers. In the process this also revealed something about the Church. People can be puzzled by talk of the eucharist making the Church manifest, but one way in which this clearly is true is the fact that all the people gathered – from presiding clergy to rulers and magistrates, shopkeepers and urban poor – are equally prophets, priests and kings, and their relationship is one of *communion*, in the scriptures, in the kiss of peace, and in sharing the Supper of the Lord. The Christian liturgy is utterly egalitarian:

we are all equal in the sight of God. Toffs rub shoulders with vagrants. This could be found nowhere else in the late antique world, nor can it be found anywhere else today.

In subsequent history the equality of all was often violated when ruling elites came to treat the church as their possession: those creepy English village churches in the grounds of mansions, rebuilt in elegant taste and run by the local gentry, are one example of this. But there has always been the gospel law by which one day they would be found wanting. The nearest thing in the early centuries to the inclusive, grand-scale participatory event of the Christian eucharist would have been public ceremonies associated with the city and the state, but there divisions would have been rife, and any sense of solidarity far from any ideal of communion. Nowhere would it have been possible to find such participatory drama, such a total work of art.

The drama of the liturgy, then, needs to be performed in such a way that it corresponds to the nature of God and is an icon of God. This way already exists, and our part is to uncover it.

4

A Strange Warping

What happened to the basilica liturgy? The period following the decline of the Roman empire is not a familiar one in the study of liturgy, and receives little attention from students of the history of worship. Most people know it vaguely as a period of liturgical decline in which a lot went wrong. There was in fact great creativity in the production of texts and the evolution of architecture and music, but also a general trend to distortion of basic principles of the gospel and of the liturgy, yet in a way that later bore splendid and unexpected fruit.

There was no particular moment when the character of worship changed. The practice of the early Christian basilicas was slowly replaced by something quite different, but it was a long process of gradual change, in different ways in different places. From the fourth century onwards we see a gradual stratifying of the Church and an increasing confusion of ordained ministry with secular power. While worship continued to be celebrated and perceived as the *action* of the People of God, it started to mutate. The tendency for clergy to become a class apart proved divisive. Education in the West collapsed from the fifth century onwards, so that ordinary folk who could be expected to know and sing a few of the psalms, for instance, became an increasing rarity. Vernacular speech changed while Latin remained what it was, increasingly difficult to understand. Among northern peoples it was never understood by many in the first place, and so in due course the Latin of the liturgy was the preserve of those with a certain level of education, making the exercise more clergy-centred, the role of the laity increasingly restricted. This undoing came mostly from the north – in the Mediterranean area the ancient approach to worship remained in vigour for longer.

Italy is a country where ancient practices and church layouts survived long after disappearing elsewhere, and the twelfth and thirteenth centuries even saw a revival of ancient basilica arrangements, still to be seen in St Clement's Church in Rome, and hosts of churches in the Abruzzi and down into southern Italy and Sicily. In the twelfth-century church of San Clemente a Casauria (Plate 6) a fine ambo stands to one side in the nave in the company of a huge paschal candlestick. Can we imagine here at this late date an ancient scenario: congregation crowding round the ambo for the liturgy of the word and then migrating to the east end of the church to gather round the altar for the eucharist? This is implied by illustrations in twelfth-century Italian Exultet rolls.[1] In the centuries that followed, Italy never knew the proliferation of screens and chantries that British people associate with the Middle Ages.

Elsewhere in Western Europe different stories are to be told. A fuller study of the fate of the basilica liturgy is likely to show great variety in the process of change. Little has been written on the topic and not surprisingly, as there is often little available information. It is possible, however, to trace an outline of the story, and for that we need to start in Rome.

The Roman liturgy

In Rome the liturgy early on evolved a particular style, simple and straightforward, probably deriving from patrician traditions of understatement and conciseness. Liturgical ceremonies were unfussy (incense for example was just carried), and prayers were of a didactic nature with little liking for imagination and emotion.[2] Here is a typical example:

> O God, who today through your only-begotten Son
> has overcome death and opened again to us the way into eternity:
> grant that our prayers and sacrifices,
> which by your prevenient grace you have moved us to offer you,
> may also be further accompanied by the assistance of your grace.

Here, according to Klauser, is a desire to express truth with precision and circumspection (notice the careful doctrine of the last two lines), according to the rules of cultivated Roman rhetoric in balanced sentences following a majestic rhythm.[3] This was far from everyday language, and average Christians may have struggled to follow its sense.

From the fourth to the seventh centuries we have little information on how the liturgy was celebrated in Rome: for that we need to go north and west, leaving Rome for a moment, to return later.

The Gallican rite

While the Roman liturgy was used only in the city of Rome and some other places in Italy, elsewhere other ways prevailed. In lands to the north and west we find something completely different, the so-called 'Gallican' family of rites. The 'Gallican' liturgy used in France until Charlemagne's time was part of a wider family including the Mozarabic rite of Spain and the Celtic in the British Isles. Gallican and Mozarabic texts tend to the dramatic and emotional, rich in imagery, often striving for effect, long-winded and flowery, more akin to oriental texts than the prim formalities of Rome.

The Gallican eucharist

All the worship that was ever offered in the first thousand years of Christianity has left precious little trace behind it except for texts and buildings, not much surviving even of them; so for a sense of what it was like to experience Gallican worship we have little to guide us. One of the earliest accounts to come down from late antiquity is a description of the eucharist as celebrated in France in the sixth century, entitled *Exposition of the Ancient Gallican Liturgy*,[4] a text that can be filled out from passages in other contemporary authors such as Caesarius bishop of Arles (*c.* 470–542) and Gregory of Tours (538–94).[5]

Sunday worship started with Vigils and Lauds, after which 'the people went back to their homes, and reassembled in church for the celebration of the mass at the third hour (about 9am). The celebration took approximately two hours as far as one can assess.'[6] Before the liturgy itself begins the faithful bring gifts to the 'sacrarium', a side room in the church. The celebrant chooses from them materials for the eucharist, the remainder being blessed and given to the poor and sick. Enter the clergy, the choir singing an antiphon. A deacon calls for silence and the celebrant greets everyone, saying 'The Lord be with you always'; the congregation answer: 'and with your spirit'. Then the *Trisagion* ('*Aius*', from the Greek '*Hagios*' – 'Holy God, Holy and Strong, Holy and Immortal, have mercy on us') is sung in Greek and Latin, ending with an Amen. According to Caesarius of Arles the Trisagion was sung by the congregation. A triple singing of the Kyrie Eleison by a choir of three boys follows the Trisagion, and after it 'The Prophecy', known to us as the Benedictus (Luke 1.68–79), is sung by the whole congregation. After the first reading from the Old Testament or the Acts of the Martyrs follows the Song of the Three Young Men or a responsorial psalm, leading to the epistle. Once more the Trisagion in Greek accompanies the bringing-in of the book of the gospels, accompanied by seven clerks with burning torches, leading it to the ambo, where the gospel is read. After it the clerks proclaim,

'Glory to you, O Lord' (in the version Gregory of Tours knew, the congregation sings 'Glory to Almighty God'), followed by the Trisagion in Latin while the Gospels are taken back to their place. A homily is given by the celebrant, and before the dismissal of the catechumens the deacon leads a litany, concluding with a collect by the celebrant, after which the deacon orders the catechumens, penitents and excommunicated to withdraw.

The second part of the eucharist begins with the deacon calling again for silence – we must imagine both noise and movement, natural things in just measure, but needing the deacon's regular touch to the tiller – the deacon here as through much of the liturgy's history comes over as a sheepdog governing the unruly flock. Then the *sonum* is sung (apparently so called from the bell or bells rung during it), while the deacon carries bread and wine to the altar. The bread is piled on a large paten, and together with a chalice containing wine and water is placed upon the altar, all then being covered with a decorated cloth.

Alleluia is now sung three times, followed by recitation of names of the dead. The cover is removed from the bread and wine. The kiss of peace is exchanged among the congregation. The celebrant sings 'Lift up your hearts', to which the congregation reply 'we lift them to the Lord'. (This is interesting: more commonly, as in the Roman liturgy, the response is 'they are with the Lord', on the reckoning that we cannot do the lifting – only God can do that. The Book of Common Prayer has the Gallican form, presumably because Thomas Cranmer had recently acquired some Mozarabic liturgical books. From him, presumably, it passed into the modern Roman mass in English.) After the preface the Sanctus is sung and followed by a collect. The celebrant then recites the rest of the eucharistic prayer. During this the clergy sing psalms with antiphons, implying that the eucharistic prayer may have been said quietly. Then the Lord's Prayer is sung by the congregation. After this the congregation come to the altar to receive communion in their hand and drink from the chalice, while the choir sing the *trecanum* chant (three verses of Psalm 33). Reception of communion, however, gradually ceased to be usual, and was eventually limited to high feast days.

According to the *Expositio* and Gregory of Tours the service then ended, but Caesarius of Arles mentions a blessing, and so do the councils of Agde (506) and Orleans (511), and most of the sacramentaries. This was not normal in the Roman liturgy – it was a Gallican innovation. These final benedictions were, as Mayr-Harting puts it, 'The perfect expression in worship of Gaulish episcopal might . . . They wind on, with heightened language, or piling phrase upon phrase, through ardent supplications and

56

sometimes opaque theology.' Pope Zechariah described them as 'vain-glory'.[7] The *Praefatio post eucharistiam* is a thanksgiving prayer said by the celebrant, and the deacon gives the final greeting and dismissal.

We have enough evidence to know that this account gives the basic content of the eucharist as celebrated in Gaul at this time, although there was no centrally recognized model and great variation from place to place and even between one celebration and another in the same place. There were growing complaints of confusion. How far this was exaggerated by those who wanted to introduce the Roman liturgy is difficult to say.

This outline of the Gallican mass, skeletal as it is, has a recognizable affinity with the liturgy of the early Christian basilica. Much of the potential for distortion is already becoming fact – the clerical takeover is well advanced, with clear signs that clerical status and power were beginning to count for too much. The eucharist was becoming less a corporate celebration by the people of God and increasingly a powerful work done by the clergy on behalf of the people of God. The practice began to appear of offering the eucharist for particular needs ('votive masses'), and we see the appearance of private masses which might even be celebrated by a priest without anyone else present. Caesarius of Arles as early as the fifth century speaks of different forms of eucharistic celebration including 'missa brevis' and 'missa publica'. The normal daily liturgy was the round of the offices: the eucharist was only celebrated on Sundays (it seems to have been daily in Lent).

At one level this description gives a good idea of what the worship was like; but there is much we can never know. How far does this clean picture fairly depict the quality of worship in parishes? How far did people engage with the gestures, texts and singing, and how far were they content to leave them to clergy and choir? Many questions we will never be able to answer, but anyone who has travelled fairly widely and experienced Christian worship in various cultures, especially outside the sphere of the modern West, would be able to see such a description as this fitting easily into a world where congregations on the whole take their worship seriously, some approaching it with a degree of vulgarity and smudging of sacred and profane sufficient to cause a nuisance to others and irritate clergy who by nature have unrealistic expectations of their people. A conscientious bishop such as Caesarius of Arles could regularly berate his congregation for inattention, noisiness, sprawling on the floor or engaging in fisticuffs outside the church door, and was not beyond coming down into the congregation to argue with them. He complained regularly of people leaving the church after the gospel without staying for the eucharist, and started to have the doors locked to keep them in. A little earlier John Chrysostom in faraway Antioch was engaging in an identical struggle with his congregation, while Augustine wrote of brawlers and drunks who treated worship as if they were at the (greatly despised) theatre.[8] The often rollicking and superficial world of new Christian nations could hardly have been otherwise, but in the midst of all this we have no reason to suppose that there were not good dedicated people who were lights of Christ in their generation, for we know there were; nor is there any reason to suppose that worship was not often edifying.

Rome about 700

And so back to Rome. We have little information on the early history of the eucharist in the Eternal City. There were numerous Christian communities, some representing different nationalities, not all of them relating harmoniously. From early times the Popes chose to go in procession on certain occasions to celebrate the eucharist in particular churches of the city. This and other stratagems were devised partly to hold before people the unity of the local church, where there was often a divisive spirit.

We happen to have good information on Roman worship at the end of the seventh century for it is our good luck to have a rare thing among liturgical documents: a closely detailed account of how a eucharistic liturgy was celebrated. *Ordo Romanus I* (the First Roman Order of worship) gives a detailed description of mass in the city of Rome as celebrated by the Pope about the year 700 on Easter day. It is the first of a series of dozens of Roman 'Orders' produced over a period of two or three centuries;[9] these guides to worship variously covered the eucharist, baptism and other aspects of the liturgy in Rome. *OR I* may be misleading, as it shows us not the normal worship of a local church, but the unique form of worship presided over by the Pope on the greatest day in the Christian calendar. It is a complex, pompous, courtly affair, but we can be sure that ordinary people will have found its basic elements familiar. The papal liturgy had by this time become encrusted with fussy practices from the court ceremonial of the Caesars, but beneath that the old basilica liturgy and its spirit are quite recognizable. Here is a fascinating insight into changes the basilica liturgy had undergone by the end of the seventh century, and the description is so vivid as to feel like time travel. Here is an outline account:

THE PROCESSION

As day is breaking the entourage gather in the Lateran Palace.
They set out walking before the Pope's horse.
Acolytes carry the Chrism before him and the vessels, linen and other impedimenta; the subdeacon has the epistle-book, the archdeacon the gospels.
The clergy have gone ahead to the appointed church, assistant bishops sitting on the left-hand curve of the apse, presbyters on the right.

THE ENTRANCE

The Pope arrives and goes to the *secretarium* (room for vesting) to change his robes.
The subdeacon places the gospels on the altar.
At the doorway of the secretarium a subdeacon calls: 'The choir!'
They answer, 'I am present.'
Subdeacon: 'Who is going to sing the psalm?'
Choir: 'N.and N.'
The subdeacon gives the Pope the names of epistle-reader and other ministers.
The signal for the psalm is given, the subdeacon cries, 'Light up!' and bearers light their candles.
They go to place themselves before the altar preceded by incense, the choir forming up in two rows either side. The Introit psalm begins.
A subdeacon walks before the Pope with the censer.
Seven acolytes with candles precede the Pope from the church entrance. Two acolytes bring pyxes containing consecrated eucharistic bread, and show it to the Pope who bows and kisses it before seeing if any surplus pieces need to go in the cupboard. The rest will be put in the chalice at communion.
In front of the chancel the candlebearers divide, four to the right, three to the left;
The Pope passes between them and bows to the altar.
He prays and makes the sign of the cross on his forehead;
He gives the kiss of peace to one of the hebdomadary bishops, the archpresbyter and all the deacons.
Then he signals to sing the *Gloria Patri* which ends the Introit;
The Pope prays for a while on a prayer rug before the altar, kisses the gospel book and altar, and goes to his throne in the apse.[10]

OPENING SONGS AND PRAYERS

The choir begins, 'Lord, have mercy'.
The precentor watches the Pope in case he wishes to change the number of Kyries.
Once they have finished, the Pope begins the 'Glory be to God on high'.
After the collect the subdeacons place themselves at right and left of the altar.
Bishops and presbyters sit.

THE READINGS

A subdeacon goes up into the ambo and reads the epistle.
A cantor ascends there to sing the respond and Alleluia or other chant according to the season.
The Pope says to the deacon in an undertone, 'The Lord be in your heart and on your lips . . .' The deacon kisses the gospel book and picks it up;
Two subdeacons with incense and two acolytes with candles lead him to the ambo, where he reads the gospel.
The gospel book is then kissed by all in the choir and taken back to the Lateran.

THE PREPARATION OF THE TABLE

A deacon throws one end of the corporal (a large tablecloth) across the altar, the other catches it and it is spread.
The Pope goes down and receives the loaves from the nobles in order;
The archdeacon pours wine into the largest chalice which is then emptied into a bowl.
The loaves are placed in a linen cloth held by two acolytes.
A hebdomadary bishop receives the rest of the loaves from the Pope and puts them in the linen cloth.
Flasks of wine are poured into the bowl.
The Pope receives loaves from dignitaries, men and then women.
The presbyters do likewise, should there be need, either after the Pope or in the chancel.
The Pope returns to his throne and washes his hands, as does the archdeacon;
The Pope approaches the altar;

Subdeacons bring loaves to the archdeacon, who arranges them on the altar.

Having made the altar ready, the archdeacon takes the Pope's flask of wine and pours it through a strainer into the chalice and water is added.

The Pope goes to the altar, reverences it and receives more loaves.

The archdeacon puts the chalice on the altar to the right of the Pope's loaf;

The Pope bows slightly to the altar and signals to the choir to stop.

The bishops stand behind the Pope.

The archdeacon stands on the right of the bishops, deacons to their left;

The subdeacons go round the altar and face the Pope in order to respond, standing upright until the *Sanctus*.

THE EUCHARISTIC PRAYER

The Pope begins the eucharistic prayer ('Canon').

An acolyte comes near with a linen cloth around his neck holding the very large paten (the size of a dustbin lid) before him until the middle of the canon, when the subdeacon goes with it before the altar and waits for the regional subdeacon to take it;

Bishops, deacons, subdeacons, and presbyters remain in the sanctuary and bow down.

At 'To us sinners' the subdeacons rise up,

At 'Through whom all these things, O Lord', the archdeacon rises.

At the final doxology, the archdeacon lifts up the chalice with the offertory-veil passed through its handles, and raises it towards the Pope who touches the side of the chalice with the loaves saying, 'Through him, and with him', as far as 'For ever and ever. Amen.' The Pope puts the loaves down, the archdeacon puts the chalice down by them;

The subdeacon stands behind the archdeacon with the paten.

When the Pope says, 'And safe from all unquiet' the archdeacon turns round and gives the paten to the second deacon.

THE PEACE

When the Pope says, 'The peace of the Lord be always with you', he makes a cross with his hand thrice over the chalice and drops a consecrated fragment [from the previous solemn mass] into it.

The archdeacon gives the kiss of peace to the leading bishop, then the clergy in order, then the people.

THE FRACTION

The Pope breaks one of the loaves on its right side and leaves the fragment on the altar:
The rest of his loaves he puts on the paten which the deacon is holding, and returns to his throne.
At the *Agnus Dei* various officials go to the Pope to receive names of those invited to the Pope's table (!) and that of the *vicedominus*, and go down and deliver the invitations.
The archdeacon gives the chalice to a subdeacon who holds it by the right corner of the altar.
The subdeacons and acolytes with little sacks come to right and left of the altar: the acolytes proffer the sacks, subdeacons hold them open and the archdeacon puts loaves in.
The acolytes pass right and left among the bishops around the altar, and the rest go down to the presbyters to break the consecrated loaves into the little sacks.
Two subdeacons carry the paten to the deacons for the fraction.
Finally only the fragment which the Pope broke off is left on the altar.
The archdeacon signals to the choir to sing the *Agnus Dei* and then goes to the paten with the rest.

THE COMMUNION

The fraction finished, the second deacon takes the paten from the subdeacon and takes it to communicate the Pope;
After partaking, the Pope puts a particle which he has bitten off the holy element into the chalice which the archdeacon is holding, making a triple cross with it and saying, 'May the commixture and consecration of the Body and Blood of our Lord Jesus Christ be to us who receive it for life eternal', 'Peace be with you'; 'And with your spirit'.
The Pope is communicated with the chalice by the archdeacon.
The archdeacon comes with the chalice to the corner of the altar and announces where communion will be given out;
He pours a small quantity from the chalice into a bowl held by an acolyte;

Bishops and presbyters receive from the Pope at his chair.

The chief bishop takes the chalice from the archdeacon to administer to the remaining ranks;

The archdeacon takes the chalice from him and pours it into the bowl mentioned above: he then hands the empty chalice to a subdeacon who gives him the reed with which he communicates the people with the consecrated wine;

The subdeacon takes the chalice and gives it to the acolyte who returns it to the sacristy.

The Pope comes down from his throne to communicate the magnates. The archdeacon gives them the consecrated wine.

Then the bishops communicate the people, deacons and presbyters administering the cup (actually, bowl with reed);

The communion anthem is sung;

Then remaining clergy and others are communicated.

POST-COMMUNION

The Pope rises with the archdeacon and comes to the altar and says the post-communion collect.

DISMISSAL

At the end of the collect one of the deacons says to the people, 'Go, mass is over!' and they answer, 'Thanks be to God.'

All process out.

Of the wealth of comment we could make here, the following points deserve mention.

The document has been hurriedly written and subsequently adapted, leaving some inconsistencies. It gives detailed rough notes intended purely for the Master of Ceremonies. The papacy was gradually filling a vacuum left by collapse of the civil power, and there was a need to impose order among many scrambling for influence. Minutely detailed prescription, pomp and ceremony made up for absence of stability in the social structures. The details are fiercely policed, excommunication a penalty for lack of compliance. This is liturgy mixed with politics and bordering on the decadent: notice the unsuitable point at which dinner invitations are sorted and given during the *Agnus Dei*.

The singing is led by the choir, responses made by a group of subdeacons: there is no indication that the congregation had much to sing, although it is likely they would have joined in the main chants, the Kyries, Alleluia, Sanctus and Agnus, and perhaps more. This is VIP liturgy: choir and clergy have taken over the lion's share of vocal participation. In the 'parish' churches this is unlikely yet to have been so.

The peace has been moved from its traditional position to just before communion. There are various theories on the reason for this, but note that the peace is given near the beginning of the service too to some of the clergy.[11]

The Pope faces the people for the eucharistic prayer.[12] Early Roman basilicas faced in any direction, but most of the principal ones had the apse in the west, the entrance in the east, and this went together with a norm of celebrating facing the people.

The corporal, nowadays a small white handkerchief of linen, was originally a large tablecloth spread at the preparation of the gifts. The paten is large too.

The eucharistic prayer is devoid of gestures until the elevation at the final doxology: no signs of the cross or other gestures with the hands, and, of course, no taking of the bread and of the cup at the words of institution – that was not to appear for another half-millennium.[13]

There is much decanting of wine, consecrated and unconsecrated (in OR III at one point the consecrated wine is poured from the chalice to a bowl and thence to another bowl). At communion they do something very surprising for us: the bowls contain ordinary wine, into which is poured a drop of consecrated wine to consecrate the whole, and from that the people receive through a gold or silver straw. (It may be more than a coincidence that the oldest eucharistic vessels in Europe, found at Water Newton, Huntingdonshire, and dating from the fourth century, include a large deep paten of a kind also found elsewhere, a two-handled chalice and a number of deep bowls. The hexameter around the rim of one bowl seems to quote the Easter baptismal liturgy used in Milan in Ambrose's time.[14])

There was no confession, sermon, creed, intercessions, Lord's Prayer, or final blessing.

The intercessions had by this period disappeared from their place at the end of the liturgy of the word to appear instead as an element within the eucharistic prayer itself.

We have no information on how things went in ordinary churches. There will have been someone to lead the singing, and at least one presbyter, deacon and subdeacon, and we can roughly picture how services proceeded from the information in OR I and what we have already heard about worship in the fourth century. The basic basilica liturgy can be seen here beneath the complexities, and will have survived better in smaller churches.

In order to understand what happened next in worship's evolution we need to turn our attention again to Northern Europe, where the liturgy of the Roman basilicas underwent a radical transformation.

The Franks

North of the Alps the Gallican liturgy gradually came to be replaced by the Roman, disappearing completely from the face of the earth by the end of the first millennium, with the noble exception of five parishes and a cathedral chapel in Toledo, where it is still used today. Its disappearance and replacement with the Roman rite is bound up with the hegemony of the Franks north of the Alps. In order to understand what happened to the basilica liturgy we need to gain a picture of these people in whose hands it underwent great changes.

The Franks originated east of the Rhine and invaded Gaul in the fifth century; not much is known of their pre-Christian religion as they had quickly adopted Christianity. As information becomes available we see them using the Gallican rite. The Franks had a love for the florid, dramatic and impressive. In their hands changes came about not only in the kind of liturgical texts used but in the overall character of the liturgy. As it went along it came to reflect changes in the structuring of society, as the way of life of the Franks in Gaul developed into the feudal system of the Middle Ages. Freemen were gradually squeezed out by the huge Gallo-Roman estates the Franks took over, and so there developed a feudal structure of lords and serfs with nothing in between. There was no modern state here, but simply personal possession by those who ruled: no notion of a public purse, nor of a sovereign state. Kingdoms were divided up in arbitrary ways on the deaths of kings; Charlemagne's will (d. 814) left his great library to be sold and the proceeds given to the poor. All his treasure was dispersed and his kingdom divided up. There could be no clearer indication that to Charlemagne the whole lot was personal and not in any sense public or corporate. Long before Charlemagne the village and its inhabitants had become the possession of the lord. Communication was nightmarish: few could read, and communication depended on verbal accounts from messengers. Counts were always being exhorted to employ a scribe in order to read the emperor's missives. Often they didn't bother, or borrowed a local cleric when really needed. In this we can see part of the origin of a sharp divide between clergy and laity that became typical of the Middle Ages, as higher clergy at least came to be associated with those who could read and govern, rather than with the governed.

Irish influence

A powerful influence on Frankish religion was Irish Christianity, whose missionaries brought the faith back to many parts of the continent where it had disappeared. At risk of distortion, it would help here to give a thumbnail sketch of some of its characteristics (noticeably different from current pictures of 'Celtic' piety).

Prayer was powerfully stimulated by fear of demons, inherited probably from a paganism never fully left behind. The cross and redemption tended to be considered as protecting powers rather than means of grace or subjects for meditation. They were necessary protection from dangers threatening body and soul on all sides. A shift of emphasis to the divinity of Christ, overshadowing his humanity (spurred by anti-Arianism in Spain, a country with considerable influence in Ireland, surprisingly), and to the Trinity, sometimes resulted in magnificent texts seeking protection against evil, such as St Patrick's Breastplate:

> I bind unto myself today
> The strong name of the Trinity,
> By invocation of the same,
> The Three in One, and One in Three.
> I bind this day to me for ever,
> By power of faith, Christ's Incarnation;
> His baptism in Jordan river;
> His death on Cross for my salvation;
> His bursting from the spiced tomb;
> His riding up the heavenly way;
> His coming at the day of doom;[15]

People seem often to have had a fear- and guilt-laden relationship with God: the eucharistic prayer, for instance, was called *periculosa oratio* (dangerous prayer). People were powerfully conscious of sin while more weakly aware of the victorious redemption achieved through Christ. The liturgy filled up with private prayers by the priest called *apologias* (formulas of self-accusation). Here is an example:

> Before the immensity of your countenance and before your ineffable eyes, O amazing majesty, indeed before your holy faces, O great God,

Omnipotent Father of great mercy and power, not without due reverence, but yet with no standing in your sight, as your utterly lowly sup-
pliant I draw near and stand before you . . . I therefore accuse myself,
without excuse, and before witnesses I confess to you, Lord God, my
unrighteousness . . . I fall low, therefore, I fall low before your unspeak-
able mercy. Spare me, Spare me, Spare me, I beseech you, merciful deity.
Listen, listen O listen to these words I pray . . .[16]

Here is a strand in North European piety which became thoroughly established, observable still in full vigour in the following prayer from the
Book of Common Prayer, even if there might be no direct connection:

ALMIGHTY and most merciful Father, we have erred and strayed from
thy ways like lost sheep, we have followed too much the devices and desires of our own hearts, we have offended against thy holy laws, we have
left undone those things which we ought to have done, and we have done
those things which we ought not to have done, and there is no health
in us: but thou, O Lord, have mercy upon us miserable offenders; spare
thou them, O God which confess their faults, restore thou them that are
penitent . . . have mercy upon us, have mercy upon us, most . . .[17]

The Franks' natural affinity was less with the Roman spirit than the Irish,
whose spirituality was a blend of 'ancient church tradition with Span-
ish-Gallic anti-Arianism and a Celtic religiosity which was still strongly
stamped by paganism'.[18] Ireland was to have a profound effect on Frankish Christianity through its missions, and one result was a reinforcing of
some of these regrettable characteristics. Rome, however, was the central
focus of the Western Church, so that in the Frankish empire there was a
confluence of two streams:

1. A Roman-Patristic stream coming from the Mediterranean world
   and the Romanized Anglo-Saxon Christianity represented by Bede.
2. The world of the Irish-Scottish monks. These influenced another part
   of British Christianity represented by Boniface, the apostle of Germany. He thought of himself as Roman, but in his intellectual and
   religious attitudes bore the stamp of Irish monasticism.

The Gallican liturgy in Frankish lands was eventually replaced by the Roman, but the liturgical result was an odd mixture: a foundational rite from
cool, clear Roman culture with added accretions and alterations reflecting a
religion of fear and irrationality deeply influenced by northern paganism.

Distortions

Christian theology in Frankish territories underwent strong distortions through these cultural processes. Joseph Jungmann claims this period saw the greatest disruption and distortion[19] of the faith in the whole of Christian history.[20] God became more transcendent, fickle and touchy. He was now 'the heavenly emperor. As his subjects, human beings owed him *servitium debitum* (due service) . . . it was to the *honorem Dei* (honour of God) that Christ had to offer his sacrifice, and it is *ad honorem Dei* that God wills the punishment of a sinner . . . earthly kings and lords were arbitrary and high-handed . . . Babies were thought to go to hell if the priest made any mistake in the baptism formula.'[21] 'To avoid damnation one must behave appropriately . . . what counted as appropriate behaviour was by no means confined to virtuous living. There were rites and ceremonies to be carried out, and the fact that provision of these was beyond the means of many gave rise to a good deal of anxiety . . . In the light of this, much religious practice tended to take on a somewhat utilitarian aspect.'[22] A solution only began to be found to this great anxiety when the Irish introduced sacramental confession by the individual to a priest.

Arnold Angenendt has painted a stark picture of changes in society and in the Church in the period from about 600 to 1100 and their devastating effect on the liturgy.[23] According to him, theology simply disappeared, to be replaced by a stringing-together of patristic texts. The classical pagan philosophy schools had been closed down in the sixth century because of their pagan roots, and from then on the role of reason went out of the window. According to Yves Congar Christianity regressed to a 'pre-mental' level: it became 'religion' full stop. In administration of justice reason came to play an insignificant part: it turned instead on tests with red-hot iron or other signs from heaven. Medical knowledge declined as religious practices took over care of the body. Religion took over the whole of life. The devil came into his own, with sin seen as invasion by devils. The inner, ethical aspects of sin faded from view. Sin was objective evil, unconnected with inner processes and attitudes, so that there was now such a thing as unwilling and unconscious sin, and a lot of anxiety about its possible existence in one's heavenly account-book. Christ was a remote divine King and instead of a God of love there sat a deity setting severe standards of human achievement. There was a strong judaizing tendency, the inner life sacrificed to external conventions, the person to the group. Reference to Old Testament texts and institutions is frequent. Seven-branch candlesticks came to stand before the altar – fine examples survive, from Italy to Scandinavia (see the enormous specimen as high as a house now in a transept in Milan Cathedral).

By the time of Charlemagne relationships in the Church were thoroughly feudal, and there was no longer any positive doctrine of the lay state. Clergy and monastics were thought to live the 'perfect life', while laity in their state of profanity had to manage as best they could to get on the right side of God. Despair was not uncommon.

All of this marked a massive step backwards. From 800 to 500 BC reason had come to be set higher than myth in Greece. In the same period in Israel the prophets proclaimed the superiority of the 'heart' and social justice over law and praxis. In the Europe of the so-called 'Dark Ages' many aspects of Christianity went back to a more primitive stage. It was only after the millennium that reason slowly began once again to assert itself in the new schools of learning. Scholasticism opened up the road to scientific thinking, and gradually the prevailing religious mentality came to be questioned. Devils were now seen to have less arbitrary power and the sense of individual responsibility increased. By the sixteenth century many educated people abhorred still-surviving primitive attitudes in the world of popular piety. It was this unregenerate popular religion that eventually triggered the Reformation revolt rather than the official teaching of the contemporary Church.[24]

Charlemagne

In the period immediately following his accession to the Frankish throne, Charlemagne (742–814) built up an empire stretching from northern Spain to the borders of what is now the Czech Republic, and from northern Germany to Rome itself. He fostered education, in the interest of having an empire worthy of the name. There was a revival of classical learning, but the same gifts were not applied to theology. Most lay people had a tenuous and patchy hold on the Christian story and faith. Clergy were hardly much better. Charlemagne laid down as a minimum that the priest know how to baptize, know the Lord's Prayer and Creed (powerful protection against devils), and be able to teach them, abstain from hunting and the game of *histrions,* and not go into taverns. There arose a deep divide with laity on one side and clergy on the other. The priesthood was increasingly perceived as a separate order, *pars electa* of Christ's body in its power to *make* the sacraments and *bring about* both the presence and the sacrifice. Charlemagne made great use of the clergy for administration, production of documents, education, as emissaries, and so on (by this we should mean higher clergy and monks). The Church was 'no longer . . . the communion of the redeemed bound together with a glorious Christ in one Mystical Body . . . [now there was a stronger sense of] the external earthly Church, its hierarchical structure of clergy and laity'.[25] Perhaps it might be more true to say that the 'holy' and 'mystical' part of the Church was now restricted to clergy and monastics. Even today in popular parlance 'going into the Church' refers not to baptism but to ordination. From this period also come phrases like 'Holy Church teaches her children', unconsciously presuming the Church to be one thing (clergy), her children another (laity).

Saints and their relics became sources of divine power much sought after. Holy bones were set in the churches, often behind the altar. Increasingly the priest came round to the front of the altar to celebrate with his back to the people. Altars multiplied to accommodate a multiplication of masses, increasingly seen as an effective work, a transaction with not a little of the utilitarian about it. The Old Testament and its spirit loomed large. 'Some scholars have pictured the religion of this period as so dominated by the OT as to be a "Mosaic Christianity" or a "Christianity of the Law".'[26] In prehistory it was natural to see other human beings as *things*: outsiders could be ill-treated without compunction, and were also treated as a corporate mass. In the Old Testament we read often of whole families being exterminated because of an offence of one of their members, or children tortured or killed because of misdemeanours of their parents. The ability to imagine others as having feelings equal to our own, summed up partly by the word *empathy*, was only gradually learned, and even though Jesus of Nazareth set it dramatically in the foreground of human living – 'love your enemies; do good to those who hate you' – his own followers over two millennia have hardly been quick to learn the lesson. René Girard has pointed out that for most of the last 2,000 years Christians have practised their faith too rarely in the key of the New Testament and too often in that of earlier forms of Old Testament religion.[27] An eye for an eye and a tooth for a tooth has often been the model rather than Christ on the cross. Vengeance in Christian Europe was routinely wrought on criminals, enemies and foreigners, violence prevailed over love, and power and might over service. These developments slowly but surely would have far-reaching effects on the liturgy inherited from the early Christian basilicas: they are a far cry from the joyful, confident faith ringing from Bishop Cyril's addresses to the newly baptized in fourth-century Jerusalem:

> Therefore Solomon also, hinting at this grace, says in Ecclesiastes, Come hither, eat your bread with joy . . . and drink your wine with a merry heart . . . and let oil be poured out on your head . . . and let your garments

be always white, for the Lord is well pleased with your works . . . you must be clad in the garments that are truly white and shining and spiritual, so that you may say with the blessed Isaiah, My soul shall be joyful in my God; for He has clothed me with a garment of salvation, and put a robe of gladness around me.[28]

This relaxed joy of early Christianity had gone, replaced by something a lot darker.

Introduction of the Roman liturgy

By the eighth century there were many complaints that the Gallican rite was in confusion. From one diocese to another, one church to another the usages varied without a central authority to regulate them. From at least 700 Roman usage began to be imitated in some places, often in a pick-and-mix way and drawing on different forms of the Roman rite.[29] Ghislain Lafont writes,

> It cannot be denied that the Rome of that epoch exerted on the Germano-Frankish world . . . a powerful attraction, fascination even; so much so that every town (and, after a while, every monastery) prided itself on being a Rome in miniature, or . . . a manifestation of the *Urbs*, the Mother-Church itself . . . [people went there] on pilgrimage and to carry away with them some of its relics, to make copies of its liturgical texts, to have recourse to its judgments and accept its recommendations . . . there looms large an almost-unquestioned faith in the Roman church as the visible centre of Catholicism.[30]

There were places which added Roman elements to their Gallican liturgy, others where the Roman rite was adopted wholesale while in all sorts of ways being Gallicanized. Charlemagne (ruled 768–814), determined to take the situation in hand, asked for a book providing an authoritative exemplar of the Roman liturgy as established by Pope Gregory. He had to wait for some time for it to come from Rome, and then it turned out to be 50 years old and incomplete (it is known as the *Hadrianum*, after Pope Hadrian I who sent it sometime between 784 and 791). There were texts for papal solemnities, no use at all as they stood for small churches; missing were any texts for Sundays after Christmas, Epiphany, Easter, Ascension, Pentecost, and all Ordinary Sundays, the Common of Saints, various blessings, consecrations and ordinations, the order of baptism and much else, and it had only a few votive masses and prefaces.

Someone would have to fill all the gaps. In this way the notorious *Supplement* was born. It used to be thought the work of Alcuin, but Benedict of Aniane (*c.* 750–821) is now recognized as the mastermind, while Alcuin composed many masses for it (i.e. complete sets of the variable texts for feasts and votive masses). These are longer than the Roman and more complex in style, and have no connection with Roman sources, but because the new texts emanated from the Palace at Aachen they were received with honour, and to these newly composed texts in Franco-Gallican style was attributed the authority of the Roman mass itself.

As well as texts, all manner of new ceremonies came in, such as the Asperges (penitential sprinkling with holy water at start of mass on Sundays), censing of the gospel book before reading the gospel, a sign of the cross on head and breast at this point (another on the mouth was added in the eleventh century), anointings in ordination, ceremonies connected with the Calendar, such as the procession of palms with 'All Glory, Laud and Honour', Tenebrae, Maundy footwashing, a more elaborate veneration of the cross with the Reproaches on Good Friday, lighting of the New Fire, the 'Light of Christ' greeting, the blessing of the Paschal Candle and Exultet, and almost all the rich ceremonial of the blessing of the baptismal water.[31] The Franks had turned it into their own kind of thing.

Britain

In Britain we find a similar story, but in a slightly different way. Augustine, sent by Pope Gregory the Great in 594 to restore Christianity to Britain, brought with him the Roman liturgy (which form of it we are not sure). The surviving Christianity in the north and west was Celtic-Gallican, which only succumbed to the Roman way after a messy struggle. Even once the matter was settled Celtic ways took a long time to die out. In 801 Alcuin in Charlemagne's court wrote a letter to Eanbald II, Archbishop of York, who had done nothing to introduce the revised Roman rite even though he had the books. He had asked Alcuin to compose an adapted mass book for his clergy to use. Alcuin drily told him to be content with the Roman books in his possession as there was no question of more books, and reproved him for dragging his feet and setting the clergy a poor example.[32] In this way Britain was the first national territory in the history of Christianity to go over entirely to the liturgy of the city of Rome.

Apart from the *Hadrianum*, perhaps the most influential document in diffusing the Roman rite was *Ordo Romanus I* and subsequent adapted versions of it. What we now see appearing north of the Alps is a transmogrified version of *OR I*. Originally found only in the city of Rome, it was now becoming a transnational universal rite.

While this liturgical changeover is often portrayed as being a response to the poor state of the Gallican liturgy, that picture should not be overpainted. For Thomas Pott the motivation for blanket introduction of the Roman liturgy was political: it did not express a new self-understanding of the Church, but justification for the reign of the new Roman emperor through a Roman cult. For Pott the liturgy had not been in any serious crisis before these moves.[33]

What was the Frankish-Roman mass like?

We are lucky enough to have what is in effect a ninth-century cartoon-strip showing the celebration of this mass, in the form of nine ivory panels carved around 850 for the cathedral at Metz in northern France at a time when its archbishop Drogo was primate of France (Plate 7). It conjures up before our eyes a fascinating picture of the mass in ninth-century Gaul. The panels show the mass celebrated in Metz Cathedral as it had been codified by Amalarius between 813 and 823.[34] The panels have at some time been remounted slightly out of order, and the following description follows the sequence proposed by R. E. Reynolds, in which panels 1 and 6 (counting horizontally) swap places.[35]

Panel 1: The bishop, led by the archdeacon and accompanied by clergy, enters the church and goes towards the altar.

Panel 2: The clergy bow to the altar. Three deacons are on the bishop's right, two on his left, and the others behind. In front of the altar are two candlebearers and a thurifer, with another behind the bishop (people's importance is indicated by their relative size!). In the background we see the famous *schola* (choir) founded by Chrodegang of Metz (d. 766) which through the ninth to eleventh centuries was, with those of Rouen and Saint Gall, the most outstanding north of the Alps.

Panel 3: The first kiss of peace, which the bishop gives to assisting clergy after he has reverenced the altar. The ciborium over the altar is the *reba* which Chrodegang had had installed . . . (Paul the Deacon wrote of this around 783, mentioning also the *cancelli* surrounding the presbytery.[36] A fine set of such cancelli is preserved in Metz.)[37]

Panel 4: The bishop kisses the gospel book.

Panel 5: The bishop has gone to his seat. In *OR I* he faced east, that is towards the congregation. French churches were built facing the other direction, but the rubric is interpreted with rigid literalism: he faces the east wall to sing the Gloria with the people.

Panel 6: The epistle: the bishop sits on his throne, the curve of the apse behind him. Three priests on his left sit on a draped bench, one of the *formulae* visible in the St Gall plan of an ideal monastery.[38] The altar curtains are draped around the pillars of the ciborium in ancient fashion; hanging in front of the ciborium are seven objects, either *philacteria* (bags containing relics) or, more likely, seven lamps to the altar.

Panel 7: Two scenes. At the left the bishop with the archdeacon on his left receives people's offerings across the barrier of the *cancelli*. The bishop takes bread on a piece of white cloth offered by a woman as she kisses his hand. Others are waiting behind her. The right half shows the bishop standing at the altar, on which lies a loaf, this time receiving the clergy's offerings.

Panel 8: In the eucharistic prayer the bishop points to the wine in the double-handled chalice usual in antiquity, and the bread in front of it. Just as Amalarius describes it, the bishop's ministers, deacons and subdeacons stand around the altar.

Panel 9: A priest receives communion from the bishop.

These panels show the bishop's part in the liturgy, which probably accounts for the surprising omission of the gospel, read by a deacon (although this does not explain why the epistle was included, except in showing the bishop had to sit). Nevertheless, the detail in these panels is very exact, the artist going to great lengths to cram details in. We gain a measure of its likely accuracy from the fact that the drum-like bishop's seat shown here, created from an ancient marble column, is still in use in Metz Cathedral (Plate 8).[39]

The covers of the Drogo Sacramentary show us worship in a leading cathedral led by the bishop. In parish churches where one or two priests and deacons would be assisted by a couple of parish clerks the event would have been more rudimentary, but we have little idea how in practice the grand liturgy was scaled down to suit, and what the 'feel' of the worship would have been like in terms of the people's participation and the qualities it exhibited.

Liturgical history has its ebbs and flows, and the ninth century was not all gloom. There was an attempt to encourage participation by all in the mass, leading to a short-lived little renaissance of the liturgy. People once more sang the Gloria, Sanctus, Agnus and other chants. The offertory procession after a period of decline was reintroduced. Most of the texts were pronounced aloud. Unfortunately this was short-lived, as the developments described above proceeded to follow their full course.[40]

It all travels back the other way

The transformation of the mass in Frankish hands eventually travelled back the other way, replacing the old liturgy in Rome itself by about 1000. Rome then was in a sad state of degradation; its churches began one by one to use the prestigious Frankish books in place of their old ones, and finally the liturgy in the papal court itself was replaced.

The later Middle Ages

In this story we see evolving before our eyes that liturgical world which in the end gave birth to the reaction of the Reformation. Many Frankish characteristics carried over into the later Middle Ages: obsession with rank, the theatrical, with sin and guilt, with what could seem the vindictiveness of a distant God and the need to make the required liturgical transactions with him, a sharp divide between sacred and profane.

But we must beware of oversimplifying. By the late Middle Ages the fabric of Christian living and devotion was highly complex, holding together a formidable picture of God with a very strong perception of Jesus' humanity and closeness to us. In a parish church sacred jostled at every level with profane, and a liturgy which in many ways was highly clericalized was at one and the same time popular in every sense of the term, and in many ways it was the laity who called the shots.[41] In a small church in the sticks the picture of an elite clergy sharply divided from a less worthy laity can hardly be imagined – the priest would be a simple man, one of the people. I have seen an Orthodox country priest during a funeral being told what to do by the laity, who were clearly in charge of the occasion. It is often simply stated that the clergy en masse became an elite and that the laity were excluded from the liturgy, but this is too simple. The old basilica liturgy was by now greatly distorted, and the people's participation limited, but it was real, especially in the ordinary parish.

It is not easy to give a description of late medieval Sunday worship because it will have varied greatly from place to place and even more from country to country. Worship in Italy or Spain, for instance, would be very different from that found in Northern Europe. In Britain we think of churches partitioned off by screens, chantry priests galore amid Gothic mystery – things that were not nearly so prominent in Mediterranean countries. The level of people's participation can be illustrated by an outline description of a Sunday high mass, but in the following description of worship in an English parish we have to bear in mind the great differences to be found across Europe.

A medieval Sunday mass

In a typical English parish church of the fifteenth century the high altar was separated from the nave by a wooden screen carrying above it a rood loft which was a descendent of the ambo. (While Southern Europe kept the raised ambo, usually with an eagle supporting the bookstand, in the north this separated out into pulpit, lectern (often an eagle) and rood loft.) There would be many side altars, perhaps screened off, and masses could be going on at them while the high mass itself was in course. The church would be a hive of activity, its statues shrines, lamps and candles focuses of busyness and devotion.

High mass began with a **procession** of clergy and servers going around the church sprinkling chapels and congregation with holy water. During the **confession** and the **Gloria** people would recite prayers that corresponded with these texts. They would bow each time the **name** of Jesus was mentioned. They would stand for the **gospel** and make the sign of the cross at its announcement. On certain occasions the gospel was sung from the **rood loft,** the whole procession clambering up there. After the Creed the priest went to the **pulpit** for the **Bidding of the Bedes**, a liturgical unit largely in the vernacular including notices, intercessions, a psalm, perhaps the gospel reading, and a **sermon**. At the **offertory** people might bring offerings up to the altar. During the **preface** of the eucharistic prayer the congregation stood. They had their own **special prayers** to say to coincide with the commemoration of the living, the Sanctus, the institution narrative and the **elevation**, the high point of the mass, when all would strain to see the Host. There was another prayer to be said during the commemoration of the departed. At the **Lord's Prayer** the congregation rose from their knees to stand again. Then the **pax brede**[42] was brought round for each person to kiss. People would pay attention to the priest's communion, the Blessing and the reading of the Last Gospel (John 1.1–14). After the mass **blessed bread** was distributed that had been presented before Mattins.

This liturgy is like a city in the sands of a desert – much of the old basilica liturgy is buried, but familiar elements protrude. The changes that had taken place in the first millennium are clearly in evidence.[43] The Frankish culture of the Dark Ages had acted upon Christian liturgy like a refracting lens or a distorting mirror. While in earlier times the rationale for all that went on would have been clear, much of the liturgy was now muddled by misunderstanding and layers of fanciful interpretation. Christian worship will always reflect its local culture, but here the influence of a culture has got out of hand. This raises in stark form a question we now need to address: that of the relationship between Christian faith and the culture of particular societies.

5

God and Culture

Of the many issues thrown up by the Carolingian episode one that immediately strikes us is the complex matter of culture, and the positive and negative potential of any engagement between a culture and the gospel. It is worth pausing to reflect on this very contemporary issue that links us closely with them. First of all, what is a culture? The word is used in four main ways:

1 **Aesthetic**, in reference to the world of the arts and education. A pamphlet for visitors to a city can have a 'Cultural life' section, giving information on concerts and arts events; we can speak of a 'cultured person', a notion that includes not only sensibility but knowledge.

2 **Anthropological:** A matrix of established conventions, habits, attitudes, institutions, symbols, rituals, that enable people to relate within a society (such as Japanese culture).[1]

3 **Situational:** Subcultures, or a mentality that has evolved in a subgroup, such as an air accident report that said an airline had 'an authoritarian cockpit culture'; or a newspaper article's comment that 'Russia is not at its strongest when it comes to safety culture'. All cultures have situational subcultures, such as that of the warriors and that of the wives within a single tribe.

4 **Biological:** Scientific parlance, as in a 'culture' of bacteria in the laboratory. It relates to agri-culture and the cultivation of the land, and so to cult.

'Culture' is a synthetic term originating in the modern propensity for abstract general concepts, and so it is notoriously difficult to define. It is an attempt to corral some motley realities of daily life under an umbrella-concept, always a slippery activity. When words such as 'culture' find a firm place in common parlance we have then to beware of using them unthinkingly or sloppily, but also to accept that if they will not go away then they are likely to indicate a significant intuition into the nature of things. In our present discussion we shall be using the word 'culture' in its societal and situational senses, and at a level that avoids the need to pay attention to finer distinctions.

Inculturation

When the British empire spread across the globe, behind it followed the Church of England, taking into the ancient culture of India or the steaming jungles of Africa the Book of Common Prayer, choir robes, harmoniums and *Hymns Ancient and Modern*, presuming these to be the gospel. A similar story is true of the other churches. Only fairly recently has it come to be recognized that local cultures have their own dignity and gifts to enflesh the gospel in their own way.[2] The Roman Catholic Church after the Second Vatican Council began to blaze a cultural trail in the wake of which other churches have followed. Roman Catholics on the whole have shown greatest boldness and imagination, producing some outstanding schemes now justly famous, such as the Zaire/Congolese rite which incorporates African music and dancing and a splendid array of local practices and characteristics. Another example would be a community of nuns in Malawi who celebrate some of their eucharists in the open air, the priest wearing robes of a tribal leader, scattering flour instead of incense, sitting behind the altar instead of standing, and so on.[3] India is a continent where inculturation has been controversial but bold: the readings for the daily offices include, for instance, optional readings from Hindu scriptures.

Ansgar Chupungco has identified a range of terms, all with their own nuances of meaning, especially *indigenization, incarnation, contextualization, adaptation, inculturation* and *acculturation*. He reckons the last three to be most commonly used. *Adaptation* has been favoured in Roman documents, reflecting their cautious approach – judicious addition of local trimmings to the standard Roman rite. *Acculturation* for Chupungco is use of compatible elements in the Roman rite not as trimmings but as matters of substance. *Inculturation*, however, as Chupungco uses the term, is a new birth brought about within a culture through the coming of the gospel, a conversion ('baptizing') of existing practices, artefacts and arts, a bringing to birth within and from that culture of its local vintage of the gospel. This should come about through an initial process of acculturation. Perhaps the most famous account of an attempt at serious inculturation is Vincent Donovan's *Christianity Rediscovered* – too bold apparently for the Roman Church, as it seems to have come to nothing.[4] In what follows I shall use 'inculturation' as a term to cover the whole subject.

Nothing new

Inculturation is always happening in Christian worship: it is impossible for it not to happen. If Christians are not aware of it, then it will happen unconsciously. The early Church quickly found itself faced with the question, and perhaps the first reasoned, conciliar decision to opt for cultural plurality can be seen in the Council of Jerusalem in Acts 15, with its acceptance that Christians of Jewish culture could live the faith in one way and Gentiles in another. In the not-so-long term this was to mean a move for everyone from Jewish into Hellenistic culture (see Acts 15.12ff). The post-Constantinian Church became adept, both consciously and unconsciously, at embracing local culture. A typical example would be the remembrance days of *cara cognatio* in Rome ending on 22 February, when households put out a chair for departed ancestors: in the Roman Church calendar on 22 February we find the feast of St Peter's Chair. There was a spree of such 'baptizing' of popular cultic practices in this period. The deep instinct for sacrifice in people led to a strong focusing on the theme of sacrifice in the eucharist, and not only there: offering of incense came into the evening office (in imitation of the Jerusalem temple) with the same theme in mind. Both of these had a theological foundation that was thoroughly scriptural, though more ambiguous were other innovations such as adoption of gestures and items of clothing from the imperial court.

In more recent times seventeenth-century Jesuits in China, faced with a proud and ancient culture, saw much there to respect, and boldly experimented with Chinese terms for Christian concepts and for God himself, association of the ancestors (very important in many cultures) with the Communion of Saints, use of Chinese robes and gestures in the mass, and other authentic attempts at inculturation. After much wavering on the subject in Rome these practices were eventually forbidden in 1742, and finally permitted again only in 1939. Revived interest in the 'Chinese Rites Controversy' has brought a spate of writing on the subject in recent years.[5]

A complex matter

In the years since the Second Vatican Council gallons of ink have been spilled on inculturation in a debate that shows no sign of abating. Anyone proposing to research the subject is faced with a formidable body of material, and as the debate goes on there is an increasing sense of the complexity of the issues. Here are a few:

1 *Liturgy may be co-opted by the culture*

Aidan Kavanagh speaks of a middle-class piety which 'draws its power more from civil religion . . . than from the Gospel; indeed, it inculturates the Gospel to middle-class values . . . such as comfort in affluence, participation in approved groups, consumerism, and a general optimism which seems to have lost its grip on reality. . . . Such an inculturation of the liturgy has been called by some an *embourgeoisement* of the Church [in which there is little counter-cultural activity].' It is not difficult in any society for the Church to become a poodle of the status quo. It is difficult for Christians to stand apart from the mood and passions of their society, particularly in times of national struggle, or when the 'tribal' instincts of a country or economic or other group get into top gear, or when deeply entrenched relationships or practices (such as slavery or apartheid) fail to be seen for what they are. Even in individual personal lives we will never be immune from bending the gospel to our own preferences and outlooks – we have already seen an example in the co-opting of the gospel to the presuppositions, outlooks and cultural deficiencies of Europe in the time of Charlemagne, when unexamined, unchallenged, unspoken assumptions had free rein. According to T. E. Hulme 'There are certain doctrines which for a particular period seem not doctrines, but inevitable categories of the human mind . . . Doctrine felt as facts.'[6] There is enormous power in such cultural phenomena for distorting the gospel.

2 *'Defumigation'*

Cultures often have to go through a period of 'defumigation' before the liturgy can take them on board. A country where tribal drum-music is associated with devil-worship means drums will be unusable until they have known some decline, which may require the wait of a generation. An example of a defumigation process getting stuck is the early banning of musical instruments from worship. In the pagan world sacrifice was accompanied by the music of a small group: so when early Christians heard lyre and flute they immediately felt the atmosphere of heathen sacrifice. In the West a later generation reversed the interdict, but in Byzantine Orthodoxy that has never happened, and instruments are still forbidden. The principle of defumigation applies even today: churches wanting to introduce modern music tend to opt for styles at least a generation out of date. Power of association brings problems for inculturation that can leave Christians preferring to dress their worship in weak examples of a cultural tradition, rather than the most lively and vigorous.

3 Adherents of local religions can resent adoption of their sacred practices

Some Hindus resent Christian use of the traditional Hindu lamp in church. Such use is now widespread in India, the lamp surmounted by a cross instead of a Hindu symbol. It can, however, be difficult to draw a distinction between local culture and local religion, particularly where the local religion continues in vigour. Is the culture being adopted or the religion?

4 The local culture may be elitist

Dalits and tribal people in India tend to see high Indian cultures as more oppressive than Western culture. Within most cultures there are sub-cultures, and the Church has often been faced with a dilemma as to which culture to choose to work with. This led to rivalry between Jesuits and Franciscans in the Far East in the seventeenth century, the former concentrating on the cultured elite for good strategic reasons, the latter on the ordinary people and the poor, for good pastoral reasons. This problem multiplies exponentially in the complex modern Western world. How does the Church engage simultaneously with many cultures and subcultures in one place, especially if any of them are in conflict?

5 Basic problems of principle

Inculturation involves a dilemma that comes out sharply in the sacraments: which is more important in a sacrament, the outward form or the 'inner' significance (usually there are several, never tidily identifiable). For instance, should bread or bananas be used for the eucharist in a banana culture? Wine or tea? Using bananas preserves the immediacy of ordinary daily food, but loses a whole array of associations with bread and wheat in the scriptures. Bread is made by human beings, bananas just grow. For any new Christians there has to be a degree of inculturation into the world of first-century Palestine, so bread might seem to be the thing. But if bread and wine are expensive curiosities imported at great expense to the detriment of needs for schools and clinics, as in some African countries at the moment, the problem becomes acute. Bible translation meets the same problems: translators are faced with a choice between word-for-word literalism, long-winded explanations, or 'dynamic equivalent'. The problem seems irresolvable.

6 Who checks it from outside?

A local culture left to its own devices could be blind to ways it is perverting the gospel. But how can those outside the culture assess an inculturated liturgy? You cannot come from outside and 'get into' a culture: culture comes forth from inside and is a whole experience. There is an ultimately unsolvable problem here about how processes of inculturation can be understood, guided and received by the universal Church.

7 All cultures are becoming westernized

Inculturation theory tends to have monocultures in mind, but all local cultures are coming under the influence of Western pluralism. Contemporary thinking about inculturation often assumes freestanding, discreet monocultures, but there are no longer any virgin cultures today. In many places the Church finds itself even trying to resurrect a culture that is dying or has largely disappeared. It is impossible for cultures to be pure today, and so we have to recognize we will usually be dealing with a hybrid, something that is on the move towards assimilation and has to some extent lost its virginity – a culture in a state of flux.

One phenomenon of today is a new resistance to globalization partly expressed in revival of elements of local culture. Inculturation can mean reviving aspects of culture that are lost or fading, and then its function may be not so much to root liturgy in the reality of people's lives as to help resurrect for them a strong sense of the local for their own health. Sometimes it can include importation: so the abundant African artefacts and clothes visible in South Africa tend to come from West Africa which is richer in such traditions. This kind of thing can slip into serving a quest for identity and the manufacture of identities – this was to be seen in the Carolingian empire, with its importation of Roman and classical cultural and liturgical items.

8 A two-way process

The tradition of the Church is made up of two cultural components. One of them we shall examine shortly: the Church's own culture passed on through the centuries (itself always expressed in human cultural forms). But the Christianity of any group will also contain elements of purely human culture, which will on the whole be transitory (such as robed choirs, or class distinctions). There will be elements in the lives and practice of the gospel-bringers that fail the test: so the many sad stories of well-meaning missionaries undermining a corporate culture that was in fact more healthy and less individualistic than their own. The Church always has something to learn about the gospel from those to whom it brings it. But the new culture being engaged with also comes under judgement: cannibals, for instance, have to give up eating people.

In contemporary life churches have had to learn truths of the gospel from the secular world: they have, for instance, been obliged by secular authority to make adequate provision for the disabled, something in which they should have been blazing a trail ahead of everyone else. There are those who say the Church needs to attend to contemporary society, and those who say it needs to be countercultural. It will really need to be both, and discerning between the two is not easy. There are no quick answers, no easy ways out of the complexity.

The culture of Jesus

This outline of the question sets the scene for an issue that centres on the person of Jesus. I have used the term 'situational culture' to refer to the way of life in a group of people such as the crew of an aeroplane. In any group particular ways of working and living together grow up – attitudes, ways of relating and practices. In our time we have become aware of atmospheres that can colour the life of groups, and ways of doing things that can give them a unique feel – in that sense even every family has its own culture: ways of living, preferences, good and bad ways of managing the challenge of life together.

This increasing awareness that every group develops its culture can give us insights into the relationship of Jesus with his followers. Among them was a smaller group often referred to as 'the Twelve'. These were more than just a group he gathered for teaching purposes, taking an opportunity for evening classes or learning to assist him in his work, like simple volunteers. They went around with him, accompanying him as he taught the crowds, healed the sick and debated with authorities; they ate with him, bivouacked with him on journeys, sailed the sea, argued with him, huddled together to talk about him. When a group of people live as closely together as that a 'way' grows up, a mode of living and talking that is slipped into when they come together: the group develops its culture.

What was the culture evolving in the group of disciples around Jesus? First we can say that life in that group was a life that transformed its members – it was a transforming culture. They were changed by being with Jesus: it was not just his teaching that changed them. The teaching went with a lot more – with particular ways of behaving, of being courteous, of taking other people seriously, ways of living that were new to them. Jesus was a role model, but like any charismatic leader he was more: he was inimitable, and it was infectious.

The heart of it was Jesus himself. His infective presence, magnetic personality, closeness to God, radiated from him. His example of love, care and endless ability to take people seriously had a deep effect – it got under the skin. The magnetism of Jesus drew the crowds. He had an extraordinary assurance, the bearing of one with authority; people were struck by his dependability. They were struck by his uniqueness. Jesus' teaching has a particular character: nothing of the like comes from the lips of anyone else. It crosses the span of 2,000 years still clearly recognizable in large proportions of the stories and sayings and in the overarching message. Shakespeare's mature writing has the same characteristic – in many passages as well as in his overarching structures there is nothing like it, either in his time or since – you can tell it a mile off. *Pericles* was jointly written with another, possibly one George Wilkins, who on the basis of the style seems to have been responsible for the first two acts. With Act Three the work obviously becomes Shakespeare's.[7] With much of Jesus' teaching as it is reported to us we recognize him straight away. All of this will have affected the spirit and tone of the group, and the group's feel for Jesus, his values and his approach.

People also saw the way Jesus prayed to the Father, and that will have had its effect on the culture of the group. His closeness to God radiated from him, and they picked it up, so that it became a shared reality within the group. It may be to this that Mark is referring when he reports Jesus as saying, 'To you has been given the secret of the kingdom of heaven' (Mark 4.11f.).

We have mentioned Jesus' lived-out message of love, his care and endless ability to take people seriously. Those are things that rub off. They become infective, and we find ourselves involuntarily imitating them. There was love of enemies – one of the things that most amazed the ancient world. That said a good deal about the culture of this group. Through the New Testament we see Jesus trying to bring the disciples to realize the extent and depth of such costly and unconditional love for all. They found it difficult to understand but they did not give up and go away – they were held by something they were unable to leave.

This group culture is not simply abstract: it developed a frame both of mind and of body. It is possible with inspiring figures to find their devotees picking up physical characteristics and modes of speech. The disciples were slow in picking it up, slow to be formed in this culture, we are told, but gradually it was to transform them. The culture grew, layer upon layer, informed by the life that was in Jesus. Going around with the Lord, listening, watching, receiving guidance, would slowly bring them to see with different eyes. As St Benedict was later to say in speaking of monastic communities, it transformed their hearts. It will have transformed their own picture of themselves. 'How he's changed / how she's changed', friends might have said of a disciple or close friend, but the effect was not only to change individuals; it was the forging of a community, breaking down divisions between people and bringing them to bond with one another in reference to something bigger than themselves. Increasingly as they came together there would be this atmosphere, this climate, this culture of the Kingdom.

By the time Jesus came to his cross it was a culture in its own right – strong in the group of the disciples, and alive too in many people and groups in Galilee and elsewhere. It already had shared memories – such as those of the two disciples on the road to Emmaus, their memories awakening as Jesus broke the bread with them.

Some things in life have to go through a fixing-process if they are not to dissolve or unravel. Photos used to be put in a fixer after being developed or they would disappear. Pottery has to be fired if it is not to fall apart, iron to be annealed to make a usable knife. The culture of the group needed a confirming process. When the difficult moment came all fell away. In Gethsemane as it came to the push, one betrayed him, a little later one denied him three times, and the rest fled.

So much for the culture of the group. But the resurrection raised it again and launched it in flight. This is portrayed in the second chapter of Acts, where Christians in Jerusalem called nothing their own but held everything in common and ate and prayed together every day in an atmosphere of love and zeal. The picture is idealized – no group is without disagreements and problems, and the rough edges of rubbing-up against one another are all abundantly there elsewhere in the New Testament documents, an unavoidable part of the process of community. Even so, these ideals are characteristic of Christianity from the start. Love of one another – life together with people who belong together. Caring for the poor, confident in the love of God the Father of all of us. In this account of the period after Pentecost in the book of Acts we see the culture of Jesus strong and well, flowering and multiplying. It was now strong enough for individuals to go off on their own or in pairs without losing its dynamic force. The apostles fanned out through the known world, taking the culture of Jesus with them.

This picture is based on what can be straightforwardly seen at work as the story is told in the Gospels and Acts. We can see it happening in the accounts, but it is also implicit in many sayings, not least in John, the evangelist of organic unity. 'I am in my Father, and you in me, and I in you' (John 14.20). 'May they be one as we are one' (John 17.11). John is not episodic by nature but organic – it is he who gives the image of the Church as a vine – he sees all this in terms of a firm, strong continuity. The saying that 'the Holy Spirit will lead you into all truth' (John 16.13) is a key to something even more striking: the close association of the Holy Spirit with baptism and the elemental life energizing the Body of Christ. The genetic life of Jesus in the Church is carried by the Spirit. If the temple of 1 Peter is built of living stones (1 Peter 2.5), its life is the Spirit.

Christianity is a genetic religion. The passing-on of the culture has been genetic – a church cannot be set up *ex nihilo* by people reading books, passing on texts, believing the beliefs – it is caught within the uninterrupted stream of the group's life down the centuries from the beginning, and is not a thing, but Jesus himself, and not Jesus in isolation but always together with the group, in the Spirit. Christianity, being such a deeply genetic religion, is a culture in its own right. The term 'genetic' has the advantage of gathering up notions of historicity, tradition and apostolic succession in a more holistic and less mechanical way than at least the latter term might imply. The word 'culture' even more so.

Is the gospel a subculture?

The notion of the Church as a culture needs exploration, for on the one hand the gospel of Christ can never be seen as a subculture (like, say, the world of horse-racing), while on the other it is clearly incomplete. It provides no framework for cultivating land or for courtship, for instance; it does not provide enough for the running of a society. Here we come back to inculturation. The life of the Body of Christ is a *metaculture*. It cannot exist on its own, but only in harness with the particular forms of human society. The gospel only becomes a present reality when it pairs up with life. Whenever there is such a pairing-up, the process is always mutual and dialogical. This is because whenever Christ comes to a group for the first time through the mediation of the Church, that Church is already the expression of a particular culture, just as the Church of England was in the jungle – it has things to learn.

On the other hand every non-Christian group have Christ among them already, even before the Christians get there. Wherever there is love in a family, wherever people care for one another, wherever they are seeking the truth, there is Christ among them. Where love is, there God is. Often recipients of the gospel have been living better lives in some respects than the bringers of it. Because of this there has to be dialogue and listening. Each side has something to learn, and from that can grow a new creation: the gospel inculturated.

'The gospel'?

Here begin the difficulties, as we have seen them already. The metaculture of the Body of Christ is not wandering around disembodied like a cloud, seeking whom to inhabit. This is part of the drawback of talking simply about 'the gospel' and the bringing of it – 'spreading the gospel'. The whole thing is genetic and physical through and through. The culture of the Church is always passed on already married to a particular people and their way of life, and they, like many missionaries of the past, need to do some discerning to distinguish what is of their own local culture from what is universal.

There is a further complication: some of the core content itself of the culture of the Body of Christ is determined by a particular culture, but irrevocably. We cannot un-make the Jewishness of Christ or the local Palestinian particularity of the scriptures. Any missionary dialogue with seekers has to be able to handle this complexity, which entails a need to be inculturated into some aspects of first-century Palestine and of other cultures of the Church's past trajectory. Any bearers of the gospel, the culture of Jesus, need to be vigilant and discerning as they seek to distinguish between those things that merely represent a particular place and time, and those that are, or have become, indispensable.

Even though virgin cultures are probably no longer to be found except in remote parts of Amazonia, all of this applies in the same way to the passing-on of the life of the Church to people of our time in their own cultures, subcultures and sub-subcultures in the complex situation of today.

The metaculture of Christ

To sum up, perhaps there are four main characteristics of the metaculture of Christ. It is:

1 Not a societal culture (on which a human society can be founded) – the traditions of Christianity lack key things which such cultures provide.

2 Like other cultures, it uses the outward forms of community, tradition, practices, physical realities, inherited ways and so on.
3 It cannot exist apart from human culture, but is designed to pair up
   with it, and is always passed on already dressed in a particular local
   cultural form.
4 It engages with culture in all its major terms, and with every aspect
   of human life.

It is within some such framework as this that we are able, indeed we
must, talk of the culture of the Body of Christ.

Understanding history

Now we go back to the Carolingians. If this culture of the Church works as
a constant guarantor of communion with Christ, with an implication that
it is indestructible, then what happened to it in early medieval Europe?

It is possible for groups of Christians to go dead on the culture of Jesus.
It never went that far in Carolingian Europe. One saving grace was the
restless dynamism of the West, unmistakeably characteristic even as early
as St Augustine. Little renaissances in the ninth and eleventh to thirteenth
centuries were signs of something that could not be kept down. In addition, the context was open, not shut – there was a looking outwards, to
Byzantium and above all to Rome. Such outward looking is an essential
part of a 'sense of the Church', which cannot be had in a closed system.
While Christianity in the time of the Frankish empire was gravely distorted,
it never lost the culture of Jesus. For instance, those great civilizing agen-
cies the monasteries witnessed to it continually. One of the central texts
of the age, the *Rule for Monks* of St Benedict, was so imbued with the
culture of Jesus that it has become popular among Christian laity today,
even as a basis of courses for training business managers. The monastic
witness to the gospel also set forth a radical model of human society
in which all were equal. Even after those second-class monks, the lay
brothers, were introduced to deal with heavy work, the monasteries were
societies run on the principle of consultation, their leaders elected as in
a modern democracy, and even where that principle became corrupted,
the vision of the second and fourth chapters of Acts remained close to the
surface. What the monasteries set forth was not simply a less hierarchical
society – they continued to witness, subject to the inevitable constraints
of their times, to the nature of the Church as a communion of human
persons with God, rather than a feudal pyramid.

Early medieval society as a whole was gradually transformed by the gospel: slavery disappeared, and then serfdom after it. The changes could have happened faster, but happen they did. The culture of Jesus went as it were through a long narrow tunnel until about the tenth century, when the gospel of Christ-presenced forgiveness and love re-emerged in a remarkable volte-face: the stern imperial Christ of the Franks started turning into the man of sorrows; *Christus Rex* crucifixes became crucifixes of suffering. Although Christianity had become deeply fearful of God, people paradoxically came to express their sense of oppression in representations of Jesus' suffering. This was lopsided, because the Gospels do not emphasize the humanity of Jesus in this way: they keep a balance between his humanity and his divinity, directing the attention through Christ to the loving God. At a certain point in early medieval Europe nevertheless attention came to be directed towards Jesus' humanity as a compensation for a bullying and arbitrary God. This 'turn to the human' was unique to the West – it is not found in the East, any more than the Carolingian distortions were, and it led to a dramatic new development in human self-understanding – human feelings were now being given a place in the scheme of things. Our humanness was becoming interesting and worthy of attention.

About 970 Archbishop Gero of Cologne commissioned a crucifix – this crucifix was revolutionary; its Christ is filled with agony and sorrow. Even Greek art at its greatest never accomplished this – typical classical sculptures regard us with a glassy stare. Kenneth Clark has said of this crucifix and similar works of this period:

These confident works show that at the end of the tenth century there was a new power in Europe, greater than any king or emperor: the Church. If you had asked the average man of the time to what country he belonged, he would not have understood you; he would have known only to what bishopric. And the Church was not only an organizer; it was a humanizer. Looking at Ottonian ivories, or at the marvellous bronze doors made for Bishop Bernhard at Hildesheim at the beginning of the eleventh century, I am reminded of the most famous lines in Virgil, that great mediator between the antique and the medieval world. They come when Aeneas has been shipwrecked in a country that he fears is inhabited by barbarians. Then as he looks around he sees some figures carved in relief and he says: 'These men know the pathos of life, and mortal things touch their hearts.' Man is no longer *Imago Hominis* [as in the stiff figures of the Book of Kells], the image of man, but a human being, with humanity's impulses and fears; also humanity's moral sense and belief in the authority of a higher power.[8]

90

A fundamental Christian truth was being discovered, but with a new intensity, as if there was suddenly a great deal of catching up to do: the rediscovered truth was that while God is the person greater than all persons, the same God has made us not simply as objects casting a shadow in his light, but as living persons in our own right. By the tenth century joyful love was around the corner again, to emerge in such a remarkable text as these words by St Anselm:

Jesus, like a mother you gather your people to you; you are gentle with us as a mother with her children.
Often you weep over our sins and our pride, tenderly you draw us from hatred and judgement.
You comfort us in sorrow and bind up our wounds, in sickness you nurse us and with pure milk you feed us.
Jesus, by your dying, we are born to new life; by your anguish and labour we come forth in joy.
Despair turns to hope through your sweet goodness; through your gentleness, we find comfort in fear.
Your warmth gives life to the dead, your touch makes sinners righteous.
Lord Jesus, in your mercy heal us; in your love and tenderness remake us.
In your compassion bring grace and forgiveness, for the beauty of heaven may your love prepare us.[9]

Words like this could never have been written in classical antiquity nor in the time of Charlemagne – the like had never been seen before – here was a new spirit that was eventually to lead to a new vision of the human person, to the Renaissance, and to the humanism of the modern era with all its gifts and failings.

This development might never have taken place had it not been squeezed out of people by the distortions of the preceding epoch. The gospel is the source of the best European humanism, and it was able to be so because the culture of Jesus, dimmed during the worst times of the intervening centuries, was eventually to resurface in this new form.

In any age the purity of the gospel will be smudged and distorted, and this has to be embraced as part of the processes of real life rather than shunned in favour of ideal pictures. While there are no short cuts past creation's groans and travails, it helps, however, to be more self-aware and enlightened than the Carolingians were, and as we ask urgent questions about the contemporary Church we are pointed inevitably towards issues to do with culture.

6

The Cross and the Font

Growing up from small seeds in late antiquity and the early Middle Ages, especially among northern peoples in Gaul and Germany, a transformation slowly overtook worship in the Western Church from about the twelfth century onwards. It is not easy to describe and difficult for us to be aware of, so long have its results been part of our makeup. In this chapter we trace this transformation, taking by way of example the story of a little-known tradition that is interesting indeed for its own sake.

Around the year 384 a religious sister from the south of France or northern Spain called Egeria visited the Holy Land and sent back reports on worship there.[1] In the Church of the Holy Sepulchre, between the rotunda containing Christ's tomb and the great church of the Resurrection, was the place of the cross. What was believed to be the true cross had been found in this place by St Helena, who concluded the spot to be Golgotha itself. The wood of this relic by the time of Egeria's visit was locked away, and in its place stood a large metal cross studded with precious stones. The main part of the daily evening office took place across a courtyard in the rotunda built around Christ's tomb. After the final blessing there was then a procession to the cross on Golgotha, where the bishop said a prayer and blessed those who were training up for baptism. After another prayer the faithful went 'behind the cross' where the same was repeated and then everyone melted away.

This little office at the cross was part of a tradition developed in response to the uniqueness of Jerusalem, where people entered into and celebrated the saving events at the places in which they were supposed to have happened. The daily evening worship in this way held together the tomb and the cross, the sepulchre and Golgotha.

This significant little practice passed into liturgical history as a major item in daily prayer. North of Jerusalem in eastern Syria we find a form of local liturgy that has preserved perhaps better than any other liturgical tradition significant elements of the Jerusalem liturgy as witnessed by Egeria, including certain practices in daily prayer.[2] Here, after the final blessing of the morning and evening offices on weekdays, there is a procession to a martyr's tomb where a small dismissal service is held. The content is as follows:

Martyrs' anthem
Each priest says a prayer
Three prayers: of Mary, of the Apostles, of patron saints
Blessing

Originally the procession was to an outdoor cross. Although the earliest texts of this daily liturgy only come from the eighth century it is probable this devotion at the end of the office is a close relative of the station at the cross in fourth-century Jerusalem, a conclusion drawn by various authors.[3] The Georgian church has similar traditions, together with fine outdoor crosses reminiscent of the 'Celtic' crosses of Ireland and Great Britain. E. de Bhaldraithe suggests that Irish high crosses were used in this way too.[4]

Constantinople

Next we go to Constantinople. Here for many centuries there was a similar practice after both the morning and evening offices each day: a procession, not this time to a cross, but to two parts of the church. The first was the *skeuophylakion* in the north-east corner of the church to the left of the altar area. Here the treasures were kept, as well as relics and the holy myrrh, the equivalent of oil of chrism in the West. In later times this developed into the chapel where the gifts are prepared at the eucharist. Thence the procession went to the baptistery, a little further around again to the north-east, for further prayer. Texts for these processions have not survived, except for a prayer and a blessing for use at each of the places visited. As in Egeria's description, at each place the blessing with a bowing of the head ('Prayer of Inclination') was given again.[5] Here it seems we have a reinterpretation of the Golgotha station at Jerusalem, as Nicholas Uspensky says, a conclusion supported by the oriental liturgist Gabriele Winkler, who concludes this practice must certainly derive from Jerusalem.[6] These processions to *skeuophylakion* and baptistery were integral to a form of the Byzantine daily office which has long since disappeared from use, the so-called 'Chanted Office'.[7] In Constantinople it fell victim to the Latin sack of the city in 1204, but survived in its last outpost, Thessalonica, until that fell to the Turks in 1453.

We are uncovering a practice of processing at the end of the evening office every day (and after the morning office too in Byzantine practice) either to a cross, martyrium or baptistery, and sometimes a combination of more than one of them. The common connection is the cross of Christ in the context of the resurrection. The font is the place where new Christians die, according to St Paul, to rise again with Christ as a new creation. Martyrs have furthermore died a physical death and gained an eternal crown, glorious signs to the Church on earth of Christ's victory over death.

Rome and the Lateran basilica

From Constantinople we now go to Rome. The basilica of St John Lateran was for long the mother church of Rome and its liturgy, and residence of the Pope. In the twelfth century a priest called Bernard wrote an account of the annual liturgical round in St John Lateran. His description includes a visit to the font and the chapel of the Holy Cross after vespers every Sunday throughout the year.[8] Bernard's reference to this weekly procession has received little attention from scholars, but here we see at the heart of the Roman liturgy what is apparently a weekly commemoration of baptism and the crucifixion at the end of evening prayer, whose similarities to the other traditions I have described ask for some explanation. There was a period in the seventh and eighth centuries when most of the Popes were Greek, and Rome contained large numbers of Greek immigrants; these exercised an influence on the liturgy. It was said of these Greeks that they had a particularly strong devotion to the font, which fits with what we have heard of the liturgy at Constantinople. One possibility is that this practice is a result of Greek influence. Bernard tells us no more about this weekly visit to the font and we are left to guess what form it would have taken.

There is yet another practice at Rome, however, that is better documented: a tradition of processing to the font and chapel of the Cross after vespers daily in the Easter octave and at certain other times.[9] This also is described by Bernard, but its earliest texts are much older, from approximately the seventh century,[10] describing a practice that seems older still. Four centuries before Bernard, Amalarius of Metz about 812 refers to short offices in Rome 'to various altars in different places, and very often to the cross and the fonts' in the week of Easter. He describes it as a 'glorious office'.[11] Anton Baumstark suggested that the procession to the font itself may derive from fourth-century Jerusalem, where Egeria, in addition to describing the procession to the cross after vespers, also described a daily procession in the Easter octave[12] to the Mount of Olives and the site of the ascension before the evening office.

Roman paschal vespers

The form of this Roman service is curious. Vespers in the Lateran basilica was followed by a procession to the baptistery, where much of vespers was repeated, including the same psalms and the Magnificat. The procession then moved on to the chapel of the Holy Cross ('St Andrew at the Cross'), where all of that was repeated yet again. The texts are paschal – the psalms for the vespers of Easter day are repeated each day – and they are texts naturally bringing with them allusions to the crossing of the Red Sea, Galilee and other themes both paschal and baptismal. The chapel of the Holy Cross was hard by the baptistery across a small courtyard. It was built in the fifth century on a similar design to the mausoleum of Galla Placidia at Ravenna; together with its splendid mosaics it was barbarously demolished in the 1580s. By Bernard's time it was known as 'St Andrew at the Cross' due to the proximity of St Andrew's monastery. A third station at St John Baptist's chapel, also opening off the baptistery, had been added by then – or it may have been to St John the Evangelist's chapel, also nearby – there is an ambiguity in the texts. This multiple procession took place as well on certain feasts such as St John the Baptist and St John the Evangelist. At St Peter's on the Vatican there was also a baptistery with a chapel of the Holy Cross, and a similar practice in Eastertide.

In this daily paschal pilgrimage we have a bundle of themes, cross, resurrection and baptism chief among them, recalling to the participants their transformation in Christ. Chrysogonus Waddell points out that for the Fathers the name Galilee means 'passing beyond', 'passing over', 'transmigration' – the procession to the font is in obedience to the angel's command to the women: go to Galilee – there you will meet him. In medieval monasteries there was a regular Sunday procession after vespers to the 'Galilee' (often a porch) about which the twelfth-century liturgist Rupert of Deutz says, 'we have to go forth into Galilee, that is to say, into transmigration, to see the Lord with his apostles, so that, namely, we may not be the man of yore, the "old" man we once were, but that we might walk in newness of life'.[13] Clearly a baptismal reference there, while the little service itself had by now been adapted to monasteries, which did not normally have fonts. But there was something else, very intriguing, which also perhaps takes us to Galilee. The service at the Lateran ended in the refectory with successive drinking of three different wines: *de greco*, *de pactissi* and *de procamu*. Waddell concludes that, going by the names given to the wines, they progressed from poor to excellent (the first, 'Greek', was wine with salt added). Was this a reliving of the drinking of that best wine saved till last at the wedding at Cana in Galilee?[14]

Although by the time of Bernard these stations at the baptistery seem to have been largely a clerical affair, for a long time they must have been very popular services, in early centuries particularly popular among the many Greeks in Rome. The venue began to be varied, the procession going to other churches on some days of Easter week, reflecting the over-blown stage things had reached by the twelfth century at a time when the traditional public liturgy of the Lateran basilica had already been pared down and to some degree distorted. This ancient tradition came increasingly to be resented by a clergy wanting to follow new fashions in simple liturgy. Here is something often seen in the history of Christian worship: clergy develop their own culture and know-how, and a particular view as to what is proper, while failing to appreciate the mind-set of the general population and religious expressions that would be natural to them. There follows a familiar pattern of clergy first taking over, then de-gutting the rite, and finally laying it aside through lack of enthusiasm.

In the eleventh century there came a movement for reform which affected this liturgy. The life of cathedral canons was often thought to be unsatisfactory, and in many places they were replaced by new communities of canons living a monastic life under vow. This happened too in the Lateran; between 1061 and 1105 the old chapter of the Lateran was replaced by a community of reformed canons from St Frediano in Lucca. These canons were at great pains to respect and preserve the ancient Roman liturgy, but where it was identical with Lucca usage, then Lucca documents were imported, from which more than half of Bernard's account derives.[15] Is there any significance in the fact that in Lucca Cathedral there stands a large and very unusual twelfth-century two-storied fountain or font?

The ramifications continue. A little way down the road from Lucca is Pisa, whose cathedral baptistery was built in imitation of the rotunda of the Holy Sepulchre in Jerusalem. This huge circular building with its great polygonal font built for baptism by submersion, stands some way west of the cathedral, the whole complex, leaning tower and all, standing in modern times in a sea of green grass. There was a particular devotion to the Holy Sepulchre in medieval Pisa. The paschaltide processions to the baptistery will certainly have taken place there, and must have been grand, given the space and majesty of the setting. But was there more? It would be interesting to see what an investigation of the medieval liturgical traditions of Pisa would turn up, for here we see a tie-up with the origins: the procession is once again visually connected with the rotunda of the Holy Sepulchre.

Milan and the Ambrosian liturgy

If we now travel up to Milan where the whole diocese still today follows the venerable Ambrosian rite (in the parishes the Roman liturgy is not permitted!) we find yet again the same tradition: a procession to the font at the end of lauds and vespers every single day throughout the year, with special prayers, a responsory, a psalm and a blessing (in the cathedral repeated at both its baptisteries on Sundays).[16] This visit to fonts after the two main daily services appears to stem from the earliest period of the Ambrosian rite, and once again a connection has been drawn with the procession to the cross in fourth-century Jerusalem. Not only that, but there is also another practice, the 'Antiphon at the cross', which prior to the 1983 reform of the Ambrosian breviary took place on Sundays in the early part of the morning office, at a point between the Sunday vigil and the morning office. In the Ambrosian office before the recent reforms, there was therefore this devotion at the cross in the morning and a commemoration of baptism at the end of both morning and evening offices at the baptistry.

The 1983 reform, under the strong guidance of Aimé Georges Martimort, moved this baptism commemoration to the middle of the offices, making a procession to the font less practical, so that it now has the meagre form of a stranded responsory. This raises a good question: what presuppositions could lead these reformers to believe that encouraging a procession to the font was undesirable or unrealistic? The answer to that question seems obvious, but we must complete our story before giving it closer scrutiny.

The Gallican liturgical family

The daily or weekly procession to the font and/or cross, and particular observances of this kind in Eastertide seem to be found everywhere we look: for instance, in the Mozarabic liturgy of Spain and the old Celtic liturgy texts are provided for processions to the font after vespers.[17] Mention has already been made of Irish high crosses. Eoin de Bhaldraithe has suggested that bosses and geometrical shapes on these crosses might be in imitation of the jewelled metal cross at Golgotha in the Church of the Holy Sepulchre. At the time of their creation these Irish crosses were a focus of liturgical processions, and an ancient monastic rule describes part of each office as being performed at the cross. De Bhaldraithe believes such practices would include a procession to the cross after the evening office, as in fourth-century Jerusalem, and in the east Syrian rite.[18] He has elsewhere drawn attention to Irish traditions of processions to wells, some of which have flights of steps down into them, suggesting they were used for baptism.[19]

The Roman rite in Northern Europe

We now return to the Roman tradition of paschal vespers. This Easter-tide custom became widespread in the West. This peculiar form of pas-chal vespers originated in the liturgical practice of the city of Rome as we have seen, but together with many other ancient Roman practices gradu-ally passed into general use in the Western church. By the ninth century Amalarius of Metz in northern France was describing it as the 'Glorious Office'. It came to be reproduced in local liturgical books, including those of medieval Britain, probably via the ninth-century Romano-German Pontifical.[20] In the Sarum rite in England processions to the font or cross took place at various times in the year. In Easter week the daily procession, following the Roman pattern, was to the font, followed by all processing to the rood, a short liturgical unit being enacted at each place.

Paschaltide vespers thus proves to be one of the great moments of medi-eval Western liturgy, a household name, as it were, now quite forgotten.

Decline

It was not until the end of the Middle Ages that this tradition entered on a long decline. In Rome itself the process started early, partly as a result of a drastic simplification of the daily offices in the papal private chapel for reasons of convenience and practical necessity. Further north in many places it survived much longer. In parts of France and Germany this trad-ition continued to be practised until the nineteenth century, and in some places, such as Nantes in France or Braga in Portugal, was still taking place at the time of Vatican II and perhaps may still be.[21] Finally, the Sec-ond Vatican Council itself produced a reformed breviary whose General Instruction recommends the revival of paschal vespers.[22]

We need to ask why it is that an element of such significance in the history of the Church's daily liturgy, attested to from early times in East and West, could disappear, and despite the fruits of modern scholarly study should still fail to be accorded the importance it deserves. It stands out as a significant action which, whether it involves the cross and/or the font, and whether practised daily, weekly or at significant seasons, brings worshippers face-to-face with the heart of the Christian experience: Christ's death on the cross and his ensuing resurrection, both of them re-presented in the waters of Christian new birth. Why did it ever disappear?

7

Swimming

In the later Middle Ages a sea-change took place in liturgical attitudes – a marked move away from wholehearted embracing of enacted liturgy. In its place came an obsession with *text* as liturgy's primary constituent. Liturgical actions tended to be reduced to what were thought basic essentials, performed by clergy alone while the people of God made do with static observation, their freedom of movement finally eliminated by provision of seats.

The Roman liturgical catastrophe

In the early centuries of the second millennium the papacy saw years of precarious living, often elsewhere than in Rome. A Pope could be absent for decades, residing in one place after another. The papal liturgy lost contact with two vital elements in local liturgy – particular places and particular communities – and gradually lost the accumulated memory and praxis associated with the geography of Rome. Life on the hoof bereft of the community, the gathered People of God, cannot sustain the liturgical drama that should enliven any normal Christian community great or small, and the rites were abbreviated for the needs of this nomadic papacy with disastrous results. Brooks-Leonard, in describing the stripping of the liturgy in late medieval Rome, says 'popular and time-consuming elements were suppressed in favour of a service that required no music, no *schola* [choir], no deacon, no presider, no baptistery, no church, no people . . .'[1] Swathes of the tradition were cut away and discarded. This coincided with emergence of the breviary and the missal, handy books giving basic texts: by their nature minimal. These handbooks for slim liturgy were popularized throughout Europe by the Friars. The fashion was now for a handy book giving all you needed for recitation of the texts of office and low mass; this could not be achieved without drastic pruning of ancient liturgical riches: texts, music, ceremonies, practices, went wholesale into the bin – many ancient traditions were abandoned, lost for ever, and among them the processions to font and cross. It is difficult for us to appreciate the nature of the loss. It was not simply of texts and practices: we are talking of a whole mindset that had been second nature to the People of God, an unselfconscious way of participating in worship with physical freedom and ecclesial unity that was consolidated and set forth in the early Christian basilica, in a strong context of liturgical geography. It all survived longer elsewhere in Europe, but the influence of this skeletal Roman liturgy was so great that eventually the rot spread universally, if not quite everywhere.

'Externals'

The first difference to notice in this medieval revolution was a change in attitudes towards 'externals'. The new worship books (especially the newly invented breviary and missal) led to an assumption, fully developed by the time of the Reformation, that worship could be divided into 'essential' elements, especially texts and human speech, and others that were optional, such as music, roles, and many actions and ceremonies. Early Christian worship had shown no sign of such a division: worship is one whole, engaging all our faculties and abilities. By the eve of the Reformation, however, any liturgical actions that continued to be seen as important tended in an instrumental direction: blessings, the elevation, certain sacramentals such as holy water, popular beliefs about statues, and so on, and these were prime targets for the Reformers' wrath.

Shrinkage of symbols

When symbols come to be seen as 'externals', that is, as belonging to the surface rather than the essence of the gospel life, then people lose motivation to devote the best of their energies to them. Because of human weakness symbols anyway have an innate tendency to shrink. If contact is lost with their significance, a common fruit of our laziness, then we start to adapt them to our convenience. Examples abound in the world's religions. The sensational rending-apart of garments in anguish at disaster and death can be seen today in Judaism in the form of men present producing tiny scissors to snip their shirt. In the Christian eucharist the corporal was a large tablecloth thrown over the bare altar by deacons at the point in the eucharist where bread and wine were prepared. We have encountered it already in the eighth-century document known as *Ordo Romanus I*. The cloth was gradually reduced to the size of a handkerchief for convenience' sake, and then irrationally had to have under it a large

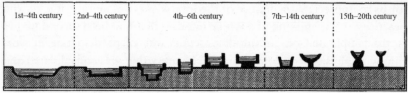

| 1st–4th century | 2nd–4th century | 4th–6th century | 7th–14th century | 15th–20th century |

Fonts rise out of the ground and contain less and less water

The changing fortunes of the font

linen cloth covering the top of the altar. Shrinkage often brings imaginative reinterpretations, so it came to be thought that those gifts that were
to be consecrated had to be on the handkerchief ('corporal'). In order to
recover this symbol the handkerchief needs to go in the bin, together with
the altar's linen cloth, both to be replaced by a large tablecloth thrown
over the altar at the preparation of the gifts. The process of symbol-
shrinking can sometimes be charted visually. The French scholar F. M.
Buhler has produced a diagram showing gradual shrinkage of the font
from river and bath to tiny bowl, as submersion in the life-giving waters
was sanitized into the sprinkling of a few drops.[2]

When we cease to see the essence of symbols we trim them for convenience, and upon our diminished understanding there then follows a
deeper diminishment of the symbol's ability to speak.

Carolingian distortions

At the time of Charlemagne we see several things happening at once:
there is an enriching of the liturgy with introduction of many new ceremonies; on the other hand there comes a stripping-down of the mass
liturgy to enable low masses to proliferate. Such celebrations show a
chronic shrinking of symbols: roles shrank down to one priest with assistant, movement and use of liturgical space and focus-points shrank to
one spot, audibility went almost entirely, music totally disappeared; the
theology of the eucharist shrank almost entirely to categories of presence
(moment of) and sacrifice. Many major symbols such as the eucharistic
prayer were gradually corrupted, their original significance either forgotten or overlaid with new interpretation.

Legal and instrumental attitudes

One reason that symbols could be undermined and the view of the liturgy as the action of the people of God lost to sight came from distorted

attitudes to God. We have seen that God became more transcendent, fickle and touchy, a stern judge, difficult to be on good terms with. The relationship to him reflected society, feudal and fear-ridden. God required due service, and his worship inevitably was now approached in a more utilitarian and contractual way. The main preoccupation was to do what was required, with an anxious eye to fulfilling those particular requirements thought to be the necessary minimum. So people came to ask what was absolutely necessary for the performance of a sacrament for it to be valid. Instead of asking, 'what is the most we can do that the worship may be the best we can offer?' Christians stood everything on its head and asked, 'what is the least we need do to ensure God is satisfied and that the sacraments work?' It is as if in giving Christmas presents to our children we were to ask, 'what is the least I can give that will satisfy the need to have given a present?' rather than, 'what is the best I can give that they may really enjoy themselves?' The latter attitude is the principle of overflow, gratuitous giving of the best we can summon up in us to give, the other an attitude of calculation and self-preoccupation.

An irreversible sea-change

In the later Middle Ages Christian worship in the West became like a household whose furniture has been moved to another house by a delivery firm: much was lost or damaged on the way, while of the stuff surviving much is in the wrong place, in a household that no longer coheres. Ritual riches of the liturgy were still aplenty, but often wrongly placed, either in the hands of the clergy, to be watched by ordinary folk from a distance, or squeezed out of the liturgy into extra-liturgical practices of an increasingly dramatic, not to say sensational, nature. As the centuries passed the medieval Church's worship lost some key elements of drama characteristic of the old Christian basilicas (such as the vocal participation of the throng) and became increasingly theatrical in a way that no longer gave true liturgical drama. Meanwhile, the clergy, now possessed of a complete monopoly on the central action, had gained a wonderful freedom to explore short cuts. If the heart has gone out of a thing, what incentive can there be to keep it in vigour? We see the creeping practice of replacing liturgical singing of daily offices with simple private recitation of the texts by individual priests: no more question of fonts or crosses here. The stage was set for the further reductions of the Reformation and Enlightenment. In the first thousand years, and in the Eastern churches until today, we find nothing on a similar scale. If a procession to a particular place is prescribed then it happens, irrespective of numbers. All of the liturgy's mosaic of contents is equally important. Worship that centres on text on the other hand is like a telephone conversation, the language of body and face edited out, leaving the participants with a more unsatisfactory, fumbling encounter.

Wholeness

We should not underestimate the depth of the catastrophe. It constitutes nothing less than a loss of core constituents of Christian worship. More than the degradation of symbols, more than the growth of legalistic and minimalistic attitudes, the disenfranchising of the People of God, or the loss of a sense of liturgy as the people's action: more than all these was a fatal crippling that came as a deeper consequence of all of them, the crippling of a reality that is not easy to describe. This reality is seen in a whole people worshipping with the whole of themselves in communion with one another and with God. It could be called the ability to take your feet off the bottom and swim in worship: it is a freedom to move in free relation with others, and even when stationary to be grouped together as a community, clergy and people together; it is about place and alternating focal points, about muscular engagement through posture, handling with our fingers interesting things before our eyes, energetic singing in respon-sory forms, perhaps jostling and apologizing for it, squeezing through a crowd, enduring hard work, sitting under something larger than us. It is about being unselfconscious, uncalculating, and perhaps above all simply aware of being at home, with all the givenness and taken-for-granted nature that the word 'home' can imply. The liturgical action is an unself-conscious language enunciated with the whole of ourselves, together with those with whom we belong. It is an awareness not simply stirring into action when we go to church – it is part of us, simply our life as Chris-tians, a mental framework we have largely lost but can know at certain moments (such as processing to the grave at a funeral or going a bit mad at the paschal vigil in the night of Easter – a kind of Christian Last Night of the Proms).

The Reformation

The Reformation happened too soon. Knowledge of ancient liturgies was not around much yet: the sixteenth-century reformers acted on their instincts and in the dark. A hundred years later knowledge began to improve, and would have given a better chance to the baby of staying in when the bathwater went out. If medieval worship was full of symbols and practices that had lost contact with their origins and become apparently 'empty', the Reformation's pruning of the tree of worship simply pressed this to its conclusion in a wholesale abandonment of symbols good and bad, now introducing a new consideration: a radical questioning of the very nature of symbol as it had been known in immemorial Christian tradition. Liturgy became words (largely a monologue by one person with added hymn singing), with two sacraments of Baptism and Lord's Supper often standing out rather awkwardly in contrast. The brilliant part of the reformers' work was a return to the Christ of the New Testament and the original freshness in particular of the crucifixion and resurrection in relation to our salvation. One of the greatest achievements of the Reformation was christological – an authentic return to the source and fountain, through the scriptures. However, it is an isolated Christ they found: the whole Christ is Jesus with his people, known in the context of the culture he shared with his followers and in their eucharistic communion. The Reformation's individualism was its Achilles' heel – a lack of a full sense of the Church expressed in a panoply of inherited memories and practices inherent to its genetic code, including worship that is integral, whole-persons worship, something the Middle Ages dimmed or distorted, but the Reformers drastically reduced or lost (in modern times things are now changing). Processions to fonts did not of course survive the reform, although research needs to be done on local forms of Lutheranism where they may have survived for a while.

Interestingly, there were lasting side-benefits to these false trails which mirror what we have already seen of Carolingian religion: there arises in particular a heightened awareness of the moral demands of the gospel and a new sense of the individual responsibility of mature human beings, which was to make a lasting contribution to the modern world.

The Counter-Reformation

Although the Roman Catholic Church retained a strong understanding of symbol, in practice there were similarities with Protestantism. The march of minimalism continued: chancel screens went, and with them disappeared all manner of ceremonies, many of them with a strong local flavour, and not ceremonies alone, but a whole liturgical spirit, except in some cathedrals, shrines and other such places. More and more the Sunday mass for Catholic laity in their parish church consisted of individual praying while the priest quietly got on with his own things at the altar. The greatest extreme was reached in Ireland and the USA. As a result of British persecution in Ireland mass tended to be stripped down to the simplest minimum, devoid of music or action, something that has survived into modern times; the Irish church was influential in the spread of Roman Catholicism in the USA, and so that approach to mass went there with it. Even in Italy, a major Catholic country that has always enjoyed its own Catholic freedom, there are parishes that make use of servers and assistant clergy in the principal mass on Sundays, but there is little movement, sense of drama, or imaginative use of the building, while the normal fare in most parishes is a one-man mass with lay folk coming up, often without preparation, to read a lesson and lead printed-out intercessions. Most of such practice is a surviving inheritance of the counter-reform that was simply responding in kind to the Reformation and deeply ingrained with medieval habits.

Practical religion

The Lutheran World Federation in 1993 set up a research project into worship and culture which included investigating the relation of ordinary people to the practice of their religion. The findings of a survey among devout Lutherans in a small town in southern Brazil are illuminating.[3] In their main Sunday service, which was the eucharist, the report comments that what is important and influences them is less what is said, and much more what is done. The people are typically extrovert in their responses: even an act of worship that the report sees as so ritually poor as is the service of the Prussian heritage, ends up having meaning and an impact on people much more by the sparse action it possesses or that the people attribute to it. The theorizings of the pastor in his sermons (more typical of the introvert) are difficult to relate to. As a rule, for the congregation religion is not something to be theorized but experienced: religion is lived, not theorized. The physical attributes of the church are immensely important. People mention a motley array in descending order: cross, altar, pulpit, Bible, pews, font, red carpet, organ, light fittings, flowers. Other things that contribute in a special way to creating the unique environment of worship are candles, altar decorations, space, cleanliness, tranquillity, friendship, bells.

There is a constant thread of inconsistency in what people say that is typical of the ordinary faithful Christian. It may reflect an inability to analyse clearly, but also an unselfconscious capacity for holding realities in a paradoxical tension, opening up dimensions of richness closed to those who analyse. If the latter is the case, then this helps us see why Christianity needs both extrovert and introvert humanity for its health.

Clerical responsibility

If we examine moments when the liturgy has become more impoverished, the prime movers are so often the clergy. It was the clergy in Rome who complained at the fuss of having font processions. It was clergy who stripped the Roman liturgy of its treasures for their convenience. In the East it was the clergy in Thessalonica who complained at the imaginative, participatory form of the Byzantine liturgy that had its last outpost there after the conquest of Constantinople.[4] It was clergy in England who presided over a Reform that signally failed to hold on to the common people. In Germany the main break came not at the Reformation but at the Enlightenment, when liturgical worship, vestments and other 'externals', came widely to be abandoned. Many ordinary folk could not stomach the changes – according to Herman Wegman the Enlightenment emptied the churches.[5] Among the Lutherans in Transylvania a wonderful survival of old liturgical traditions was subverted by clergy during the Enlightenment, and the result can be seen in the cathedral in Hermannstadt (Sibiu) which had to be divided in half to adapt to reduced numbers.[6] These are all examples of a 'paradigm shift' taking place mostly among the clergy, with hapless laity left at their mercy.

Pores and head

It was Thomas Kuhn[7] who coined the phrase 'paradigm shift' to describe a moment when a common mindset changes: a society shifts from a particular constellation of meanings, values, methodologies, etc., to a new one. People may not recognize the change, or they may deny it, but even the denial will be in terms of the new paradigm.[8] We have been describing such a shift from 'whole-persons worship' to 'worship with your head'. Head worship was to see more than one moment of propagation, first in the Renaissance and Reformation, again a little later in the Enlightenment, and yet again in the twentieth century.

There is one thing to notice in these developments: the people lost a strong participatory experience which the clergy in some ways continued to enjoy. In a Western church today the clergy at the front can have plenty to engage their interest: things to do, see, handle, engage in. They are sitting in the middle of an interesting scene that engages their bodies and senses without intermission. The same can be said of servers and other ministers at the front. The laity meanwhile sit in rows looking, perhaps through a forest of heads, at a distant tableau with little to engage their whole selves in any comparable way. Much of the detail can be lost to them, there is much less immediacy, and the experience easily becomes simply boring. Even what little corporality survives today is now coming under the assault of laziness – the people catch it from the clergy. Often a congregation simply sit through most of a service. That kind of sitting shows a lack of confidence in taking an active part – it expresses sitting back, non-involvement of the body (the part of our humanity that exposes us most). The sitting comes from me, while in real worship my body will be responding to a call from outside me to join in a common bodily activity.

Bodily worship

Simultaneously, however, there are signs of a turn in a different direction, as we rediscover whole-persons living. Ronald Grimes, an American scholar who has specialized in work on the phenomenon of *ritual* has commented that, 'As philosophers of religion and theologians push at the limits of religious language and belief, metaphors that once identified the sacred with height, depth, or inwardness seem to be giving way to ones that allow for a positive evaluation of surfaces, exteriority, and overt action.'[9] An example of the turn to the physical in human relating would be a funeral for a young man in a small town killed outside a night club by an aggressive group of teenagers. The local clergy moved quickly to accompany their pastoral care in the town with a hastily arranged memorial service. The church was packed, many of those present being young people. The first part of the service was fairly straightforward, but after that people were given opportunity to visit various parts of the church where there was something for them to do: light a candle, write a prayer, and so on, while on a large screen pictures of the town were projected, a town suddenly conscious of itself and shocked by what had happened in it. The service in the end lasted several hours, as people stayed in the church to pray or think, stand vacantly, or talk in small groups.

The term 'kinesics' was coined by Ray Birwhistell (1918–94) to cover all communication not conveyed through words. The memorial service for the young man was an example of what could be called 'kinesic communion'. This is a communion among people and God incarnated by every aspect of our being: mental, artistic, emotional, physical, bodily, corporate: being with others in significant space, being free to move and make gestures, and simply to be there together, conscious of the others' presence and, for Christians, conscious of the divine framework and involvement. Birwhistell's 'kinesics' strictly speaking refers to bodily movements and gestures, and would need to be complemented by other terms such as 'proxemics' (the study of space, nearness and distance in the ways people relate), but I use it here as an umbrella epithet to cover the whole range of human corporate communication and being.

A hundred years ago it was assumed that the main business of relating to God was private and inward. Today we are rediscovering the role our bodies and the objective and outward – icons, candles, rituals, recovery of the ancient tradition as in the Holy Week ceremonies – but also a new awareness of the layers beneath such objectivity. The process is complex, for action is not only self-expression – it is also formative of us. The actions, arenas and transactions of worship have a role in forming our inner life. An altar server will often be affected by the serving, and formed in holiness through contact with holy things. Very numinous worship can be full of activity. I remember a solemn mass in Soweto in South Africa with dozens of immaculate servers kneeling as quiet as mice during the intercessions, the whole service reminiscent more of worship before Vatican II than the 1990s, except that all present, from the celebrant to the persons at the back of the church, danced in the gentle African way throughout service; the congregation was given to moments of exuberance too, all mixed up with reverence. At the end all processed out onto the street to continue dancing with the passers-by. In an earlier chapter I have used the word 'vulgarity' in a wide sense of sheer ordinary human pleasantness, humanity, exuberance. Vulgarity in this sense is part of the life-breath of kinesic communion – living with our pores is a fruit of freedom and also an agent of it: freedom to feel at home in our Father's house, to speak with our bodies our natural vulgar tongue. Sometimes we can be unaware of any deep interior dispositions that accompany such action, but that does not matter so much – significant things often happen in our deeper layers without our being aware of them. There are occasions in daily life where the participants are content simply to act, without necessarily needing to reflect or feel anything. There are times when something simply needs to be done and seen to have been done, for us to be at peace. Sometimes kinesic communion can take apparently banal forms, such as a visit to a relative in which little conversation takes place; but it is important for both parties that you have been, shared a cup of tea and a few pleasantries, and then gone your way. Worship often works at that level, and as much by design as by default. Ronald Grimes even talks of 'the epistemological primacy of the body', in which should be included places and spaces, different ways of unreflective proximity, and music, seasons, objects and art-works.

Rediscovering our confidence

While we have suggested that clergy have often been responsible for de-nuding worship of these things, today the roles can sometimes be re-versed, as shepherds may try to encourage their flock to become more 'kinesic', in the teeth of their resistance. The fact is that in the West, in different degrees according to the country and the people, we have lost the art. It needs new ways, as in the memorial service for the young lad, to enable a rediscovery of confidence. Practice often fails because of our stumbling self-consciousness, for kinesic communion only begins to be effective where it comes naturally and is taken for granted, as a mode of being with which we are totally at home, like swimming. Marcel Mauss has written of people who have 'a sense of the adaptation of all their well-coordinated movements to a goal, who are practised, who "know what they are up to"'.[10] Talal Asad illustrates this with the professional pianist, whose '*practised hands* remember and play the music being performed'.[11] Our physical participation in the liturgy has to become as second-nature as that. Mauss goes on to say, 'I think that there are necessarily biological means of entering into "communion with God".'[12] Asad makes a telling observation about embodied practices which form a precondition for re-ligious experience: 'The inability to "enter into communion with God" becomes a function of untaught bodies.'[13] Communion with God needs the participation of our bodies, and that participation needs to be unself-conscious and second-nature; and it needs to be learned, as the pianist practises the piano. Our bodies are untaught, and once they have been taught and have practised, and are engaged in the liturgy, Sarah Coakley suggests that at that point 'the individual "body" has found its place in a divine drama, and can cease from its anxious self-examination'.[14] Once that is happening, mere talk of inward and outward, which in fact dis-torts what we are trying to identify, will have been transcended. There is no division between inner and outer; both are two facets of one reality. For the art historian E. H. Gombrich,

what we mean by expression in human behaviour and particularly hu-man art implies some kind of correspondence between inwardness and outward sign. How often have not religious leaders and reformers de-cried ritual when they found this correspondence wanting . . . In the study of animals I am sure this very distinction would be invalid. Profes-sor Lorenz rightly insists that for the goose the friendship ritual is the friendship. We cannot separate the behaviour and its inwardness, as it were.[15]

Contemporary complaints about lack of reverence in worship come from a real sense of a loss of inner engagement with the divine presence. A call for a more contemplative and reflective approach to the liturgy is not alone the answer, however. As far as the eucharist is concerned, if John Zizioulas is correct, the celebration by its very nature is the place where the church is made manifest, and one of the ways that comes about is by being the place where people from all types and backgrounds worship together, the contemplatives with the active, the cultured with the vulgar, old with young.[16] It therefore has to manifest a little of everything, from contemplation to action.

Swimming around the font

At a time when renewed attention is being paid to the focal place of bap-tism in Christian living there is an increasing practice of placing a full-submersion font in a prominent position in the church building. Many parishes now have catechumenate programmes for baptism and confirm-ation candidates. The two traditions we have uncovered, of a daily observance at the font, and a paschal office there in Eastertide, seem natural candidates for revival both in larger churches such as cathedrals, and in parishes. But that seems out of the question. Few people go to evening services nowadays. Only small groups of Anglicans if any go to daily evensong in their parish church, and such services are usually minimalistic – mere sedentary recitation of texts. Any proposal to revive such a tradition lacks plausibility. Not only do we worship with heads, not pores: in antiquity churches were crowded, and faith could be pas-sionate. There was little to compete with the church, and the excitement of participating in hugger-mugger worship and its attendant processions could be a highlight of the community's week, as churchgoing of any sort continued to be for many until Victorian times. Today we have endless other attractions to fill our time and take up energies: this style of wor-ship is a different proposition altogether. Our bodies, in addition, are not only untaught but ill-equipped: until the nineteenth century people had tough legs fit to take them long distances regularly and work long hours on their feet. They were also more psychologically robust – even though we are capable of shopping for hours, we can flop in church after ten minutes if asked to be without a seat. Even though we are seeing today a new interest in symbol and ceremony, and even though our culture is more favourable to reviving ancient liturgical practices, our church culture has moved so far from one where the congregation is content to be free and mobile, and our desires go so much for peace and having no demands made upon us that the fuss, organization, time and energy needed to perform something like processions to fonts or crosses, with what normally today will be small numbers, can seem simply unrealistic.

For an answer to such objections all we need to do is look at the local gym and the other ways we seek to keep our bodies fit and active. The problem is an indication of the degree to which our horizons are constricted by 'untaught bodies'. Is it possible for us to gain once again a lively frame of mind that treats such practices as normal and matter-of-course, something simply there and given, accepted practices that we give ourselves to? This would require us not to assess them by what we think we may gain from them, but simply to do them because we do them, speaking to us, as they do, with an effortless authority.

Our mental programming runs deep, and to see it better for what it is we now need to give some attention to that marvellous liberty of the human mind people discovered at the time of the Enlightenment. The gradual rediscovery of reason in the Middle Ages was a motor for the Reformation. It took a little longer than that for this rediscovery to play out its forward march, however, bringing a further revolution on both sides of the Reformation divide, in the sea-change of the Age of Reason.

8

The Enlightenment

Once reason had gone out of the window in the early Middle Ages, recovery was slow; but after a slow climb back, beginning in earnest with scholasticism in the thirteenth century, reason began to race ahead, turning eventually into a newly discovered wonder to fill people with delight. This led to a period that could hardly have contrasted more with that of Charlemagne. Roughly between the seventh and the seventeenth centuries there was a gradual but dramatic shift in the outlook of western Europeans: at the beginning of this period the main foundation and central focus of life was God, around whom human life revolved. A thousand years later the situation was being reversed. Without wholly realizing it, human beings were sensing themselves more and more to be at the focus, the vantage-point from which they could attempt to scrutinize God 'over there'. Human beings were developing a strong awareness of personal subjectivity, autonomous persons looking out at the universe from their own standpoint and even at God as an object of study over against them.

The Enlightenment

It is sometimes suggested that the Enlightenment started in Protestant milieux and spread to Roman Catholic countries under their influence. On the contrary, however, it seems clear that it would have come anyway, even without the Reformation. According to Charles Taylor, Protestantism hastened a process already happening in West and Central Europe.[1] In the medieval world the seeds of the Enlightenment were already there in scholasticism and the beginnings of scientific enquiry. By the seventeenth century the progress of human rationality was leading to reason's supremacy. Creation came to be examined like a machine; so-called 'Deism' envisaged a clockwork universe set in motion by a dispassionate God who then withdrew to let it run its beautiful course. People had a new confidence in human capacity to discern the truth. Sin slipped from sight as folk came to assume that, given reasonable conditions of life, human beings had a natural and effortless capacity to be reasonable, good and benevolent.

Roman Catholic worship

There were similar developments on both sides of the Reformation divide. In Roman Catholic areas of eighteenth-century Europe Enlightenment attitudes held sway among the well-educated; they came to determine the mental atmosphere in which governments operated and the Industrial Revolution developed commerce and industry. The old world continued to hold sway, however, in ordinary life and popular attitudes and religious belief. A German book entitled *An Easy and Sure Way to Heaven* (written by a priest) gives an idea of popular piety at the time. If magic is suspected, he recommends a priest bless the place and then sprinkle it with 'Ignatius-water', or 'Three-Kings' water (blessed on St Ignatius' day or the Epiphany) or St John's wine – or 'what is more powerful, a mixture of all three'. Then the first verses of St John's Gospel should be read. If a cow is bewitched, it should be given blessed bread or salt and fumigated daily with the smoke of blest sulphur or palm branches or herbs. This book went through ten editions by 1771.[2]

The atmosphere [in church] . . . was not silent. Men and women moved about, freely, in and out, simple worshippers ejaculated, groaned, rocked to and fro, beat the breast, or prayed their private prayers aloud, sometimes too loud. To the horror of intellectuals who cared about the atmosphere of devotion, bags were passed to collect money . . . Dogs followed masters or mistresses into church and made messes and noises . . . Boys were . . . noisy, lovers inclined to use their eyes, babies were discouraged but still came. In one Italian diocese parents who brought babies under two years old into church were excommunicated. In many towns and villages young men insisted on crowding in the porch to hear mass.

. . . Spitting in church was not uncommon. In Padua diocese they provided that a spittoon should be placed on the steps of the altar, and cleaned eight times in the day. This was partly caused by chewing tobacco, which people took to masticate and others to use as snuff: authority continued to be against all forms of tobacco in church but [only] succeeded in preventing [smoking]. Even celebrating priests could be observed to take snuff; and were not thought irreverent . . . In a crowded city church a man of property needed to beware. Burney, when he visited Italy to study its church music, suffered . . . from pickpockets in church . . . Italian confessors . . . needed to argue whether a thief who stole a handbag from a worshipper who was rapt in prayer committed only the sin of theft or also the sin of sacrilege.

Where the choir gave no musical rendering, the people joined in singing the Nicene creed. This and the Lord's Prayer were the only parts of
the liturgy where in a majority of churches people joined with priests.[3]

It is not difficult to imagine a clash of mentalities between this world and
that of educated people (including the higher clergy). The Age of Reason
brought in another guise the same reaction to 'superstition' as that of
sixteenth-century Reformers, and in consequence we see widespread attempts in Roman Catholic countries to change things. The gap between
mental habits of the educated and illiterate was widening. The eighteenth
century saw the emergence of a world operating on two paradigms, for
the educated and the uneducated. Clergy belonged increasingly to the
former group – the classical education they now received made them see
how badly the medieval Latin texts of the liturgy compared with Horace
and Virgil. Laity, on the other hand, even if uneducated, were nevertheless becoming more capable of participation in worship.

Scholarship

In Germany and France in particular there was from the seventeenth century onwards an impressive advance in theological, historical and liturgical scholarship. The Benedictine Congregation of St-Maur edited and
published a vast amount of ancient and medieval texts for the first time;
Mabillon published such texts as the *Bobbio missal* and the *Ordines Romani*. These opened a door to another world: the world of Christian
worship in the first thousand years, and the liturgy of the early Christian
basilicas. The early basilica began to be seen as a model (Plate 9). Some
came to realize the possibilities for worship were far wider than they had
imagined, and than the sixteenth-century Council of Trent had presup-
posed. Reform was in the air and impossible to avoid.

FRANCE

The most famous instance of liturgical reform in this period was the local
diocesan reforms in France (often perhaps misleadingly called 'Gallican'
or 'Neo-Gallican'). As in England, lower clergy were coming more from
the landed classes; the Church of France had vast numbers of them. A
collegiate church could number its clergy in hundreds. Cathedrals and
collegiate churches had a sophisticated musical life

and, especially at high mass, there was such splendour as has probably never been surpassed in France. There were [also] wrangles, insults, jostling for precedence, to add a note of comic incongruity . . . One contemporary legal treatise says: It is astonishing that men bring their love of distinctions to the very steps of the altars . . . But whatever the intrusive incidents . . . worship was dramatic, its choreography precise and measured, the vestments glittering, the display of gold and silver ornaments and reliquaries opulent.[4]

In Enlightenment France there grew up a unique liturgical partnership between reason and splendour. Picturesque traditions, however, could grate with refined Enlightenment minds, and some pruning went on. At Chartres in 1700,

> the chapter ended the installation of a 'boy bishop' on Holy Innocents' day; in 1765, the release of a pigeon during the liturgy of Pentecost was abandoned – organizing the pigeon-man and keeping him sober had proved difficult, and the fluttering distracted the choirboys . . . In 1784, the reformers suppressed the wearing of wreaths of flowers by the choir during the octave of Corpus Christi . . .[5]

In contrast to other parts of Europe, however, there flourished a love of ceremonies, and an increasing desire to arrive at what was judged a refined balance. The Church reforms of the Council of Trent were embraced energetically, but after a brief period of general use they began to be regarded less enthusiastically – compared with the worship French people were used to, the Tridentine missal was thin. Many ancient local usages were proudly maintained, such as the Rouen rite (related to the English Sarum Use); particularly venerable and unique was the liturgy of Lyon, some of its uses having affinity with Eastern liturgies. Trent had laid down that local liturgies more than 200 years old could remain in use, and this left scope for French dioceses to retain and even develop their traditions.

The social situation

The situation was very complex. Government was absolutist and inefficient, but times were changing, with a growing gap between traditional structures and contemporary life. In the earlier part of this period France was a very religious country where most people went to church, but by the mid-eighteenth century this was in decline: a more secular mentality was growing; it can be seen in the names of merchant ships: from the early sixteenth century to about 1630 the Blessed Virgin Mary and the Saints predominate. By 1686 at Dunquerque they were down to 60 per cent; by 1770, 20 per cent. In *Ex votos* (paintings made in votive thank-offering) there was a gradual transition from pictures of people beseeching the Virgin to those depicting the human struggle at sea. Statistics of illegitimate births in Toulouse tell their own tale: 1675: 1 in 59; 1719: 1 in 17; 1751: 1 in 7; 1788: 1 in 4.[6] Non-churchgoing became widespread and open. Atheism perhaps was rare, but the common abandonment of churchgoing was new. Paris was worst of all. After the mid-century, while in Rouen only a quarter to a half kept their obligation to communion, in the parish of St Sulpice in Paris it was one in ten.[7] Migration and consequent rootlessness seem to have been among the main causes.

> There was a continual stream of migration into the big towns, accelerating from the mid-century. Towards the end of the *ancien régime* 40 per cent of the population of Bayeux and Nancy and 50 per cent of Caen had come from outside . . . In the Faubourg St-Germain in Paris 78 per cent of the men had been born outside the capital.[8]

It seems clear that urban defection from religious practice preceded industrialization as a product of rootlessness rather than unbelief. It is possible to see with hindsight how the way was prepared for revolution, and how hopelessly traditional and corrupt the Church was; but the Church also had good and conscientious people in it, and there was a real desire around for moderate reform of worship. The reforms we are now to examine need to be seen in that light – inadequate to the situation that was brewing, but at the same time full of good things that would presage the renewal we have seen since the mid-twentieth century.

Problems with the liturgy

While there was not much enthusiasm among the French for the reforms of the Council of Trent, there was dissatisfaction with what they had inherited as well. For instance, in the breviary (daily office) many of the biographies of saints to be read on their days were contrary to reason: the account of the beheading of St Denys had him getting up and carrying his head. Educated clergy were uncomfortable with non-scriptural antiphons, crude hymns in poor medieval Latin, and uneven distribution of the psalter caused by constant repetitions of offices for saints' days. The mass came in for as much criticism: provision of readings was not always logical, texts did not relate, people were unable to participate.

Diocesan liturgies

The development of the unitary nation state at the time of the Renaissance had fostered in France an independent pride over against other countries in the political sphere, and a sense of independence in relation to Rome in ecclesiastical affairs. There was talk of 'Gallican liberties'. As early as the fifteenth century a principle had been established that a council is a higher authority than a pope, and that papal bulls could not take effect in France unless signed by king and parliament. Further claims were made by Louis XIV from 1682 onwards. Individual dioceses began to feel they had liberty to carry out liturgical change. Some claimed apostolic foundation, giving them unique authority to do so. Unilateral reforms started to appear, the first in 1678 with the Vienne breviary, quickly followed by a reformed missal. In 1680 came the Paris ('Harlay') breviary, followed by a missal in 1684 (this, especially in its 1738 revision by Archbishop Vintimille, was enormously influential – at least 50 dioceses adopted some form of it). Others followed rapidly, in a process that continued into the nineteenth century, the last new missal appearing in 1845 (Carcassonne). At the height of this phenomenon over 80 dioceses had their own rite, and only 12 followed the official Roman liturgy. In the mass and the daily office this did not affect the basic forms, which remained Roman: it was the variable texts that underwent change, as well as ceremonies and the manner of celebration. More far-reaching changes were to be found, however, in other forms of liturgy such as marriage.

Aims and principles

Some principles emerge repeatedly in these reforms:

- Preference for scriptural texts for antiphons, responsories and the like.
- Care for language and its style.
- Reform of hagiographies (lives of saints).
- Spreading the psalter through the week (without repetitions of Psalm 119 and the compline psalms).
- The importance of Sunday: 'It was not right that the day of Sunday consecrated to the Resurrection of the Son of God, through which he

has emerged, to speak with St Ambrose, from the womb of death, like a rising sun which scatters the shadows and darkness . . . should be obscured by the office of the dead.'[9]

- Participation with understanding (including interesting experiments with periods of silent prayer).[10]
- Liturgical catechesis.
- Moderation of devotion to saints and the blessed sacrament.
- Recovery of old local diocesan usages (that is, much of the material in the Rouen breviary).

The texts in the mass that were affected included the introit, collect, gradual and communion chants, the secret, preface and post-communion. Epistles were also subjected to change, while the Sunday gospels tended to remain Roman.

To illustrate the varieties of approach, Franco Brovelli has compared the missal of Troyes (1736) with that of Poitiers (1767).[11] Both missals take a thematic approach, but in different ways: Troyes bases its Sunday themes on what is common to collect, epistle and gospel. Some texts and prayers are replaced by others fitting the theme, while others remain Roman. The Poitiers missal is more thoroughgoing: the theme is always based on an element in the gospel reading, and is extended to all the variable material, including collect and epistle themselves, so that in most cases little Roman material remains. Troyes on the other hand had some radical rubrics, including: the eucharistic prayer was not to be said silently but only in a quieter voice; the priest was not to repeat silently to himself the public prayers and readings; cross and candlesticks were to be kept off the altar; prayers before communion were suppressed; it was forbidden to give communion outside mass; devotion to the Blessed Virgin Mary and prayer for the Pope were reduced.[12] The bishop, J.-B. Bossuet, had appointed Nicolas Petitpied as kingpin of the commission producing this, and he, a professor at the Sorbonne, had also worked with a notoriously imaginative reformer, Jacques Jubé, in his Parisian parish of Asnières, of which more see below.

The following examples from the Paris missal of 1738[13] illustrate this thematic approach:

EPIPHANY IV

Introit Lord God of hosts, who is like you? You rule the raging of the sea, and still the surging of the waves . . . (Psalm 89.9).

Offertory Let them give thanks to the Lord for his mercy, and the wonders he does for his children . . . (Psalm 107.31).

Gospel The stilling of the storm (Matthew 8).

Postcommunion *May your providence always restore us, we beseech you, O Lord; renew us by your mercy, protect and order our weakness amidst the tempests of this world, and lead us into the eternal harbour of salvation.*

EPIPHANY V

Introit . . . go from me, wicked men (Psalm 119).

Collect *(Roman).*

Gradual (about those who do evil).

Epistle (Colossians 3) Live as the chosen of God, holy . . . bowels of mercy . . . humility, modesty.

Alleluia . . . the meek shall inherit the earth . . . Psalm 37.

Gospel (Matthew 13) The kingdom is like one who sowed seed and enemies sowed weeds among it.

Offertory Defend my cause, O lord, against an ungodly people (Psalm 43).

Secret *Plant in our hearts the good seed of your word, O Lord, and by the power of this sacrifice may it grow to the day of harvest; that we too may be found good grain to be gathered into your barn, through . . .*

Communion Do not count me, O Lord, among the sinners (Psalm 27).

Postcommunion *Grant to your faithful people O Lord, whom you feed and quicken with the food of your word and your heavenly sacraments, so to advance by such good gifts, that at the consummation of all things, they may be separated from the reprobate, and be worthy to be counted among your elect. Through . .*

Pierre Jounel writes:

The bishops, as eighteenth-century men, were more concerned about morals than dogma. The themes proposed were of a moralizing nature: 'On Sundays,' says the Bishop of Le Mans, 'one theme is proposed, which is taken from the day's gospel, and is able to help us observe some particular virtue and to make the corresponding vice flee.' Themes tend to be abstract ideals. In the Poitiers missal of 1767 that of Pentecost 8 is 'fraternal charity and alms', while Pentecost 15 proposes 'spiritual death and resurrection'. The choice of themes tends to be subjective.[14]

1 Typical layout of a fourth-century basilica with clergy bench round the curved apse, the bishop's throne in the centre, canopied altar, chancel barriers, and an ambo in the nave.

2(a) and 2(b) The basilica at Sabratha in Libya. Typical of many North African churches, the altar is placed well down in the nave, while the apse, raised on a flight of steps, seems almost a separate chamber. Here a low wall encloses a large part of the nave: worshippers would be gathered on three sides of the altar in the side-aisles and rear nave. (Author's reconstruction.)

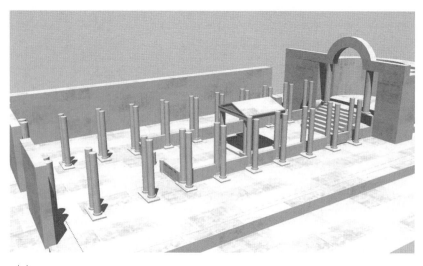

2(a)

2(b)

3(a)–3(c) Fourth-century lamp in the form of a basilica, found in Algeria.

3(a)

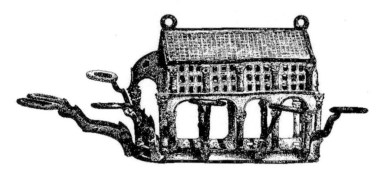

3(b)

3(c) Bishop's throne in apse.

4(a)–4(c) Cross-shape in wall plaster in Herculaneum.

4(a) As found.

4(b) Restored.

4(c) The wall plaster.

5(a)–5(i) Celebration 'Facing the People'. Examples up to the 14th century.

5(a) Melchisedek as an OT type of the Eucharist. Mosaic, San Vitale, Ravenna.

5(b) Mozarabic.

5(c) Drogo Sacramentary, Metz, 9th century.

5(d) Saint Basil celebrates the Divine Liturgy. A miniature from 1429.

5(e) Fresco in San Clemente, Rome, c. 1080.

5(f) St Martin celebrating, Lucca Cathedral facade, 12th century.

5(g) Pontifical Mass, Mainz, 10th century. (The choir is in front, deacons behind.)

5(h) St Mark celebrating the Eucharist. Antependium, St Eufemia, Grado, Italy, 1372.

5(i) Transubstantiation miracle. Fresco, Orvieto cathedral, 14th century.

6 Ambo and paschal candlestick in the 12th-century church of San Clemente a Casauria, Torre de'Passeri, Abruzzo.

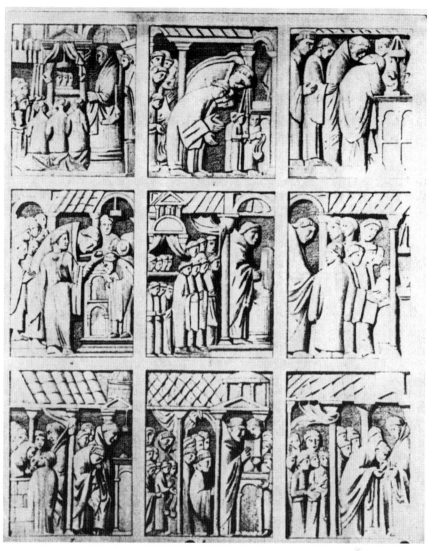

7 Ivory cover of the Drogo Sacramentary. Metz, 9th century. (Artist impression.)

8 Merovingian bishop's throne, Metz Cathedral.

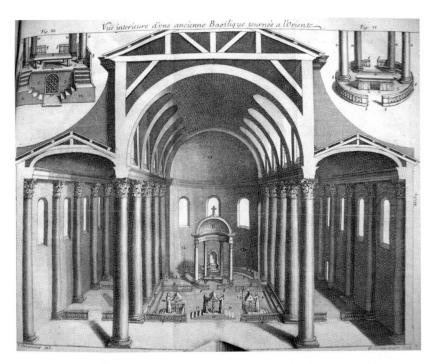

9 An eighteenth-century picture of an early Christian basilica.

10(a) and 10(b) Two pages from F. G. Lee, *Directorium Anglicanum*, London, 1865.

10(a)

The Vestments.

"Myrrha et gutta et cassia a vestimentis tuis, a domibus ebur-
neis: ex quibus delectaverunt te filiæ regum in honore tuo.
"Astitit regina a dextris tuis in vestitu deaurato: circumdata
varietate." Ps. xlv. 9, 10.

HE ordinary dress of all connected with the Church down to
Choristers is (1) the Cassock and (2) Square or College Cap.

The Eucharistic Vestments are (3) the Amice (*Amictum*);
(4) the Alb; (5) the Girdle; (6) the Stole; (7) the Mani-
ple; (8) the Chasuble.

Besides these there are the special vestments for the assistant Ministers of
the Altar, viz. (9) the Dalmatic for the Gospeller; (10) the Tunic for
the Epistoler.

These are also worn together with (11) the Mitre, (12) Gloves, (13)
Sandals, (14) Pastoral Staff, and (15) Ring, by Bishops; and with the
(16) Crozier, and (17) Pall, by Archbishops.

1. To the Daily Office—(18) the Surplice, and the Academical Hood,
or (19) the Tippet (in the case of non-graduates); and Birretta.   (20)
The Amys (*Almutium*) may be worn instead of the Hood or the Tippet.
Choristers and Acolytes wear over their cassocks a cotta or surplice.   (18.)

2. In Processions, and therefore, strictly speaking, at funerals, (21) the
Cope should be worn over the Surplice, and always (22) the Birretta.

---

1. The Cassock,[1] or Priest's Coat, is single breasted, and fastened from the throat to the
feet by numerous buttons, extending the whole length.   At the back the Cassock is very full,
from the loins downwards, and sometimes trails a considerable length on the ground.   It has

[1] A Cassock of black cloth or serge, either single or double breasted, is very suitable for clerics when engaged
in ordinary parochial work.

11 Fr Friedhelm Mennekes celebrating the White Mass in St Peter's, Cologne.

12 Benozzo Gozzoli (*c.*1421–97), Sacred Conversation,
National Gallery.

Their ethical focus was on the individual; there was an incipient sense of the liturgy as based on the communion of the People of God, but these were early days.

The Church of England experimented with themes for the Sundays of the year in the *Alternative Service Book 1980*, and it is interesting to compare those for Sundays after Pentecost with those common in French missals – the strongest contrasting factor is the sense of the Church as the People of God:

French eighteenth century

Love of neighbour
The divine mercy
Growth of the Church
Love of enemies
God providing for our needs
Seduction by false prophets
True wisdom and almsgiving
Recognizing God's goodness with humility
Having lips that will speak only good
The need to give thanks
True riches
Forgiveness
Worthy receiving of communion
Obedience to authorities

Anglican 1980[15]

Judgement
The people of God
The life of the baptized
The Church's mission to the individual
The Church's mission to all men
The new man
The more excellent way
The fruit of the Spirit
The whole armour of God
The mind of Christ
The serving community
The witnessing community

The suffering community
The family
Those in authority
The neighbour
The life of faith
Endurance

Such a comparison reveals the danger of fitting scripture and prayer-texts to prearranged themes, which if we are not careful will force the scripture to fit the presuppositions of the age.

Music

Renewed music was an important part of the reforms, the congregation's singing often accompanied by a serpent (a wooden precursor of bass brass instruments) or the organ. Little by little various elements of the orchestra crept in, till in the end the whole thing was there. Secular music crept in too. Organists excelled in exhibitionist dexterity. In Rouen the whole corpus of plainchant was revised, and accompanied throughout its first year in the cathedral by two serpents – we should not imagine the chanting was often very ethereal; notes tended to be hammered out heavily and mechanically. In parishes of the diocese there are reports of hearty congregational singing of the chant. In many churches in Paris the congregation sang with the choir, but if they failed to keep with the choir a prominent bell was rung, at the sound of which the congregation had to fall silent for a spell.[16]

Many hymns were either rewritten or replaced, and some of these new hymns became popular later in Britain. Two outstanding hymn writers were J.-B. Santeul ('Captains of the saintly band'; 'Disposer supreme') and Charles Coffin ('On Jordan's bank'; 'The advent of our God'; 'O Holy Spirit, Lord of grace, eternal source of love'). In the opinion of Henri Brémond these hymns were traditional, biblical, didactic and popular.[17] But how could ordinary folk join in Latin hymns? Brémond suggests that the Latin, perhaps above all in the hymns of Santeul and Coffin, is so French and Christian that it was not difficult to follow their gist.[18] People found them easy to sing, especially the extremely popular sequences (*proses*), of which many were written. A. F. Ozanam (1813–53) said of the *Stabat Mater* that it was so simple that 'women and children understand of it half through the words, and the other half through the music and the heart'. Chevalier adds, however, that music was the weakest element in the reform.[19] Perhaps there are parallels here with modern reforms and attempts to create new music in a hurry. Two examples from Santeul:[20]

Eighteenth-century French hymn tunes

Many fine metrical tunes have found their way into British hymn books, however, such as those for *The lamb's high banquet we await* and *O blest creator of the light*.[21]

Translation

The idea of celebrating mass in the vernacular was around, but although France had had a Catholic translated Bible since the sixteenth century, the possibility of the vernacular in the liturgy was not widely supported. Abbé Royau warned that 'The Church would be inundated with defective translations and the faithful exposed to dangerous errors in faith and morals.'[22] The struggle between Protestants and Catholics in France was long and painful, and the vernacular was particularly associated with the Reformation.

Even though services remained in Latin, there was talk of reciting aloud some of the prayers and other texts normally recited silently by the priest, and in some places this was done. There was controversy over the rubric in the Troyes missal of 1736 for instance which bid the priest say the canon not silently, but less loudly than the other prayers. Later, in the wake of the French Revolution, some strong calls were made for vernacular services. 'The *cahiers* of 1789 of Paris *extra muros* and of the parish of Fosses (Seine-et-Oise) asked for all the services of the Church to be conducted in French. "Most of the inhabitants cannot read", said the redactor at Fosses; "that means they do not understand the prayers read out in church, so they get bored and gossip as if they were in the street". At this time a curé called Carré published his *Culte publique en langue française* addressed to the new National Assembly; now we have political liberty, he said, let us exercise our right to use our own language – this would be liturgical reform as a demonstration of patriotism.'[23] Nothing, however, was done.

Against this it has to be said that the French Church was streets ahead in providing French texts to its people. Unlike Catholics elsewhere, the French had had the Bible in their own language since the sixteenth century, and from the seventeenth there were translations of the missal for people to follow in church, all of this in the teeth of opposition, often fierce, from Rome itself. McManners says that 'The Gallican church moved into the eighteenth century with a growing class of educated laymen attending its services with intelligent comprehension.'[24] Small books known as *Paroissiens* became a household item, giving all the services in French for people to follow, and providing copious music to sing.[25]

The liturgical arrangement of the church building

Progressive publication of historic liturgical documents, especially from the seventeenth century, enabled the first stirrings of liturgical scholarship. The true form and function of the eucharistic prayer were beginning to be appreciated (as among Anglicans too in Britain), and that revealing guide to ancient liturgy, the layout of early church buildings, was making some scholars ask new questions about original liturgical forms. Some talked of westward celebration.

The most famous among liturgical pioneers of the seventeenth century was Jacques Jubé, parish priest of Asnières, at that period a small place near Paris on the west bank of the Seine. Jubé became famous, notorious even, for his innovations. Among other things he:

- Affirmed the public and collective character of the mass.
- Never used the high altar in his church except on Sundays and feast-days.
- Restored the old Roman usage (which had endured longer in France than in Rome itself) of placing the linen cloth on the altar only just

before mass, and of having no other cross or lights on the altar than the processional cross and tapers, which were set in place at the beginning of mass.

- Began mass by saying the psalm *Judica* and the *Confiteor* along with the people.
- Sat down on the epistle side of the altar and listened to the epistle and the gospel as they were sung by the assistant ministers, after having sung the collect himself (normal practice was for the priest to say these silently to himself without attending to the public reading).
- Sang the Kyrie, Gloria and Credo along with the people, instead of saying them in a low voice by himself.
- Restored the offertory procession (which had never entirely disappeared from French churches).
- Had offerings of all kinds made in this procession which he later blessed at the *Per quam haec omnia* at the end of the canon, according to original practice.
- Never began the canon before the Sanctus had been sung in full.
- Said the canon loudly enough to be heard by the whole congregation.

'In other words, he wanted once more to make the readings, the singing, the prayers, the offertory real, rather than merely conventional acts; he wanted to have the . . . full . . . participation of the Christian people.'[26]

Opposition

The changes were not without opposition. On the eve of the Revolution someone commented: 'Our bishops are veritable weathercocks. They seem to count all the ancient tradition for nothing and flatter themselves they will start new traditions dating from the mid-eighteenth century.'[27]

The new rites were accused of being tainted with Jansenism. Jansenism was a response to the laxity and compromise of the times. It could almost be called a Roman Catholic equivalent of Calvinism. It was austere, demanding and moralistic. It gained a strong following, but also fierce opposition. It is true that some Jansenist sympathizers had a part in the writing of new liturgical texts, but no one has ever succeeded in showing any trace of theological bias in this direction.[28]

Not surprisingly, Rome was not happy. There were protests and attempts to dissuade the French from going their own way. Correspondence between Paris and Rome to do with the 1736 Paris breviary reveals the machinations going on. The phenomenon should not, however, be seen as anti-Roman: the French remained totally committed to the papacy – they simply saw themselves as exercising legitimate freedoms within the framework of the Roman Catholic Church.[29]

Support

There was also praise and gratitude for the new liturgies. The services were much richer than their Tridentine equivalents, thematically worked out and theologically more profound and wide-ranging, with a rich recovery of the treasures of the calendar. They tended to draw on a wide range of sources ancient and modern. The 1781 *Missal of the St Vanne Congregation*, for instance, included texts from the Gelasian, Leonine and Gregorian Sacramentaries, the Ambrosian, Gallican and Mozarabic liturgies, and even Eastern liturgies.

There was a strong pastoral drive. Brooks-Leonard says of the 1744 marriage rite of Coutances that

the increase of details in rubrics, directives for audible recitation, and the preface-form of the nuptial blessing reflect a concern for the didactic and participatory nature of the liturgy and a desire to have the ceremonies performed correctly and with dignity . . . Rubrics for silent prayer before and after the betrothal rite . . . and correction of texts reflect the scholarship of the age in its recovery of ancient forms, an increase in the use of scripture, and a concern for the interior involvement of priest and people in the ceremonies as they are performed . . . All of the changes in the marriage rite can be seen to reflect this new emphasis on the couple and God.[30]

The desire for good teaching and to attract people to the scriptures can be seen in the effort devoted to producing thematic Sunday eucharists. Often, as in the reforms in Rouen, there was a desire that ordinary people should be able to participate and understand what they were participating in.

Disappearance

It is not possible to make simple judgements on these reforms as some authors do. The state of the French Church in the eighteenth century was a complex mixture of an overblown, overweight and corrupt tradition in its autumn, together with widespread vigour and conscientiousness in encouraging the Christian laity to live their lives and worship with intelligence and commitment. Bishops on the whole genuinely desired a better-informed and better-ordered Church, and were concerned about quality, not to say good taste in worship. But they were also gratified to see their grand coats of arms and long-winded titles appearing on the title pages of their diocesan liturgical books. They tended to be spoilt and corrupt, obsessed with precedence and privileges. Although seminaries did not get off the ground until towards the end of the eighteenth century, a better-educated clergy were tending to be more conscientious in their duties. Reasons behind the reforms are bewilderingly varied: an abbess could take a bishop to court for trying to introduce the unfamiliar Tridentine liturgy; clergy were exercised by the need to win over Protestants; Jansenists could press for a reasonable and pure religion; a famous reformed missal such as that of Paris could be taken up in another diocese because the books were available and cheap; a king could want to bolster the independence of France, and so on. The good, the bad and the questionable are all mixed up together in the multitudinous boiling pot of the culture of an old and sophisticated nation.

The quality of much of the liturgical work produced was so impressive, however, as to be drawn upon widely in the Vatican II reforms. The story marks a key moment in the development of worship in the West, and even though its works were destined to pass out of use, it stands as a significant waymarker on the path of European cultural and religious development, foreshadowing in an almost uncanny way many issues that were to emerge again in the twentieth century.

The French liturgical experiment lasted almost exactly 200 years. From the 1830s onwards Prosper Guéranger spearheaded a campaign for abolition. The first diocese to return to the Roman rite was Langres in 1839, and the last Orleans in 1876 – a story told in the next chapter.

GERMANY

Enlightenment liturgical reforms were not confined to France. In German-speaking countries they were just as widespread, but of quite a different character. R. W. Franklin has produced some surprising reading for anyone who has a different picture of Counter-Reformation Catholicism.[31] There was widespread opposition among clergy, intellectuals and politicians to popular devotions, processions, pilgrimages, shrines and the like. In some places, especially in Austria-Hungary, there was closure of monasteries. To plunge us in the deep end, it is difficult to believe that views such as the following could commonly be found in the Roman Catholic Church in Central Europe (the page numbers refer to Franklin):

- Worship is service of our neighbour carried out with a careful eye on God. (174)
- The rosary is taken over from Lamaism, and absolutely contradictory to the spirit and teaching of Jesus. (207)
- In Patristic times no Christians called upon the saints or built churches and altars in their honour. (214)
- Veneration of Jesus' fleshly heart is to be fully rejected. (216)
- Brotherhoods, indulgences, novenas, processions, veneration of relics, etc., are abuses of Christianity, and all lead only to superstition with little edification. (225, 226)
- The physical consumption of bread and wine at the Lord's table can not alone quicken a spirit and be food for eternal life, without that which our understanding thinks and our heart experiences there. (244)
- A form of liturgy is justified when it clearly shows the truths and duties of religion and leads to a corresponding transformation of life. (268)
- There was a time when public worship was seen as giving due service to the deity . . . now, rather, its first aim is as a religious exercise giving ethical enlightenment to the understanding. (192, 193)
- Teach ethics from the pulpit! Let the paintings on the walls of our churches proclaim ethical teaching! – ethical teaching the statues on the altars – ethical teaching the ceremonies and usages in the holy place of the mass and in the distribution of other mysteries! (191)
- To pray is the most noble duty of every person, but only insofar as it serves to make our earthly occupations lighter, more pleasant and more blessed. (262)

These views come from a variety of authors in the Catholic German-speaking Enlightenment of the eighteenth and nineteenth centuries. They are from its fanatical wing, but numerous enough, and one has to ask what kind of a state Catholic worship could have been in to produce extreme views of this kind. The picture painted at the beginning of this chapter in fact was so pervasive as to fill enlightened minds with exasperation. A populace given to mechanical and superstitious practices was in need of strong therapy, and thinking people of the time, whether as extreme as those represented above or more moderate, tended to emphasize the functional and moral nature of worship, and the need to relate it to reason. New faith in the human capacity for reason in fact tended towards a religion more human-centred than God-centred.

The Aufklärung

The German term for the Enlightenment is *Aufklärung,* and where Catholicism in German-speaking countries was influenced by the Enlightenment it is commonly referred to as *Aufklärung Catholicism.* While in France the reforms were carried through by bishops in their dioceses, in German-speaking countries they were often pushed through by the state or offered to the public by individual private enterprise in adventurous publications.[32]

Characteristics of Aufklärung Catholicism

The Aufklärung was didactic and moralistic. Peter Conrad in Trier said that a *Vesperandacht* (evening devotion) should replace Latin vespers on Sunday: it was to consist of church hymns and Bible reading. The readings should encourage 'obedience to the authorities', and 'encourage people, parents and children, gentry and servants, husbands and wives, to fulfil the duties of their class, to earn their daily bread through diligence and manual work, and to live honestly', with simple needs, patience in suffering, and active in charity towards the needy. In other words, the Bible texts should give useful teaching 'about the manifold duties of Christians'.[33] There were many experiments in reform of the daily offices: the story of the German breviaries, simplified breviaries, devotional services, vespers in German, or mere catechism to replace vespers, has already been told in my book *Company of Voices.*[34]

At its extreme Aufklärung Catholicism seemed to advocate abandoning the very notion of worship. Priority was given to understanding. There was a desire to foster community (in the sense of a desire for the liturgy to be communal and participatory) but in essence this approach shows an individualistic understanding of human improvement. It aimed at moral instruction and motivation. One remarkable feature was its ecumenism: it promoted tolerance towards all, including Protestants (but not, apparently, those people who continued to support traditional Catholic practices).[35]

The mass

There was opposition to private masses (this proved problematic, as in some places daily celebration for a priest would become impossible without the possibility of solitary celebration). According to Benedikt Peuger (early nineteenth century), 'A mass should never be celebrated in which at least several of the faithful do not communicate along with the priest.'[36] Some spoke in favour of frequent, even weekly communion, and communion in both kinds. Mass was unofficially celebrated in the vernacular in some places, though usually not the whole rite. In some dioceses the readings and some other elements were obliged to be in German. Unlike their French counterparts, however, the Germans produced no reformed missals.

Here are some reform regulations for Sunday high mass in eighteenth-century Trier:

- No masses can be celebrated at side altars at the same time as the high mass.
- There can be only one high mass, and no masses are allowed in subsidiary churches and chapels.
- People should not go off to other churches for their festivals – church dedication festivals have to be held on the same one day throughout the diocese.
- In towns, monastic houses must not open the doors of their churches until the morning services in the parishes are over.

The reformer Peter Conrad ruled that:

- Mass should start at 9am with *Asperges*.
- The celebration should be accompanied by congregational singing of German songs (this never worked: at the most the choir sang them).[37]
- Baptism and extreme unction were performed in German.

Music

German church song was encouraged, including the use of Protestant hymns. Newly written hymns tended to reflect moralistic attitudes found also in France. Subjects of hymns could include, for example:

- Reading the Bible with understanding.
- Love for virtue.

- Growth in virtue.
- Knowledge of oneself.
- Overcoming faults in charity.
- Avoiding pious pride.

One hymn by Christian Weisse began: 'What does it help me to be a Christian / If I do not live like a Christian?'[38] Sentiments of a kind to appear again in hymn-texts of the twentieth century.

The example of Wessenberg

In a very varied picture, it will help to concentrate our attention on one example. We will take one of the most famous, not to say notorious, proponents of Aufklärung Catholicism, Ignaz Heinrich von Wessenberg (1774–1860), who was made vicar general of Constance diocese in 1802, ordained priest in 1812, and in the teeth of Roman opposition remained diocesan administrator until 1827.[39]

The vernacular

Wessenberg was cautious in his radicality. While promoting widespread use of German in the liturgy he never supported wholesale performance of the mass in German. He supported the singing of German hymns and proper texts of the mass, an Aufklärung practice that was widespread and popular, and has survived until today. (One can be surprised today to find oneself at mass in Germany singing a hymn instead of the Gloria, Sanctus or Agnus for instance.) He insisted on public celebration of vespers in German on Sunday, another tradition that has survived until today. The pastoral offices, baptisms and the like found in the book known as the *ritual*, all tended to be done into German and adapted in the process. Under Wessenberg the diocese produced a rite for baptizing children of Protestant parents, a rite for mixed marriages including both ministers (even that fruit of Vatican II is nothing new!), and obligatory German forms for the Ash Wednesday and Corpus Christi processions. Germanization went ahead gradually, but only after he had been finally ousted from his post did he publish his *Ritual*, which became tremendously popular and influential. In it he aimed 'to lift the spirit and the heart of those present to God and to make an advantageous and effective impression on their feelings which would lead to the improvement and sanctification of their lives'.[40]

Good celebration

Wessenberg was concerned, like many liturgists today, about the good celebration of the liturgy. 'What the liturgical leader can never impress too
deeply on his soul is this: the effect of liturgical ceremonies, forms and
words is very much limited by the dignity, vitality and propriety of the
personal conduct of the liturgical leader . . . The holy must be handled in
a holy manner! Then it will also arouse holy sentiments.'[41] Trapp says of
its texts that they are 'worked out with particular love . . . In general the
Ritual contained many things of great beauty and value . . . Wessenberg's
Ritual is one of the richest of the Aufklärung.'[42] Wessenberg was a poet
and wrote many hymns. Among prizes he set up for authors, one was
for a book on 'what means are most to be recommended to the pastor to
overcome the mechanical spirit and luke-warmness of his congregation at
religious services, especially in the hearing of holy Mass?'[43] It was common
for a sermon to be preached before mass, but that meant many people
would turn up after it. Wessenberg was one of many who gave directions
that the gospel reading was to be read out in German after its proclamation
in Latin, and then the priest was to preach on it. A great emphasis was put
on preaching and teaching. He and other Aufklärung clergy were particularly keen there should be teaching on the Bible. He strove to eliminate the
practice of giving communion only after the mass was ended, encouraging
people to make their communion within the eucharist itself.

The breviary

It is not surprising that supporters of the Aufklärung had problems with
the breviary. It is hard to see how Enlightenment minds could have
thought otherwise of such a voluminous compost-heap of texts of all
sorts with a heavy quota of psalmody designed for monastic life not the
parish, not to mention the element of the weird and outlandish. Many
reformers proposed it be replaced by study of the Bible, and that that
should be the only obligation on clergy. However, there were successful
attempts at reforming the breviary, especially the daily office produced
by Thaddäus-Anton Dereser, a book whose use Wessenberg supported.
This is an old story repeated in many countries. In the sixteenth century
the simplified breviary of Cardinal Quiñones was used by Catholic clergy
throughout Europe for many years before it was sidelined. The success
of the Anglican reform of the daily office speaks for itself. Even a trad-
itionalist prince-bishop of Würzburg used a reformed German daily office himself and allowed his clergy to do the same.[44]

Popular religion

Wessenberg, again typically of the Aufklärung, was very concerned about the decadent state of popular piety. The rich panoply of practices that folk loved to indulge in was closer to secular folklore than living the gospel, riddled with superstition and greater faith in nonessentials than in central verities: processions of saints, elaborate dressing of statues, all kinds of strange local practices, delightful in themselves, but causing people to lose sight of the straight message of Christ and its moral implications. As reformers often do, the Aufklärung activists tended to go too far in their attacks on all this, just as traditionalists who eventually ousted them went too far in the other direction. In 1809 Wessenberg issued regulations forbidding celebrations at pilgrimage sites unless presided over by a priest and forbidding the sale of pilgrimage booklets or the leaving of votive pictures and items. On Mary he wrote, 'The life of the Blessed Virgin Mary cannot always be preached upon because the Holy Scriptures do not give us a detailed account of the life of Mary, but rather only a few fragments.'[45]

How did it all go down?

When he was eventually forced to leave his post, Wessenberg wrote to his clergy:

> Beloved brothers, colleagues, and friends in the Lord! When I review with calm earnestness the twenty-five years during which it was given to me to provide leadership for your struggles and efforts, it gives me a great deal of inner joy to be able publicly to bear an honourable witness to you that the condition of pastoral care has within that period of time improved itself immensely in many regards. The public veneration of God has received a more worthy form, a greater seriousness and order, [particularly through] the spread of a general song and devotion book ... the preaching of the Divine Word has been brought into closer relationship again to the holy sacrifice of the Mass, as was the original intention and order of the Church.
>
> [The parish act of worship as the common bond has been promoted and thus] has the worthy celebration of the Sundays and Holy Days essentially improved ... By means of Vesper devotions in the vernacular, congregational church prayers, litanies and hymns, by the reading aloud of appropriate portions of the Scripture during afternoon devotions and prayer hours and processions, the soul-killing mechanical spirit has been confronted and the spirit and heart have been raised up in inner, joyful

and edifying adoration . . . The salutary reception of the Sacraments of Penance and the Eucharist has been effectively fostered by appropriate liturgical celebrations . . . This is particularly so in the case of the celebration of the Eucharist for children [nothing new again!] . . . Likewise in the administration of the other holy Sacraments the understanding and power of edification of the ecclesiastical rites and ceremonies has received a certain happy increase . . . because they were administered with appropriate German instructions, prayers and hymns . . . Live up to your high calling . . . do everything for the sake of the Gospel, hold fast and unshakably onto that costly treasure, the Faith delivered to the Church which has been entrusted to you! Listen to and love accordingly the Church, as loyal, teachable children who with the greatest certitude walk with their hands in that of their loving mother![46]

Deep-felt expressions of gratitude and affection came from clergy of almost all the Chapters throughout the diocese.[47] More widely, a similar response is found to most local Aufklärung projects for liturgical reform; they were on the whole highly regarded by large numbers of clergy and laity. The vast majority of Aufklärung Catholics were moderate reformers; that is, they wished to reform the Roman Catholic Church and emphatically rejected any idea of breaking with it. When in the mid-1840s a small group of left-wing Catholics broke away to form what was known as 'German Catholicism', they were for the most part rejected by Aufklärung Catholics, with Wessenberg in the forefront of the rejection.[48]

The backlash

Wessenberg had been supported by his bishop and the local government. Rome did not have the power to remove him, but managed to scotch every attempt to have him ordained a bishop. Furthermore, with the passage of time clergy of a traditional stamp were gradually placed in key positions, and the diocese of Constance was gradually broken up and divided among the neighbouring dioceses, plus a newly created diocese of Freiburg, depriving Wessenberg of his base. In 1827 the States of Baden agreed to his final removal.

From the 1830s onwards most of the Enlightenment's innovations were swept away in a conservative backlash. The French Revolution and Napoleon's conquests and revolutions throughout the century produced a Catholic panic. The Aufklärung ended up expunged and vilified, down to the present day.

Reality on the ground

The Aufklärung in German-speaking areas had a good crack of the whip but never got all it wanted. The German diocese of Trier gives us a good example of the mixed outcome of reformers' efforts. Trier resisted longer than most places in Germany the pressure to abandon its eighteenth-century liturgies and return to the Roman rite – it did not finally complete the replacement of all its liturgical books until as late as 1894, under a bishop who was still in office in 1921. Here is a description of a typical 'Enlightenment' parish mass in the mid-nineteenth century:

> Holy water was blessed and the congregation sprinkled. In Eastertide the Paschal Candle and decorated Easter Cross were carried in a very popular procession around the church. Left and right of the altar a dozen or so singers were arranged in choirstalls: on behalf of the congregation they made the responses and sang all those parts of the mass that originally belonged to the congregation, while the people mostly looked and listened, except for singing hymns at various points. German hymns were gradually introduced at this time (their fortunes in Trier varied with different bishops) for example after the words of consecration or as a paraphrase while the priest said the Creed. After the Creed the priest removed his chasuble and ascended the pulpit. After introductory words and the sign of the cross he gave out the theme of the sermon together with the text on which he was to preach. He invited the congregation either in a hymn or a Lord's Prayer and Hail Mary, to pray for a fruitful hearing of the Word of God. He then read the Gospel in German and preached for about half an hour. Then came notices followed by a general intercession composed by St Peter Canisius and provided in diocesan books. Each week one family by turns brought bread that was blessed at the offertory and distributed at the end of the service. On the four great festivals and local feasts, and at weddings and funerals, there was an offertory procession. This could on certain occasions include the things of ordinary life: dried meat, wool, flax, wax, eggs, honey, corn, chickens, sheep, 'Saint Anthony's piglets'. This usually only started as the priest began the Preface! During the moment of consecration the comings and goings [but not the clucks and grunts] were interrupted. The collected money was placed on the epistle side of the altar. All of this was accompanied by singing of hymns and chants of the mass. Texts were provided for people to pray during the eucharistic prayer and the communion, or they prayed

the rosary. After the blessing and dismissal the faithful collected their blessed bread on the way out.[49]

Is this a rationalist affair, or is it something you would expect to find in the Middle Ages? It straddles the divide, an illustration of the mix that could result from a struggle between intellectuals and embedded popular tradition.

ITALY

In those times of unofficial rationalist reform not even Italy was exempt, and indeed the most famous and radical reform programme of them all originated in the Grand Duchy of Tuscany.

The synod of Pistoia (1786)

The synod held in the Tuscan town of Pistoia in 1786 produced a document that heralded the most radical reform programme of any part of the Catholic Church in Europe in the eighteenth century. Its decrees covered all of church life and worship, among which the following:

The liturgy is a common action of priest and people.
The priest is to say mass audibly.
The missal is to be reformed – the liturgy should have a more simple form.
It should be in the language of the people.
People should be encouraged to communicate each time they attend mass, and at the proper point in the service.
Any priest who discourages this is guilty of sin.
Communion should be from elements consecrated at the same mass.
Mass stipends are abolished.
There is to be only one altar in the church.
No flowers or relics should be on the altar.
Bible-reading is encouraged.
Certain French books on scripture are to be made available.
There is to be a reduction in the number of feasts, processions, novenas, etc.
There is to be a new, reformed breviary, and people are to be encouraged to attend the offices.
Catechumens and children born in the period from Maundy Thursday to Holy Saturday are to be kept for the solemn baptism of the Easter ceremonies (or for the baptism at Pentecost).[50]

This reform came to nothing: its proposals were too radical for it to be cred-ible for long, and its major proponents had eventually to flee the Grand Duchy.

ENGLAND

There was a parallel phenomenon across the Channel which has been called English Gallicanism. It centred around some of the old Catholic families of the country. On the one hand it was suspicious of Italian forms of catholicism, and on the other had a practical and missionary concern that resulted, for instance, in vespers in some places being per-formed in the English of the Book of Common Prayer.[51]

On the Anglican side, the liturgical projects of the eighteenth-century Nonjurors reflected a maturing awareness of ancient liturgies resulting from the availability of ancient texts.[52]

Conclusions

There is a noticeable difference between Enlightenment reforms in France and those in German-speaking countries. In France various aspects of it sometimes work together, sometimes not. One is an educated, patri-cian desire to update (so medieval churches could be turned into classical temples); another is a valuing of medieval traditions as signs of French uniqueness; a third is the passion of some aristocratic prelates to pa-rade their grandeur; last but not least was a frequent pastoral and so-cial concern to enable people to enter more into worship. Some local reforms were strong on one, some on another. A measure of pruning had been needed; at the pastoral level the fruits for people's participation in worship seem to have been considerable, not only for laity but also the spiritual lives of clergy; new riches were added to the storehouse of liturgical texts; and a new awareness of liturgy as such and its history and monuments was fostered. The eighteenth-century reforms brought to bear necessary insights from contemporary culture and life, with many positive results. Particularly in German-speaking lands there was a new resistance to accepting things simply on grounds of unquestioned tradi-tion or prescriptions of authority. There was a new, potentially healthy, hermeneutic of suspicion. According to Rowan Williams,

What the European Enlightenment revolted against was precisely the sense of having your identity and capacity prescribed by a this-worldly

Other that claimed other-worldly sanction, claimed a kind of identity with the disinterested perspective of God. Enlightenment protested against what seemed the *arbitrariness* of the mediators of the sacred; and it sought to deliver human beings from the slavery of being defined unilaterally by the religious Other *made concrete* in the institutions and conventions of (supposedly) revealed faith. It is one thing to say that we find our identity in relation to or in transparency to an Other outside the systems of need and desire; something else to find that your identity is prescribed . . . by the . . . gaze of an Other who is in fact as historical and contingent as you are.[53]

This critique of some forms of religious authority is as needed today as ever it was.

At the same time some aspects of these reforms prompt questions. The confrontation between reason and popular piety was a conflict between highbrow and lowbrow. Highbrow holds the reins and wants to force lowbrow to become like itself. The cleft between savants and ordinary practitioners has been there a long time – in different forms in the Middle Ages, the Renaissance and the Enlightenment. It can partly turn on taste; in the eighteenth century 'good taste', *le bon goût,* held an effortless predominance but did not reach far into low life.

Cultures grow like plants, and can be damaged when disturbed. Counter-Reformation popular piety – devotions of various sorts like the rosary, attachment to particular places, statues, the making of processions and pilgrimages, all manner of other weird and wonderful practices and beliefs – had flourished on such a scale partly as a compensation for people's exclusion from participation in the liturgy. Had the liturgy been less elitist people would have been better able to express their religious faith, and have it fed and formed, within the liturgy. But it was not, and so ways of praying had to develop outside it. However unfortunate the often garish flowering of popular piety was, the patrimony that grew up was a real culture, of a type that cannot be replaced overnight by another culture. Cultural revolutions engineered from the top can simply alienate the common people by depriving them of the familiar and dragooning them to embrace the alien – the Trier example shows how great their powers of resistance could be.

Among educated people the 'common sense' of the time was a powerful driving force. Some were determined that the cerebral and ethical should have absolute ascendancy over physical practices and the mystical dimension. This mentality was fiercely human-centred, very confident in humanity's ability to put its house in order through its own unaided powers. The age had received a special gift, a new measure of healthy mental clarity at a time when the Church's grip on the principles of its life was less confident, riddled with bad practice and contradictions; so the Church of the time was a sitting duck, and hunters endowed with skills but unaware of their limitations gladly took potshots. It is easy to imagine mocking conversations in the chancelleries of Middle Europe where folk confident in their rightness bolstered each other over a glass of wine in what to them was absolutely clear common sense – folk traditions should be abolished, monasteries closed, worship made more reasonable. Blind to the manifold levels of human perceiving and communication, they strove to replace unreflective tradition with what was self-evidently reasonable.

Few would deny the centrality of reason to our modern understanding of the human person. The problems start when reason enthrones itself oblivious to other dimensions that must be its necessary companions. The doctrine of the Trinity for example cannot be grasped through reason alone: faith, logic, doubt, emotion, loves, intuition, tradition, have to make their contribution and then stand back as we let the Trinity breathe, as we let the music play. Accepted 'common sense' always has its limitations and needs careful discernment. The limitations in due course came out. Reason's admirable quest for human freedom and dignity was in the end shown up to be yet another path to manipulation and slavery, with some claiming the right to tell others what to do. Rowan Williams again: 'as the Enlightenment itself collapses under the weight of its own aspirations, it too is seen as potentially a discourse of slavery . . . the construction of a normative, rational subject over against sensibility, barbarity, the foreign and the physical'.[54] The efforts of the German Aufklärung in particular underestimated the place of ritual and praxis in our human makeup, and the genetic 'culture of Jesus' which has more elements to it than the purely rational: it includes the mystical nature of the Church and our capacity for immediate communication with God within that Mystery, as opposed to the mediate dimension of reason. But they also missed something else, something that fatally undermines the sovereign claims of the Enlightenment.

Something Promethean in the human cupboard

The Enlightenment marks the coming of age of the conscious mind. It celebrates, revels in, our *consciousness*, investing in it nothing less than everything. It assumes all of our mental activity to be *conscious*, and that we can come to understand all that moves within us simply by inspecting inside ourselves. It was Freud who visited upon all this a *coup de grâce* with his discovery of the unconscious. If bitter experience has been one thing that put reason in its place, Freud was another. We are now aware that almost all of our mental activity is unconscious: inside our head is a vast internal world from which only the tiniest amounts leak to the surface: a random selection of unconscious life surfaces to the conscious mind, each time taking about a thirtieth of a second to do so. According to Michael Gazzaniga our conscious mind is always the last to know! Our unconscious has already done the work.[55] Nor do these things come through just to the conscious mind – we have many levels of relative consciousness, and tiny amounts from our vast unconscious world are all the time seeping out at every level of our many-layered makeup – in intuitions, in uneasy feelings, in our response to the arts, in unrecognized influences on our judgements. Traffic goes in the other direction too – the unconscious takes in through all our cracks the teeming multitude of experiences, perceptions, encounters, that make up our life of every day. Once inside, they start doing things we cannot see.

The fruits of this discovery have been immense, in healing, in human self-knowledge, and in understanding of life. One thing this new knowledge about the unconscious does is to take reason down a peg or two; but it is also a flashback to the early medieval world of Charlemagne's time, to the primeval, the world of archetypes. It is powerful stuff, and in the early decades of the nineteenth century it burst upon the late world of the Enlightenment like a volcano blowing its lid.

9

The Movements of 1833

The year 1833 was amazing. On 11 July Prosper Guéranger in France began a monastic revival at Solesmes, setting in train a Church reform movement in France. Only three days later on 14 July John Keble preached his assize sermon in Oxford, thereby launching the Oxford Movement which was to transform the Church of England. Another eight weeks, and in September 1833 a row broke out in Germany over a book by Johann Möhler entitled *Symbolik,* 'Symbolism', launching a similar movement in the Roman Catholic Church in Germany. Something was astir in the entrails of the Church of old Europe, transcending denominational boundaries.

ENGLAND

The eighteenth century saw gradual change in the Church of England's orderly, pious quiescence as it became increasingly decadent, while the world around it underwent unheard-of transformations. The industrial revolution and Enlightenment were rapidly producing a new world. By the early nineteenth century a transformed world-view was surging forward with unbounded confidence. An old world of rural peace and landed gentry operating hand-in-hand with a sleepy and fairly ineffective Church now found itself under brutal assault from a new paradigm: Enlightenment rationalism, property, efficiency, profit, the rational common sense of the ruling class. Paternalism in employment was replaced by transactional relations, the power of the state was growing, individualism, break-up of community, and a new rootlessness for masses of people displaced from the countryside into newly fledged industries meant that old values were disappearing fast. Jane Austen's novels reflect mournfully on these changes.

The Church of England felt threatened and demoralized: 'the decades which followed the close of the Napoleonic wars were a period of great unsettlement and alarm. There was an intense consciousness of a rapid movement forward in every department of human activity, not only in speculation and learning, but also – perhaps more frightening – in technology

141

and in the ability of man to conquer nature and thereby to increase the material comforts of life. This was a generation of men who were living through the greatest industrial revolution hitherto experienced in the history of the world, who had witnessed the most terrifying political cataclysm in France, and who saw all around them the signs of intellectual ferment, the cracking of the very fabric of society, a new and purposeful *onslaught* on hallowed institutions . . . Expressions of fear and hope, often curiously intermingled, were common to reformer and reactionary. All were fired by a sense of urgency. Something must be done *now,* or else the opportunity will be irretrievably lost. Tomorrow may be too late . . . "The world is gone mad", James Stephen wrote to his wife in the early 1830s. "It is useless to enquire what is to happen, but it is difficult not to apprehend . . . formidable calamity on the earth" . . . The sense of impending catastrophe may be felt in the writings and sermons of churchmen of every party during this time . . . [Newman composed his] "Lead, kindly light, *amid the encircling gloom."* The mood expressed is precisely that of the Evangelical H. F. Lyte's famous hymn "Abide with me" (written in the next decade), with the mournful note of "*Change and decay in all around I see*".[1] Dr Arnold wrote, "The Church of England as it now stands no human power can save."[2]

This sets the scene for Keble's sermon.

Keble

John Keble, high churchman and country priest, was already known as author of a best-seller, *The Christian Year* (1827), which brought a moderate touch of Romantic sensibility to the old high-and-dry Anglican tradition. As he ascended the pulpit steps to preach his assize sermon, the government was putting before parliament a proposal to abolish some obscure Irish bishoprics. The sermon was on national apostasy. The nation was departing from the faith. The Church was a pawn in the stratagems of industrialists and scheming politicians. The Church is not a department of state, but the presence in this land of a great and holy mystery. It is God's Church, not parliament's. It is Catholic, extending beyond the bounds of this little island to encompass the Body of Christ on earth and in heaven. It is apostolic, built on the foundation of the apostles, of whom the bishops are the descendants.

The tinder was ready for the spark, and up it went. The rest is familiar – Tracts for the Times – Tractarianism – 'Ritualism' – an almighty battle set to last over a hundred years. It left the Church of England transformed in every field, from doctrine to clerical dress, from pastoral work to liturgy. Out went three-decker pulpits and humble tables; in came marble and alabaster altars. Some enthusiasts showed the excitement you might have for a new toy: curious productions like Lee's *Directorium Anglicanum*, with their elaborate prescriptions for performing and beautifying the liturgy, have the air of playing at doctors and nurses (Plate 10). Changes started happening in the liturgy that did not constitute a reform in the usual sense, happening as they were from the bottom up.[3]

The incarnation

The doctrine of the incarnation played a central role in the approach of followers of the Oxford Movement. They contrasted the elitism of gentry and establishment with the humility of Christ, who emptied himself to take the form of a servant, siding with the poor and outcast. There evolved a peculiarly Anglican theology of the incarnation that drew a connection between humble self-emptying service, practical help to the needy, and a sacramental understanding of worship which emphasized its external, physical practices and traditions. This inspired a line of dedicated priests who spent their lives at the service of deprived areas of industrial cities, combining a social gospel with beautiful and lavish worship. This social gospel drew its inspiration initially from E. B. Pusey, further developed by the Lux Mundi school and the writings of F. D. Maurice, Charles Gore and others, and on to Willliam Temple.[4]

There was a strong romantic side to the transformation they brought. The attempt to recover the Church of the Middle Ages, wantonly brought to an end at the Reformation, was a part of wider romantic stirrings epitomized in much Victorian art or the writings of Sir Walter Scott. These verses from his 'The Lay of the Last Minstrel' give a taste of the attraction of Gothic mystery.

> ix
> By a steel-clenched postern door,
> They enter'd now the chancel tall;
> The darken'd roof rose high aloof
> On pillars lofty and light and small:
> . . .
>
> The corbels were carved grotesque and grim;
> And the pillars, with cluster'd shafts so trim,
> . . .

x
Full many a scutcheon and banner riven,
Shook to the cold night-wind of heaven,
Around the screened altar's pale;
And there the dying lamps did burn,
Before thy low and lonely urn,
O gallant chief of Otterburne!
. . .

xi
The moon on the east oriel shone
Through slender shafts of shapely stone,
By foliaged tracery combined;[5]

The Oxford Movement stressed the holiness of the Church as a divine society in contrast to what they saw as the Church of England's subjection
to the state. Their interest in worship led to a flourishing of scholarship
that made the Church of England world-famous for liturgical studies in
the nineteenth century. All shades of churchmanship were affected by the
transformation of church interiors and the worship going on in them. A
famous example was Leeds Parish Church (founded by E. B. Pusey), a
centre of innovations some of which in time became characteristic of the
later Liturgical Movement.[6]

Some of the earliest signs of the international Liturgical Movement
actually appeared in the Church of England. In the eighteenth century
scholars were already becoming aware of the ancient liturgies and their
principles,[7] and those dissident Anglicans known as Nonjurors even began to put that into effect in new liturgies based on those of the early
Christian basilicas. Eighteenth-century architects began to take the primitive basilica as a model, and even that Anglican curiosity the three-decker
pulpit, which was almost universal in churches until the nineteenth century, was seen as taking up the ancient tradition of the ambo.[8] Until the
Oxford Movement changed it all, this 'ambo' was the focus for the daily
divine offices, and for the liturgy of the word of the eucharist, after which
the congregation migrated through the chancel screen (which survived
the Reformation – new screens were even introduced where they were
lacking) to gather crowded in the chancel for the liturgy of the eucharist.
Among the fruits of the Oxford Movement which swept this away was a
restoration in many places of high mass (usually non-communicating) as
the main Sunday service, but with the major difference of being in English and fully participatory, the Ordinary and other texts being sung and

said together by all. This was closer than anything any other church had so far produced to the basilica model.

The other unique contribution of Anglicanism was a movement for a participatory eucharist with general communion suitable for all ages, and held at a time when most could come. The 'Parish Communion Movement' started early, the first example of its type appearing around 1890. It was to have enormous success into our own day.[9] The Anglican picture as a whole had surprising similarities to the contemporary situation in France.

FRANCE

France had once been a very religious country where most of the population went to church, but by the mid-eighteenth century religious practice was beginning to decline as we have already seen.[10]

The 1830s

Between the 1790s and the 1830s the Church in France had passed through a series of great woes, including revolution, Napoleon, counter-revolution and a right-wing reaction. It had plummeted from a privileged place in society's fabric to a humiliating one of defensive marginalization. The weaknesses in Enlightenment Gallicanism were exposed, but there was also courageous witness to the faith from many clergy who had been formed by it – large numbers of them were carried off to the *pontons* (hulks), where their diocesan breviaries helped sustain them through appalling experiences. A large part of the Gallican Church, however, compromised with the Revolution and with Napoleon – so-called 'Constitutional' clergy swore an oath to the Napoleonic regime.

The Revolution strengthened some of the worst aspects of rationalism: after 1789, French governments, like their German neighbours, favoured a policy of suppressing popular liturgy; the Organic Articles of Napoleon severely restricted the number of public processions; the only feasts that could be celebrated publicly on weekdays were Christmas, Ascension Day and All Saints; people were forbidden to leave work to attend weekday services; commemoration of all apostles was restricted to the Sunday nearest St Peter and Paul's day; martyrs to St Stephen's day.[11] There was now confrontation between a militantly secular society and a persecuted Church. Rationalism was everywhere in the parishes, and in the country at large widespread indifference and opposition.

A good rationalist parish

Franklin gives a description of what might be thought a good rationalist parish near Paris. The priest, Dufriche Desgenettes, had attempted to meet the needs of his people with rationalistic methods. On Sundays there were three sermons, in Advent and Lent a series of lectures. To increase the level of religious education he began an association for propagation of good books. However, he failed to revive his parish church by these means. At the Revolution of 1830 he was expelled – he had no support from the people. The parish records show that less than a quarter of the population came to communion even once a year.[12]

There was liturgical chaos in French dioceses after Napoleon. Most had their own liturgy, but Napoleon redrew the boundaries to coincide with civil boundaries, thereby creating many dioceses with more than one liturgy. In the diocese of Nevers, for instance, 30 parishes used the Nevers rite, 183 that of Paris, 45 that of Auxerre, 18 Autun, and 6 the Tridentine Roman liturgy.[13] It was not easy to make this situation uniform – to the difficulty of changing people's habits was added the expense of replacing books. In France as in England the problems were demoralizing. There were worried questions: could the Church survive? Was its situation not hopeless?[14]

Guéranger

Into this scene stepped Prosper Guéranger (1805–75). He had served as a priest in the rationalist parish just described and had been repelled by it. As if on the rebound he developed a passionate interest in monasticism, which after 1792 had ceased to exist in France. Guéranger talked of reviving it. In the teeth of fierce opposition he bought some medieval priory buildings at Solesmes, and there on 11 July 1833 monastic life began again on French soil.

There are interesting parallels with the English situation. Here too in France monasteries were seen as things of the past, places of superstition and fanaticism. Earlier on, Guéranger had cooperated with Lamennais in working for a renewal of society through the Church. The founding of Solesmes marked a new phase, when his interest turned more to scholarship and the quest for sanctity. Guéranger's friend Lamennais 'objected that in this Order there was to be the choir; and I answered that it was precisely that which made me choose it and that my associates had the same attraction'.[15] Guéranger thought to revive ancient monasticism, but his was a strange version of it, imitating a high-blown late medieval form with romantic additions. Solesmes was to be dedicated to scholarly study and editing ancient manuscripts, which bore plentiful fruit in a great series of scholarly editions, especially the series *Gallia Christiana*. Solesmes also grew into a major centre for revival of Gregorian chant. Guéranger's aims were strikingly similar to those of the Oxford Movement, including:

- Renewal of society through the Church.
- Restoration of a sense of community lost in recent history.
- The Church as not simply a community but a divine society. While the rationalist view of the Church was static – an instrument in human hands – the traditional view was dynamic – the Church will always escape human attempts to tame it.
- The Church's freedom from the state. (Here Guéranger differed not only from current secular governments, but from the *ancien régime* as well.) We can understand Keble's plea in nineteenth-century Britain that the Church should not be governed by the state, but it may surprise us to see the same battle fought in continental Europe by Roman Catholics.
- The liturgy was the way to renewal. The liturgy stands at the heart of the Church's life. The debilitating effects of liturgical plurality and confusion made Guéranger realize the liturgy's central importance.
- Participation and understanding for all classes. The Church of the past had been in the hands of gentry and the ruling elite. There was a gulf between these people's Christianity and the piety of common people. After the Revolution the division continued, except that now clergy were often more united with their people by common suffering. The new desire was for a Church for all people, and this meant a move, conscious or unconscious, in the direction of the religious world of the common people. Popular piety and devotional practices began to be taken more seriously.
- The importance of the arts of the Church and the revival of plainsong. The Enlightenment was not a period strong on religious art: now the senses were to have their birthright restored in the *visual*, the *musical* and the *aesthetic*.
- Incarnation – again as in England the incarnation was central. Guéranger later wrote of the effect on him of reading Philippe Gerbet's *Considérations*:

My eyes [were] opened on a great number of points. The mystical sense had been awakened, the narrow tendencies of false criticism had disappeared. My intelligence was awaiting a signal . . . It was the liturgy which gave me this signal . . . I envisaged the doctrine of the *incarnation* as the centre to which I had to relate everything, and [I envisaged] the doctrine of the church as enclosed in that of the incarnation. The sacraments, the sacramentals, the poetry of the prayers and of the acts of the liturgy, all this seemed to be more and more radiant.[16]

- Holiness – the quest for a holy life was pursued through prayer and worship but also through asceticism, self-denial, and an ideal of sacrifice that contrasted dramatically with the sober and reasonable temper of the eighteenth century. For the Enlightenment the world was to be improved using God's gift of reason. For the ecclesiastical revolutionaries of the nineteenth century that was an impossible ideal – it failed to recognize our continuing human depravity (let any in doubt look to the excesses of the French Revolution). We cannot reason our way to God – the way to God is found in the quest for holiness, and only that quest can give the Church life.
- Liturgical teaching – 'Next after our faith, the thing which unites us all into one family is the church's liturgy'; it can solidify people torn by economic stratification; the laity need to be taught about the feasts, ceremonies, even rubrics, to attend to the whole of the liturgy, attend the daily office, join in the psalms and hymns. Guéranger regularly used the verb 'uniting' for coming together to worship, presupposing by that a purposeful corporate involvement.[17]

Renewal of parishes

Parishes renewed under Guéranger's influence stood out. The battle for renewal of worship in the parish included that for people's equality before God – as in Britain it meant among other things a battle against pew rents. An inkling of the fruits comes from a story about World War I. The line of the trenches ran constantly through the eastern part of the diocese of Troyes: priests attached to the ambulance corps discovered a remarkable village in the valley of the Vanne, not many kilometres west of Troyes. It had been observed that it was the rule in the churches of the district that men did not attend services, and the sacraments were abandoned except by small groups of pious old women during Holy Week and Easter, but at Mesnil-St.-Loup the offices were frequented on Sundays and feast days by the entire population, who sang the Gregorian settings and received communion together as one body. It was rumoured that this had been the state of religion for 65 years.[18]

An extremist campaign

Guéranger was an extremist. He spared no one whose opinion differed from his own. For example, he wrote in his *Institutions Liturgiques*:

About 1725, [the priest] Francois-Nicolas Vigier ... took it upon himself to compose a breviary following the latest ideas ... This obscure person was to be the instrument of the greatest liturgical revolution the French Church had seen since the 8th century. He gave birth to the breviary of Paris ... Fr Vigier belonged to a body deeply gangrened by Jansenist heresy ... [On the hymn-writer Charles Coffin]: We acknowledge his great merit as a hymn-writer ... and it is all the more sad therefore to show how far he went in prostituting it. Coffin ... was a notorious heretic.[19]

The vitriol knew no bounds – all-out war, ranting and raving without restraint. Guéranger was not interested in compromise: the neo-Gallican liturgies must be expunged root and branch, utterly cast out. The ancient rite of Rome (as he saw it) was the only possible rite for Catholics to use, and the Church of France in its weakened and demoralized state could not long resist this vigorous, fanatical and confident campaigning.[20] So in 1848 the Bishop of Carcassonne, seeking to bring some order to the confusion of his people, 'enforced the forms of prayer of the centre of the Christian world'; the Bishop of Tarbes in 1849 established 'the ancient, universal, unchangeable Roman rite' as a means to arrest a chaotic situation over which he was losing control.[21] There were tremendous battles in some places; in Paris the diocesan rite was seen as a national treasure, and only finally abandoned in 1873. Orléans was the last to go in 1875.[22] There were massive rows with Solesmes' local bishop (Le Mans).

Gradually the reformed liturgies of the dioceses of France all passed into oblivion. The loss was tremendous: away went beautifully constructed and balanced breviaries with splendid hymns and biblical riches; clergy found themselves now reciting a tangled and repetitive hotch-potch with no evident rationale; back came St Denys carrying his head, and other medieval tales for the credulous.

Beginnings of the Liturgical Movement

Guéranger thought that by promoting historical study of the liturgy Christians would come to embrace wholeheartedly the ancient Roman liturgy as a wonderful deposit of tradition. In the long term this backfired. Scholarly study revealed more about liturgical history than Guéranger had bargained for, a process that led in due course to the liturgical reforms of the Second Vatican Council – the doings of that body would have caused Guéranger an apoplexy had he lived to see it. His unintended contribution to the emergence of the Liturgical Movement was enormous. Even he himself came to see that the Middle Ages provided an inadequate model for worship, and began to take the pre-medieval liturgy of the time of Gregory the Great as the perfect model, the liturgy of the time of *Ordo Romanus I.*

There are those who say Guéranger and his supporters were elitist and out of touch, and that the real impetus for reform came from elsewhere, especially the *Centre de Pastorale Liturgique* of the Dominicans.[23] 'Guéranger's passion was to glorify the old (that is, medieval) Roman liturgy and to suppress whatever was in conflict with it. In a short while the neo-Gallican renewal was radically uprooted . . . Guéranger was a papal *Zouave* for the defence of the Roman liturgy! His restoration of the Roman Liturgy did indeed do harm and for a long time blocked its development'.[24] After 1848 he became increasingly conservative and obscurantist. So Lord Acton came to the opinion on Guéranger that he was 'the most outspoken adversary against modern knowledge'.[25]

Contacts

Given their shared interests and sympathies, it is not surprising to find there was contact between Guéranger and the Oxford Movement. When Solesmes was in dire straits Guéranger sent Pitra to England. The Roman Catholics refused to help, but Anglicans had no problem. Pitra was given the use of Lambeth Palace library.

Cardinal Pitra . . . [a great scholar and editor of texts] . . . went to England in 1844 . . . he was shown the curious liturgical books of the new Anglican school and the works of Pusey. . . . Pitra [was taken] to a 'Puseyite dinner' at Oakeley's house, and . . . visited [various Tractarians] . . . in London . . . The visits and contacts between Solesmes and Oxford, before the many Anglican conversions to Roman Catholicism

in 1845, moulded English ritualism in a model set by the Benedictines
. . . The nurturing influence of relations between the English and
French churches continued to be important to Pusey throughout his
career. Other links with France prepared Pusey for his conversion to
ritualism and had an impact on the elucidation of his spirituality and
ecclesiology.[26]

Guéranger himself turned to people of the Oxford Movement for financial help, manuscripts and moral support. In France, both sides in the
battle claimed Anglican approval: Guéranger said the Tractarians ad-
mired the Roman breviary; Henri Brémond on the other hand pointed
out that the neo-Gallican hymns of the Paris breviary had been so ad-
mired by Anglicans as to have been published in English translation in
1839, that Newman used the Paris breviary and that Isaac Willams had
set about translating the hymns of Santeul and Coffin.[27]

The similarities between the French and English (Anglican) situations
are fascinating, but the differences equally so. The same is true in a different way yet again for Catholicism in Germany.

GERMANY

In the early part of his life Guéranger had moved in more liberal circles.
The same can be said of Johann Adam Möhler (1796–1838). Möhler
grew up in the Roman Catholic Church in Württemberg. His bishop
sent him to study under the famous Protestant scholar Friedrich Schleiermacher in Berlin. The Church of the Enlightenment in German-speaking
countries often had good contacts with Protestantism. The Archbishop
of Salzburg regularly sent students to study under the philosopher Kant.[28]
In this way Möhler went to Berlin to study under Schleiermacher, from
whom he picked up a notion that German Protestant Romantics were
beginning to talk about: a sense of the Church.

Another of the teachers in Berlin was Johann Neander (1789–1850).
Pusey studied under him and became his friend. Neander's teaching led
Möhler to a renewed vision of the Church as a divine society, a mystical
body. For Neander:

A great disaster had occurred. The *Aufklärung* had turned the faith into
a natural and rational ideology. Equally dangerous had been the Evangelical development of the German pietists who eschewed the material

aspects of Christianity. The classical view had been that the Church conveyed divine power to humankind through material means. The central theme of the thousands of pages Neander wrote is the incarnation, God joining matter and spirit and the human and the divine through Jesus Christ.[29]

This vision of the Holy Church Catholic that Protestants were feeling drawn to came to reinforce in the Catholic Möhler a reaction against Enlightenment Catholicism. Möhler wrote in 1827 that the Church was in danger of disappearing. 'Christians were, for the first time in 1500 years, living in a continent of unbelief and materialism without spirit. This soulless situation was most advanced in England where an overemphasis on machines and factories was crowding out the world of the spirit. Möhler wrote an article in which he described England as a desolate place where factories were being built during a time of feverish economic activity, but not churches.' The existing parochial machinery was not able to provide for 'the Christian needs of the new English towns, although the bishops were rich. The challenge to Christianity in England is shown to have implications for all of Europe.'[30]

Paradoxically, having learned these things from Protestants, Möhler ended by producing in 1832 a book showing why Catholicism was right and Protestants wrong. It was entitled *Symbolik*, or 'Symbolism'.[31] He looked at Lutheranism, Calvinism and Zwinglianism, but also Methodism and other smaller movements. (Amazingly, given his earlier comments, he ignored the Church of England.) He shows in this book why all of these are wanting in comparison with the Catholic Church:

[In Protestantism] The sacraments [are] now no longer used as channels of grace which *convey* an internal sanctifying power and *proffer* it to man; their effects [are] necessarily confined to the subjective acts of the individual at the moment of reception . . . Hereby, therefore . . . the objective character of these means of grace . . . [is] of necessity rejected; and everything drawn down into the subjective.[32]

[The Church is] the visible community of believers, founded by Christ; by means of an enduring apostleship, established by him, and appointed to conduct all nations in the course of the ages back to God[;] the works wrought by him during his earthly life . . . are . . . continued [in the Church] to the end of the world. Thus to a *visible society* . . . is this . . . . mysterious work entrusted. The ultimate reason of the visibility of the Church is to be found in the *incarnation* of the Divine Word. Had that Word descended into the hearts of men, without taking the form of a servant, and . . . without appearing in a corporeal shape, then only an *internal*, invisible church would have been established. But since the Word became *flesh*, it expressed itself in an outward, perceptible, and human manner . . . so Christ established a community.[33]

The definition of the Church as the continuation of the incarnation is found in Pusey's writings too. While Möhler might appear to be un-ecumenical and conservative in his statements in *Symbolik*, we need to be careful how we place him. He was a scholar: he knew his church history. Therefore his message took the form not of a return to the *ancien régime* but to Christian antiquity. Franklin is able to say of him that he was 'the first Roman Catholic theologian for a thousand years to argue that the ground of the Church was not the clergy or the state, but the communal life of all believers.'[34]

Opposition

In 1833, in September, Möhler came under fierce attack from Protestants for the polemical tone of his *Symbolik*. He was also attacked by Aufklärung Catholics, but he was no Guéranger – he led no campaign against the eighteenth-century liturgies. In German-speaking lands restoration of the Roman rite went ahead without a figurehead. Enlightenment clerics were gradually removed through fair means and foul, under strong and sustained insistence from Rome.

After years of revolution, destruction and uncertainty, the cry now became, 'back to authority, the Faith, and the Tradition'. The liturgical reformers were all heretics, the only thing that counted was what had been before them, what was established by authority, what the letter of the law required.[35]

All of this was going on but Möhler does not fit with it. He represents a combination of some ideals of the Catholic Restoration Movement and other ideals gained from scholarly study. In one way he was an Enlightenment Catholic: he wanted use of vernacular and restoration of the chalice, and believed in the priesthood of the people and the vision of a communal Church that went with it. Möhler's theology was taken out to the parishes by his students. It bore the seeds of future renewal and the Liturgical Movement, in building up the parish as a community fit to face modern industrial society[36] – and parishes under Möhler's influence thrived.

Stirrings within a world culture

A new culture emerged in the West as a result of the Enlightenment and the Industrial Revolution. It brought social upheaval, economic revolution and clear agendas. Human history has repeatedly been battered by people's agendas – agendas lived out with total conviction, ignoring life's deeper complexity. These agendas drive people to a point where the spirit rebels, giving birth then to an oversimple counter-agenda. Across Europe in this period establishments came under fire from new political agendas, as well as artistic and religious ones. In religious, artistic and political revolts of the time we see a quest for recovery of community, a new fascination with tradition and history, and a yearning for the mysterious and intuitive in reaction against purely practical and utilitarian reason.

Our three movements had a deeply romantic agenda, seeking a religion of the heart to balance the head. The liturgy was like a work of art. Guéranger believed the beauty of ritual, as well as the verbal content, had the power to awaken the religious sense, for 'the splendour of the services, and the magnificence of the chants, will open our hearts . . .'[37] The visual arts were priorities not only because of romantic sensibilities and attraction to the aesthetic, the evocative and the numinous; art was central to the life of the liturgy, which engages not only the head but all faculties and senses. Incense and candles, beautiful churches populated with images, the liturgical life and its ancient given-ness provided order, colour, beauty, entertainment, emotional release to populations denied the antique festivities and state rites of the *ancien régime*. An emphasis on singing added joy to the lives of multitudes.

There was a fascination with the transcendent, a conviction that there is more to life than what immediately meets the eye, more than reason alone can grasp; an affirmation of the hidden dimension, the supernatural, the otherness of the world around us. Splendid rites located Christian belief in the senses. 'There is no doubt', says Franklin, 'that the liturgical advocates had discovered an elemental form of discourse.'[38]

There was a new sense of the Church as a divine society ultimately beyond our understanding, a mystery. Authority over its life rested not with human calculation but with the sovereignty of God. Champions of this approach reacted often with ferocity against rationalism, the gentry, state control of worship and the Church, undermining of monasticism, mundane estimates of the liturgy and its perfunctory performance, and there was a deep dislike of industrialization and most of what it stood for. The struggle was against bishops, governments and academic establishments. In both Britain and Germany clergy went to prison. This dramatic fate befell none less than the Archbishop of Cologne, and later a Polish archbishop, for refusing to implement government orders on liturgical practices.[39]

Rejection of the establishment fortified a desire for closer association with the common people and an incipient social gospel. Struggles for justice, equality, social reform, community, could take swashbuckling forms, such as a delight in challenging convention and the status quo. 'Justice began to flow from the eucharist. Funds for workers' compensation, funds for worthy burial and distribution centres for clothing, food and other necessities.'[40] Lydia Goehr has said that in the early nineteenth century artists generally felt allegiance to two ideals, 'art for art's sake' and 'art for the people'.[41] This can be turned into a Catholic Romantic statement by substituting 'God' for 'art'. Such down-to-earth social involvement did not mean these movements were very good at listening to society and the world's wisdom – with their clear agenda they were too busy rebelling against them, against revolutions political, social, scientific and industrial, to be able to take what was going on in society as seriously as it deserved.

Achievements and ambiguities

It is fascinating to see the close similarity between the various countries involved, across ecumenical boundaries. As Möhler observed, 'What takes the lead in one of the members [of the European collective] must by necessity insert itself soon into all the others.'[42] In each of the churches to which they belonged the movements of 1833 brought a transformation. The effects in the Church of England were almost unbelievable: completely changed church buildings; return of the liturgy to mainstream catholic tradition (although still varying in degree and kind from place to place); renewed church government and pastoral care; a boom in liturgical and other scholarship; and a renewed confidence and drive.

The movements had wanted to reverse the effects of rationalism and restore a mystical understanding of the Church; and yet they were children of the Enlightenment in giving a high place to reason and scholarship. The revival of Gregorian chant gives us a good example.

Romantic and rational

The old art of singing the Church's chant had been lost. Two monks of the Abbey of Solesmes engaged in a celebrated struggle to establish the best method for recovering the way Gregorian chant should be sung. Both of them were romantic in their methods, and both scientific at the same time.[43] Dom Joseph Pothier (1835–1923) saw the chant as having one true form. He invested great labours in finding a typeface for the chant that would help singers reproduce this true form. He believed the true form of the chant was so divinely inspired that there was something instinctively right about it. So he laid great weight on the role of intuition – in judging which manuscript had the correct version of a melody, he trusted his ear. Dom André Mocquereau (1849–1930), on the other hand, thought there was no finally definitive form, and he published photographs of hundreds of medieval manuscripts to prove it. When readers turned from Pothier's supposedly perfect productions to Mocquereau's photographs and his dozens of parallel columns setting side-by-side the same chant in so many versions from manuscripts from the eighth to the fifteenth century, they saw two things; sometimes a majority of the manuscripts contradicted Pothier's liturgical books, but often also there was a degree of variation that could not be resolved. They saw before their eyes a reality that was in small but significant ways unstable and shifting, in fact a living tradition. There was no one 'true' form of the chant. One could only gain a sense of the character of this tradition by looking at the scientifically produced evidence and letting it find the right levels in the mind. Mocquereau may seem the more scientific of the two, but he had highly romantic ideas about the flow of the music being discovered through bodily movements that accompanied it, mapped out in beguiling twirls sketched above the music.

We can see in this tale a paradigm of nineteenth-century romantic catholicism; a belief in one true and definitive tradition apprehended at a level that was intuitive as well as rational, but containing a struggle between various notions of how far it was possible to resolve the picture definitively. For Pothier the one true tradition was there waiting to be captured by trained instincts; for Mocquereau the factual evidence meant that we will never reach a totally definitive point. Final resolution will always be deferred and in this he foreshadowed Jacques Derrida (1930–2004). In coining his term 'différance' Derrida brought together the two French words for 'differ' and 'defer'; the otherness of truth will always be Other, different, and the gap will never be finally bridged, final resolution will always be deferred. One thing some people came to realize in these reform movements was that in seeking to recover 'the Tradition' we should expect to find something that is shifting and alive. Anything that can be reduced to static formulas and a fixed system was not true tradition but a caricature of it.

Swimming towards the tradition

One of the main problems with the romantic catholicism of the nineteenth century was too static a notion of the tradition. Children of the age of Romanticism, its advocates were fired by a vision they deeply and passionately loved; the one, holy, catholic and apostolic Church of immemorial faithfulness. This had and still has in it for many an element of the absolute, as an eternal and unchanging container of the deposit of faith. This faith consists of propositions but also an innate sense of the quality and flavour of this truth, as lived out in many holy lives and supremely in the liturgy – the Church is ultimately indefectible and viewed with passionate love and allegiance.

Just as unbridled reason has to be challenged however, so does this when it is too unreserved. Newman's 'Holy Church as his creation and her teachings as his own' is easily absolutized into a great romantic love, when we are not free to go that far. We have to stay with the more testing struggle, straining to understand a mystery greater still, always held among many things in tension. As human beings we are not capable of finding the point of ultimate rest where everything is right – there will always be the need to move on further.

The Enlightenment was a source of life when it came, and many of its proponents were right to do what they did, but it was in thrall to an *idée fixe*, a particular agenda, too unnuanced, incapable of holding a range of slippery realities in tension. The romantic reaction was better equipped for that, but still not enough. Perhaps it can be said that God's truth for us is a fine, invisible line weaving among immense complexities of life and faith. We usually wander from it in one direction or another and need to learn to dance between the signs that are vouchsafed us, without ever plumping for a final spot.

It is a paradox that both rationalism on the one side and romantic catholicism on the other, where they wander from this elusive path, begin to look human-centred. Rationalism obviously enough, but romanticism too, when it may seek to manufacture synthetic experiences of the strange and other-worldly, in a wishful thinking, an 'as-if' approach to worship. Guéranger was often accused of this, and it is certainly true of a strand of ritualism in the Church of England. A self-conscious conservative celebration of a past form of the liturgy can be as human-centred as anything the Enlightenment or the 1960s could devise. The faith once delivered to the saints and preserved in the one, holy, catholic and apostolic Church, is called to go forward balanced forever wobblingly on the narrow line of truth. This line is partly mapped by reasoned questioning and openness to unexpected developments, but never so totally clear that we can take a static position upon it and cease struggling; it is also mapped by that love of which I have spoken – you cannot have truth without love, and you cannot love without confidence in that in which you are placing it. Here is a sharp question that affects our worship today over inability to embrace women's ordination, but not only that. If we look back at all the ages we have passed through in the last nine chapters of this book, we can see that this has to be said of any age: all of them had gifts but none found the definitive truth – they look now to us more like stumbling explorations in a process of growth that goes ever on and on.

This can sound like trying to hedge our bets: on the contrary, it is possible still at the same time to have faith in the truth of Christian teaching within the Catholic tradition. It is also possible through the process of holistic apprehension to have a confident sense of the Church's indefectibility, a sense of God's faithfulness to the Church and the grace that enables it to be faithful; and to see it as something to be loved. But God's truth cannot be reduced to simple categories simply grasped. The battle of the 1833 movements was a great and moving battle strewing glories in its path, but warfare, even in a 'just war', can breed unbalanced patriotisms which in the area of the liturgy still impede the journey towards the worship that goes on eternally in heaven, waiting for us to join it. It is worth asking the awkward question: why, in the midst of the great success of the campaign originating in 1833, is there also an eloquent failure? Why did the Second Vatican Council have to undo much of the work of 1833 in an urgent quest for pastoral effectiveness? Why, despite all the organizational fruits of the Oxford Movement, did the Church of England continue to fail to grasp the imagination of the common people?

The message of two centuries

The two contrasting stories of, roughly speaking, the eighteenth and nineteenth centuries repay our close attention. Like two sides of a coin, we see in each an archetypal drama marking out two bearings for our future journey, while in their smaller detail they have left an abundance of riches that have something to give to any age. Not only are they two sides of one coin however – they sometimes appear as two sides of a face, merging so much at some points that it is difficult to tell the difference between them.

For Anton Mayer writing in 1930,[44] the restorations of the nineteenth century were largely formed by rationalism. The unselfconscious abandon of the Middle Ages was not recovered. The nineteenth-century experience was in some ways simply rationalism taken further. The old catholicism was pursued methodically, and along a rigid path lacking the Middle Ages' enthusiastic and unselfconscious abundance and waywardness. It was programmatic, it emphasized preaching, teaching and scholarship, the liturgy of the word, vernacular song, and self-conscious cultivation of what it saw as the tradition; it continued use of the vernacular and other forms of participation (especially in Anglicanism, where conscious participation and the vernacular reigned as they never had done in the Middle Ages). This rational strand in the makeup of romantic catholicism was not according to Mayer capable of leading to the heart of the liturgy, and in his judgement catholic restorationism failed to get to the heart of the liturgical life of the tradition. We might think him over-harsh, but the work that needed to be done in the mid-twentieth century shows us some of the ways this restoration failed. Joseph Jungmann comments on the attitudes inherited from Guéranger and his world that,

> the liturgy is praised as a finished art-product, a wondrous work of the Holy Spirit . . . in such a treatment of the liturgy we recognize the expression of a time grown tired . . . accustomed, with every technical skill, to measure the tasks of intellectual culture, not by an independent judgment of things themselves, but by comparison with certain finished patterns which thus passed muster as an unalterable canon.[45]

On another level there is an uncanny sense of déjà vu in the eighteenth and nineteenth centuries. Rationalism was followed by a return to the imagination and the intuitive; just so is the rationalism of the twentieth century now followed by a renewed taste for the imagination, the artistic and the experiential. The Enlightenment and the romantic movements of 1833 are inseparable twins, archetypal characters in our twenty-first-century spiritual wrestling-matches, caught as we ourselves are in struggles, passions and profound changes, with no rest. We never find what we want – that is, a five-star Church. God waits for us to stop trying to organize everything according to our simple agendas for which we show such passion.

The Church is like a listing ship. The cargo is loaded either too much to starboard or to port. One generation shifts the weight too far and the ship then lists in the other direction, waiting for another generation with insufficient nuance to start shifting things too far back the other way. The task is more complex than people realize or than human passions care to have patience with. The ship can list in all manner of complex ways and the cargo, besides needing to be organized with an infinitely fine balance, also needs careful adjustment in an up-and-down direction, as well as backwards and forwards. The task of discerning God's truth is infinitely complex and unfortunately lies in the hands of sinners. One habit that certainly helps here is to try to see the good in the opposition – hard to do in the heat of battle.

Vision upon vision

As we cast a backward glance over the succeeding visions of the centuries we can gain an impression not only of destructive lurches, but also of layer laid upon layer. As an artist adds brushstrokes, stops and stands back and then returns to adjust the picture in an iterative process of revealing what is waiting to be discovered, and then, once it is complete, ruthlessly reconstructs large areas several times (as X-ray techniques have revealed with many masterpieces), so Christians have restlessly sought to discover the Other, an Other so different that a final resolution of the quest is always deferred – there is always more to be discovered. This layering of vision upon vision is like the layering of a human person's psyche, where the accumulated experiences of a life lived thus far make for a person who may be integrated and balanced, but nevertheless deeply complex. In the history of the Church the myriad changes of direction, the incalculable loss through destruction, the energy lost in battles that to another age may look so unnecessary, all go together with the riches that every age produces for our enlarging, building up treasures in a storehouse for which we can be profoundly thankful. The constant succession of vision upon vision is in such ways as this always both negative and positive.

The Liturgical Movement

By the beginning of the twentieth century dissatisfaction with worship was growing yet again. People were learning enough about early Christian history to realize how imperfect their liturgy was, carrying with it so many of the mistakes of the ages it had passed through. There was a sharp sense among many in the Roman Catholic Church that a venerable, much-repaired and adapted monument no longer measured up to scholarship or pastoral need, while at the same time the churches of the Reformation were sensing a new urge to rediscover a tradition now known to go back to very early times and so to carry a greater authority than had been realized.

Out of this stirring emerged what came to be known as the Liturgical Movement at the beginning of the twentieth century. Its early founders saw an obvious need to return to the principles of the primitive liturgy. This became a paradigm for most liturgical thinking in the years to come. None of the early figures of the Liturgical Movement foresaw, however, what would come of it in the reforms issuing from the Second Vatican Council: they were at its beginnings still living in a romantic key. Ildefons Herwegen blazed a trail at Maria Laach Abbey in Germany with basilica-style masses in the crypt – he wanted to reform the staging of the liturgy according to the principles of early Christian worship, motivated by a vision that was both scholarly and pastoral. But these experiments were still in Latin, in which he thought the faithful should be given classes!

The Second Vatican Council surprised even its participants by the lengths to which reform would be taken. Other denominations have their equivalent story. No one realized what was to happen to worship from the mid-twentieth century. Little did the early figures of the Liturgical Movement realize either what sort of a world their movement was to fall into. Not only that, but not even the contemporaries of Vatican II could imagine what kind of world the Church would find itself in, in the twenty-first century; nor would they be able to foresee the ways in which the world of the twenty-first century would have deeply problematic consequences for worship.

Part Two

WHAT KIND OF WORSHIPPERS
DO WE NEED TO BECOME?

Another World

The situation Christian worship finds itself in today in the developed world is unprecedented. We know more about liturgical history and principles than any other generation. There is more variety and creativity than ever before; but there is an unprecedented loss of interest and sympathy for it in the population at large. The quality of worship is patchy; while there is good worship around, indifferent or bad worship abounds. Quite a lot is now being done to equip people to design and perform worship better, but good as that is, it is not enough – something fundamental is being widely avoided. In order to probe this avoidance we need first to take a look at the contemporary culture that flows through our veins, powerfully conditioning our living of the gospel.

Many authors in a wide variety of disciplines could be called on to paint for us something of the nature of our present society. It will be sufficient for our purposes here to pick two, one who gives a brilliant portrait of the problems but offers little in the way of solutions, and another who, as a committed Christian, rounds out this picture and offers some ways of responding.

The world according to Zygmunt Bauman

Zygmunt Bauman has vividly depicted the contemporary predicament in a range of books.[1] His picture goes something like this. Before modern times rural society had solid structures. People knew their place and had a sense of where they belonged. God was in his heaven, religion helped us relate to God, we were close to the land, and there was a direct connection between the work we did and our daily food and necessities. There were problems to do with injustice, poverty, uncertainties of weather and disease but, all things considered, you knew where you stood.

Then came the Industrial Revolution. Peasant life was destroyed, large numbers of the population were herded into towns to be little better than slaves in grim factories, with appalling physical and social living conditions, and a new form of life severed from the old roots. This was in its turn a solid framework, but a more grim one for large numbers of people. It had its codes of behaviour to be adhered to, governing family life, use of money, respect for 'betters'. In the workplace there reigned the newly conceived 'work ethic' claiming the virtue of work for the work's sake, and a delaying of reward as a value in its own right. For workers the work they did was a kind of god to be honoured and treated with respect. For employers on the other hand the work and the profits it produced were in a similar way set up as absolutes, fundamental ideals that had to be honoured for their very selves, irrespective of the happiness or welfare of workers. 'Business is business.' Gradually more enlightened approaches appeared leading to the welfare state, but the supreme reason for treating your workers well was that it improved production. In this new world generated by the Industrial Revolution people knew where they stood, just as they had done before in the rural world. It was a solid framework with familiar landmarks – you knew how to behave, what to believe in, what you owed to whom.

Liquid modernity

That solid world has in its turn collapsed. In twenty-first-century Britain the work ethic has faded away, notions of authority and hierarchy are suspect, and there is a profound sense of all being equal. Anything whatsoever that is expected of me first of all has to prove itself – nothing can be taken for granted. Consequences in the workplace have been dramatic. Part-time employment and short-term contracts, flexible hours and strictly contractual relationships mean first of all that work is uncertain and potentially short-lived. Employees are as easily dropped as taken on. Increasingly for many working people their job is a strangely characterless affair. You are tied to an assembly line, or to computer networks and electronic automated devices such as check-outs, and tend to be treated as expendable, disposable parts of the economic system. Bauman goes on to say that neither particular skills, nor the art of social interaction with clients, are listed in the job requirement. Where employees have no incentive to engage positively with clients, their workmates or employers, they will see little point in developing attachment or commitment to jobs, or lasting associations with workmates. To avoid frustration they tend to be wary of any loyalty to the workplace. Unsurprisingly, this can result in poorly made goods and patchy service, not fully the case everywhere, but a situation that is progressively spreading.

As for those in charge, their life has changed too. According to Bauman, instead of straightforward systems of authority and command we have a new global elite who as it were dance around among a flurry of projects, possibilities, networks, teams and coalitions. Now the aim is not so much control, leadership and management, but influence. Everything is looser, more diffuse. Organizations can be put together, dismantled and reassembled at short notice or without it. The world of business is increasingly fast-moving, fuzzy, plastic, uncertain, and even chaotic. Solids have gone, melted into liquid. Everything is turning to liquid; in today's business the less solid and the more fluid it is the better. Since he has written we have begun to learn some of the shattering consequences of this, not least in the world of finance.

Uncertainty

This style of living affects everything, from education to politics, from religion to personal well-being. How is it affecting you and me? The first way, one of the most obvious, is in uncertainty. If people have no strong sense any more that they will be in their job or field of work for life, and if that applies also to family life and marriage as well as the nation and our sense of who we are, then one key fact about our present state of mind is uncertainty. For many there is a feeling that our hold on life is now a game of chance where nothing can be depended on. For instance, a generation that thought it could be guaranteed an adequate pension for its old age is now discovering as old age approaches that there is no such guarantee and great uncertainty about the future. Once we felt we knew where we stood in the neighbourhood where we lived, with the work we had for life, in a nation that knew what it was and where it stood. Now increasingly we are nomads, never completely sure where we stand or what the future holds.

Another part of our uncertainty stems not only from not knowing where we stand, but also not knowing where we are going. There used to be a sense of travelling towards the Kingdom – there was progress towards a happier society. In personal life you had an idea of the shape your life would have. Now people are no longer sure whether God is there; old-fashioned Victorian pie-in-the-sky-when-you-die religion has been discredited, and in a universe thoroughly scanned by scientists it is difficult to imagine where heaven might be. You don't have to be an atheist to have a measure of uncertainty about the end of the journey, and while here on earth, our old-fashioned simple belief in progress has more or less collapsed, too many terrible things have happened for us to be able to simply to believe in straight progress towards the good life. The image of a happy society painted in the 1940s and the heyday of the setting-up of the welfare state now looks a pipe-dream in a world where most have what they need yet are not particularly happy, and are increasingly conscious of further benefits they still need (even though no society has ever had them, such as universal health treatment without gaps or waiting-lists). We still have a sense that many aspects of life continue to be improved – scientific knowledge still advances, and increasingly amazing gadgets appear in the shops, but there is much less sense of getting anywhere, working towards a place that we long for. The great economic crash of 2008 has now left this uncertainty both exposed and magnified.

Reason's fall

Then there is the collapse of reason. From the eighteenth century it came to be believed that education and reason could eventually solve all the world's problems: it only required more and more people to approach life on the basis of reason for all society's problems gradually to melt away. More recently have come the horrors of two world wars, Auschwitz, and all the ghastly and unmentionable events of the twentieth century, brought about by 'reasonable' modern people. We are realizing that reason is not enough – there are things within us that reason cannot control that can wreak havoc.

Then there is the loss of faith in words. We no longer trust what people say – we want to see the proof. Reason and words are no longer reliable, and so we have come to an age of suspicion – all claims must be treated as suspect until proved true. Politicians are treated as suspect, church leaders, most people in public life. We are not prepared to swallow claims by anyone until we have tested them. This healthy suspicion has the drawback of leaving us unable to trust anything. If there is no sense of progress towards a goal and no vehicle we can trust to transport us to the goal (as reason used to be trusted), then unsurprisingly we feel wobbly. As we now travel through life without any idea of a destination to guide us, Bauman concludes that we are left not quite sure what in our society makes us listless, and with a strong feeling that we do not understand the position that we are in.

Self-making

If you can't trust anybody and can no longer trust society, politics, religion, employer, pension fund or spouse, then obviously the only person

to trust is yourself. The uncertainty of modern people leads to individualism. Before I can accept anything I have to be able to verify it for myself.
I am the one to decide, I the one to choose. Hence the politicians' talk
about choice – that is all we are left with. A collection of individuals each
faced with making their personal choice. In such a situation the choice is
just for me, not for anyone else. Therefore I do my work for me – I don't
concern myself with the others. I get married for me, to fulfil my desires
and needs, and as soon as they stop being met by my marriage I move
on. People now make *themselves* the centre of their own planning and
conduct of life. If I treat anything as an authority I have to choose it as
an authority first – it depends on me for validity. If I decide to follow a
religion, I need to have chosen it first from among the many possibilities
on offer, and any obedience I give to it is an obedience I as an individual
have chosen to give. We are losing the sense that we create each other –
that I am created by other people, and other people live in me. My own
mother lives in me for example in many ways – she has deeply influenced
the sort of person I am. The word for this is co-inherence. We are all
rooted in each other, and without each other we are diminished as human beings. Many people no longer know who they are because they do
not know who they belong with. It is commonly said that many young
people today cannot give themselves to anything, one reason for this being that they do not know who they are. If you do not possess yourself
how can you give yourself away?

The cyber-world

Into this uncertainty, lack of knowing where we are going, and drawing
back into ourselves, has walked the technological revolution. Now we
cannot even be certain of the earth on which we stand. Geographical
space has collapsed as cheap flights and the internet hop us instant-
aneously to any part of the globe or to any information we want wherever it is. Bauman describes sitting with his wife in an airport while at a
nearby table two men talk, each on his cellphone.[2] They continue for
over an hour while Bauman and wife watch. Both men were physically
there with the other people in the airport, but in effect were elsewhere,
talking to people on the other end of their individual cell phones, wherever those people might have been. The two men – where were they? It
is a good question. We don't know where we are; because we can hop
anywhere, the point where we are now feels less fixed. There is a weaker
sense of the local, local bonds, local place.

Consumerism

Few of us nowadays are ever satisfied. In former times it was possible to attain a deep satisfaction in family life or in achievements in either work or interests, and to rest in that satisfaction. The work ethic was linked with knowledge of a big reward at the end of the journey; a major experience of gratification and satisfaction. The disappeared work ethic has been replaced by the consumer drive, unable to stop consuming, we shop till we drop. Yes, we attain the satisfaction of buying something we want, but the satisfaction is momentary as we quickly forget the achievement and move on to the next desired object. Incapable of resting in contentment, we are driven forward by a nervous desire to attain new forms of satisfaction. You could say therefore that in the old days people worked through their lives towards the vision of a grand gratification, while nowadays we hop from one gratification to another like stepping stones. With each new thing we find a pleasure of which we quickly tire as we hop to the next thing. It is as if we have moved from standing four-square on the ground to being a disc spinning in the air, or ping-pong balls atop a column of water, bobbing up and down without coming to rest. We never stop to tap down into the deep roots of the satisfying things of life, always wanting to move on to the next entertaining object or experience. We are so insecure we dare not stop, cannot face ourselves, cannot be alone. In former times people could happily get on with their work in silence and homes could be silent places where the only thing to be heard was human conversation. Now every empty moment has to be filled, with music or television or sound of some sort, a symptom of the difficulty we have in being alone with ourselves, such is our insecurity.

This picture does not apply across the board – the variety in our society is enormous as we all know, and old lives in all kinds of ways side-by-side with new; but what Bauman paints is without doubt a partial portrait of the public face of our society, a picture becoming increasingly widespread, especially among the younger generation.

On the other hand . . .

The problematic picture painted by Bauman leaves us open to living double lives; wringing our hands about the modern world while happily enjoying its wonderful benefits. There are, however, too many good fruits of modern society for even the most critical of us to contemplate going back to a former age. If we were given the choice to live in the 1880s or 1930s or even the 1950s it is unlikely many would choose any of them –

we would opt for the 'now' that we know with all its benefits. Neither could there be any reproducing or restoring of lost aspects of life such as community or a sense of belonging, or knowing where we stand. We cannot conjure up such hard-won things with a magic wand. The past can never be reproduced – it is gone for ever, the way to it barred by an angel with a flaming sword. Rather is there a new world waiting to be discovered, whose ideal form would still have the best of modern life's benefits while other good things we have lost – such as community and a sense of knowing where we are – will have been born again in some new form. This is a recurring pattern – something important to us as human beings disappears or is lost, only later to be received back in a different form, the old having been now lost for ever. We are in a time of painful gestation – either to come through to some better place or to a worse one; in the meantime there is plenty to bewail and plenty to be thankful for. One of the reasons for our uncertainties is that modern communication holds before us such a disparate variety of things that we have great difficulty holding them all together in our minds and emotions – but on the whole it is better, it is an advance, to know rather than not to know. So long, that is, as we keep our heads and remain aware of the limitations of this kind of knowing – not a virtue always practised by addicted surfers of the internet.

Exile

Where next do we go? For most inhabitants their relation to their language is one of unconscious immersion. As the Chinese say, fish are unlikely to have any notion of water. Our immersion in our language is total, and most of the time we do not reflect on our use of it. This means that speakers can fail to see beyond the standard habits of thought and discourse of their national culture. A country, with its history, culture and language, is a universe in itself, with fairly distinct boundaries, and with firmly established plausibility-structures of its own. In *Liquid Modernity* Bauman describes the experience of a writer living in exile, at home in one language but also fluent in that of his or her adopted home. Such a person belongs in neither country, but is also at home in both in a way that gives unique insights. The unique knowledge of the person in exile 'allows him to bring to all the countries involved gifts they need badly even without knowing it, such gifts as they could hardly expect to receive from any other source'. Bauman draws on Christine Brooks-Rose, who sees in the exile a 'refusal to be integrated – a determination to stand out from the physical space, to conjure up a place of one's own,

different from the place in which those around are settled, a place unlike the places left behind and unlike the place of arrival'.[3] Constitutive
features of exile include a resolute determination to stay 'non-socialized',
non-integrated; resistance to the overwhelming pressure of the place we
are in; and an embracing of ambivalence.[4]

What might Christians make of this notion of Bauman's? We know
from scripture that we, the Body of Christ, are in exile. Our citizenship is
in heaven. Through baptism and celebration of eucharist and sacraments
we participate in heaven, but are not yet of it. But our citizenship is also
in this world – in the world but not of it. We live at a crossroads. Bauman quotes the French philosopher Jacques Derrida: 'Building a home
on cultural crossroads proves to be the best conceivable occasion to put
language to tests it seldom passes elsewhere, to see through its otherwise
unnoticed qualities, to find out what language is capable of and what
promises it makes [that] it can never deliver.'[5] Christians are in such a
relationship with the world, but also – and this is not always easy to see –
we are in such a relationship towards the Church. Those who live at the
crossroads see that the Church too must come under judgement: just as
the world, whenever it encounters the gospel, is judged, so the bearers of
the gospel, when they engage with the world, also themselves come under
judgement from the world's insights. Bauman's exile includes a necessary ambivalence; the ambivalence is important lest Christians believe
they have cornered the God-market. God's presence and activity are not
confined to the Body of Christ – they are more likely to be found in the
interaction between it and its surrounding society. The question, conse-
quently, is one of beefing up that lifegiving interaction.

Does this mean we are to have a cautious bearing towards the Church
as well as towards the world? Do we have to hold the Church always in
suspicion, as many Christians do today? Do we have to steer a middle
path between a questioning attitude towards the world and a questioning
attitude towards the Church? It is not the job of Christians simply to opt
for middle paths, and neither can we ever be capable of it – all we are
capable of is an illusion of it. Our contemporary culture and our world
are already inside us, determining our thoughts and perceptions in ways
difficult for us to recognize. In the twenty-first century the world is the
dominant partner far more than ever we realize, like the water for a fish.
A corporate body such as the Church can lose its way by not recognizing
the embedded voices of its contemporary culture within it. For example,
it has rightly learned much from contemporary psychology, sociology
and other human sciences; their fruits are deep within us. In such a situation the Church's task is not simply to seek an equal balance between

human scientific insights and the Christian tradition – in order to do that we would need already to be in possession of an impartial standpoint, but we are not. We are possessed and colonized by our culture in all manner of ways that we do not perceive. We are unconsciously immersed in our culture, patterned through and through by its indomitable character. What we need is a counterbalance. In the end we are stewards of the world only secondarily. The world can look after its own secular insights, and doesn't need the Church to be protector of them. The primary task of the People of God is to be steward of the other pole of the spectrum, witnessing to God's holiness. The Church's task is to take more seriously its own differentness. I used to have singing lessons from a woman with a voice like a bunch of razor-blades. As an opera singer she said she needed a voice that could rise above the orchestra. The Church needs to remain aware of all the music going on around it but also to make sure its irreplaceable contribution is heard loud and clear.

If our state as believers is that of exiles, we are not, however, without roots, not without a home country, and we are not standing still at the crossroads – we are on a journey towards our home. Our contemporary culture is within us and its effects need to be counterbalanced if it is not to drown us. So the two things that in fact we need to hold together are an openness to the world and its insights, but also a confidence and secure rooting in the Body of Christ.

We pray in the midst of a world that questions the plausibility of our prayer; but we are in a complex position, for we need to listen to the voices of that world in order to learn from it, while at the same time standing apart, exercising a resolute determination to stay 'nonsocialized'. The German cardinal Karl Lehmann recently said something similar. 'We have to be more resolute, but on the basis of open dialogue and tolerance. That's not so easy.'[6]

The quest for experience

While our culture questions the possibility of prayer, it is also a culture where many experience a great and growing thirst for the things of the Spirit. How can our status as exiles help such people? The contemporary thirst for 'spirituality' can often rise from an ill-informed quest for personal experience and self-fulfilment. In a liquid culture in which individuals float around without roots the only possible point of reference is the self, but precisely because of this terrible isolation the self, we are told, for many people is becoming decentred, so that even in the heart of us it is not certain what there is to refer to. People feel empty inside, and the only way to deal with that is to rush around. Bauman again:

> 'Fragile individuals', doomed to conduct their lives in a 'porous reality', feel like skating on thin ice; and 'in skating over thin ice', Ralph Waldo Emerson remarked . . . 'our safety is in our speed'. Individuals, fragile or not, need safety, crave safety, seek safety, and so then try, to the best of their ability, to maintain a high speed whatever they do. When running among fast runners, to slow down means to be left behind; when running on thin ice, slowing down also means the real threat of being drowned. Speed, therefore, climbs to the top of the list of survival values.[7]

All around us is a mad quest for experience, physical, aesthetic, sexual, and even religious; but the seekers assume that Christianity has nothing to offer. When they give it a try they can come away dissatisfied, often precisely because they are expecting immediate experience. Worship is judged on the effects produced here and now. Even the more sane and less self-orientated members of society can find it difficult to have confidence in religious practices that are not immediately self-authenticating. Many Christians who are trying with integrity to pray have the greatest problem doing so, with a strong sense of not experiencing anything. Our culture is so much part of our fabric, like the dye in a cloth, that we have problems with the plausibility of prayer. Many Christians do not pray; many clergy do not pray. Prayer can seem like trying to strike a match under water – empty, impossible. South Africa is a very religious country in comparison with Europe, but a recent television programme found there just the same problems. A man interviewed in the street said about church: 'I go in empty and I come out empty.' A woman once approached me in Milan Cathedral and said she went regularly to mass, but she just stood there 'like a tree-trunk'. What should she do to get something out of it? She always came away empty. People are looking for experience, and we have to start with them where they are before we can lead them to deeper things. How do we help one another? Teaching is not enough. Preaching through the example of our social service is vital but not enough. People need to have the experience of going to live in another country – they need to be introduced to the life-giving effects of exile. The place of exile here is the Church: there is a need to lead people into the environment of the Church.

Climate

We can trace the beginnings of this environment to Jesus. We are speaking of what in ecological terms is called a microclimate, the climate of Jesus-with-his-people. Microclimates are small areas where special conditions prevail, enabling particular flora and fauna to flourish. An example could be the inside wall of a well where ferns grow that are not otherwise found in that place. A very different microclimate would be the contained conditions of a nuclear reactor – large-scale and powerful, but still a microclimate. The microclimate of life with Jesus in the small group of the disciples was a living reality, and since then it has been passed down through the centuries as the climate, the biosphere, of the Church.

The Church has always operated on the principle of the microclimate. It is as small and vulnerable as the ferns on the inside of a well, but also akin to a nuclear reactor as an instrument of God's mighty works. It is an *environment* that enables release of powerful forces normally repressed. This environment can be seen as a culture – filled with life by the Holy Spirit and passed on through every generation since Christ first nurtured it among his disciples. Repeatedly through history Christians have smothered or emasculated the climate of Jesus. On the other hand this climate of Jesus cannot be passed on without a genetic, corporate memory, the memory of a people. It can only be fully manifest where it is passed on by the Body of Christ. In order to pray we have to learn to stand apart from the climate of our society in order to situate ourselves in the climate of Jesus. Without that, unless you have been blessed with a special gift, prayer can be like trying to strike a match under water.

There is an important and obvious corollary to this truth which further explains why people can find it difficult today to pray. The climate of which I have been speaking presumes a group. Our culture meanwhile presumes the individual as the starting-point. This is a problem, for prayer is no individual matter. The Lord's Prayer was given to us in the plural: 'Our Father in heaven . . give us today our daily bread . . .' Private prayer is a secondary matter for Christianity. Important yes, but flowing out of something more fundamental: a praying community. The community is the climate, and this climate is in fact the 'experience' that the experience-seeking people of our time really need.

'Monastery'

British television has given an outstanding example of this. Through three transmissions it followed the experience of five volunteers, none of them

Catholic, one of them in fact a professed atheist, who spent 40 days living the monastic life at the Roman Catholic Benedictine abbey of Worth.

> One worked on the fringes of the soft-porn industry . . . while a second was a former Protestant paramilitary from Northern Ireland who had spent many years in prison. A third was a retired teacher. There was a Cambridge PhD student with experience of Buddhist monastic life and a businessman from a legal publishing company . . . three of them had little previous contact with religion . . . [they] committed themselves to the monastic disciplines of silence, obedience and humility for 40 days. They joined in the daily round of the abbey, eating with the monks, working in the grounds, attending mass, and joining in the hours of the daily office, from Matins to Compline. They handed over their CD players and their mobile phones. The new arrivals were sceptical at first . . . and [at one point] two of [them] broke the rule and went for an outing. As you may imagine, the exercise was not without tension, conflict, and even drama. Each of the men in turn came to a moment of crisis where his presuppositions could no longer bear the weight of the reality they were now experiencing. For the young PhD student this was provoked by a visit the group made to the Carthusian monastery at Parkminster. He observed that 'The degree to which the monastic life is either truly sane or absolutely bonkers is pushed up to the absolute limit and you really have to decide what's what . . . And the scary thing is that the place made a lot of sense.'[8]

In different ways for each of the five, the stay in the monastery produced a conversion of attitudes and a movement towards faith. The monastery had been a microclimate of such potency that those who entered it found their presuppositions, their 'plausibility structures', beginning to crack. The cause of this was more than a holy atmosphere: the process was embodied in the monks, who were themselves going through this process every waking moment for life. The daily conversion of the monk or nun is a continual process in which his or her own interior climate is remade. It was tough for the visitors because it is tough for the monks: particularly tough at the level of challenge to self, having to face yourself, other people and life, and so being brought face-to-face with God. Monasticism comes as a huge contrast to Bauman's world; its fundamental equality is lived out within solid structures and consultative but clear authority. There is a fundamental security that comes from faith in God, knowledge of oneself and trust in one's companions. There is a powerful sense of the end to the journey, as well as a confident trust in the good use of human reason and the ability of words, of the Word, to be life-giving. Not all members of religious communities have attained to wholeness and secure self-knowledge, but in a healthy community they will be receiving help and encouragement on the way. While it is not part of monastic life to sit back in satisfaction, it is possible to know a certain repose and confidence in what the group is doing. Renunciation of personal possessions is rarely total in monastic life, but there is little scope for consumerism or continual acquisitiveness. Above all there is the givenness of God's presence and love – found particularly clearly in the silence and the climate of the place where the group lives.

It is often imagined that the life of the monk or nun involves a journey inwards. Indeed it does, and it would be impossible without the hours of silent individual prayer essential to it. The strange thing, however, is that the journey inwards is a journey outwards. Because you are committed to the daily worship and there is no getting away from it, it becomes relatively immaterial whether you feel at the time that you are receiving something from it. For long periods it may feel barren or blank, but that matters little, it is enough that you are in it. The journey inwards leads to a great *objectivity*, where all you need is to stand with your companions in the worship. You don't need special experiences or signs or consolations – you don't need to *feel* anything particularly, and that is because you have an innate sense of being deeply rooted in it. The life of faith drops from the surface level down into the foundations. This would never be possible if you had not started on the journey with confidence in what is to be gained from sitting under the tradition, seeking to be obedient ('listening') to it.

The monastery is a strange place, different from daily life, and this might be thought a disadvantage; but it attracts ever-increasing numbers of people who come to participate for a short time, going-apart into another world in order to see one's own world from a different standpoint and go away strengthened and enabled. It is a positive microclimate, a piece of ground held by a group in which another world is held in fragile being by the Holy Spirit. Visitors come into this climate and find themselves changed by it. Today many people are drawn to monasteries as to pools in a dried-up river bed. While this has always happened, many communities are coming to realize in a new way that such an encounter is one of dialogue and exchange of gifts. Visitors come seeking God and a sense of the climate of God, while monasteries depend for their part on such encounter in order to have their eyes continually opened to contemporary wisdom on what it is to be human. One instance of this is the use many communities now make of the skills of the human sciences. This is an example of the culture of the Church encountering secular culture in an exchange where both grow in truth about themselves.

There are increasing numbers of people who believe that monastic life and worship hold one of the keys to the contemporary predicament, without always being able to say why. Tantalizing is an observation by Alasdair MacIntyre in his magisterial work, *After Virtue*. Near the end of the book he writes, 'the barbarians are not waiting beyond the frontiers; they have already been governing us for quite some time. And it is our lack of consciousness of this that constitutes part of our predicament. We are waiting not for a Godot, but for another – doubtless very different – St Benedict.'[9] One element in this intuition about monasticism is the practice of self-limitation and the embracing of constraints. Ours is not a world that wants to hear about self-limitation, and yet this very notion is coming to the fore at the moment in an ecological agenda whose parallels with monastic simplicity of life are not difficult to see.

The ecological agenda

In the biblical accounts human beings are destined for mastery over creation. Humans give animals their names, they put earth's wildness in order and till it, they kill and eat. At the same time the glory of God is seen in creation, God's creatures sing his praise and are an object of wonder (as in Psalm 104). There is a balance between utilization of nature and reverence for it.

This balance began seriously to be damaged with the advent of the Enlightenment. If in potentiality all things were reasonable, then they could be organized at will by the exercisers of that reason, human beings. Thus began a transition from a God-centred to a human-centred universe. The inevitable result was the industrialization of the nineteenth century – nature became a thing to be exploited, the world's resources were plundered unthinkingly, toxic debris and detritus poured back into it. Meanwhile reverence for nature all the time continued to be held up by Romanticism in defiance of this rampant materialism.

Now, in our own time, partly out of a new awareness of our human limitations and of anguished gaps in us that can seem deeply assuaged by contact with nature, and partly out of sheer self-interest as our cavalier treatment of nature now threatens our very existence, a new sense of the awesome otherness of nature is taking hold of increasing numbers of people, as well as an urgent sense that nature is to be protected in ways that will limit some of the things we at present enjoy.

Old habits die hard, however, and there are many ways in which we remain unaware of small actions in daily life that have become habitual and need disciplining. Unnecessary printing-out of computer documents, throwing away of paper printed only on one side without using the reverse, leaving lights and electrical equipment switched on, eating food produced or transported in a way that damages the atmosphere, discarding food that can be reused, replacing face-to-face conversation with obsessive use of mobile phones. Sustainable use of resources is in our own interest. But there is more; for Christians it also has to be part of our relationship with God. Ecological awareness and sustainable living are potentially a form of love, and therefore of worship. In learning to reverence the creation, to be open to its otherness, to sit under it, we are making first steps in learning to worship in a non-human-centred way.

This is of the stuff of the monastic tradition. Throughout history monasticism has spurned waste of resources and undisciplined satisfying of desire. St Benedict in his Rule bids the monks treat implements and utensils of the monastery as if they were vessels of the altar (Ch. 31). The emphasis is on reverence rather than negation. The famous balance and reasonableness of his Rule shows no puritan rejection of the good things of nature – they are to be enjoyed in a balanced and disciplined way. Monasticism at times in its history has descended into rigorism, a negative approach to the good things of life, but that is not the way of Benedict, nor of the breadth of the early monastic tradition of which his Rule is a summing-up.

This element in monasticism is not motivated out of enlightened self-interest, nor by a pantheistic love of nature for its own self, but is simply one aspect of the community's whole relationship with God, where God's gifts are to be used with discernment and reverence, within the larger enterprise of following Christ in the quest for the Kingdom. It aims to be God-centred, not human-centred. Whoever embraces such discipline out of mere self-interest will see it as a necessary evil. Where it is motivated by God in us, it will be a praxis of love, loved for its beauty. Bauman's world could hardly be further away.

It belongs to the whole Church

If the contrast between the contemporary world and monastic life is a strong one, the aim in making such a contrast is not to encourage everyone to become monks and nuns nor to claim that monastic communities have the real gospel – far from it. The point is that some things essential to the life of the whole Church are now hard to find except in religious communities. Contact with them can therefore be illuminating – it can help us recognize ways in which worship today has been invaded by Bauman's world, and can prompt in us a realization of what we might be avoiding.

Naively Presupposing

Our second author, Charles Taylor, has in his writings sought to trace the origins of how we Westerners tick, and his book *A Secular Age* offers insights particularly useful in trying to understand what is going on in our worship today.[1]

In contemporary Western society the overall outlook, mindset and attitudes of people seem to be self-evident and natural – 'common sense'; they seem so, but in fact they are peculiar if not strange in cultural terms. As Albert Einstein once remarked, our notion of what is common sense is 'a deposit of prejudices laid down in the mind before you reach 18'. Taylor demonstrates with a disconcerting clarity how what we take to be obvious and self-evident is often not self-evident at all to people from other cultures. Attitudes we take as 'normal' can in fact look rather peculiar from other standpoints. Taylor's findings have considerable implications for Christian worship, laying bare both the remarkable achievements of our culture in the quest for human freedom and fulfilment, but also its debilitating blind spots.

The independent self

First of all Taylor shows how in a slow process originating in the Middle Ages our consciousness has shifted from a corporate one where each is dependent on all for a sense of self, to the modern 'buffered self'. The buffered self sees a boundary between me and everything outside, and that boundary is treated as a buffer. I am independent of everything outside – nothing need 'get to' me; whenever I want I can disengage from whatever is beyond the boundary of my self.[2] Although I may enter into various kinds of commitment with other people, this self can if it wishes override any of my commitments, so that commitments entered into nowadays remain such only so long as my buffered self wishes it – commitments such as marriage, community, church or employees. They can be dropped, and even while I am still in them, I may live them out only so much as I choose. The weak commitment so widespread in our congregations is an obvious example.

A society of buffered selves has built up a buffered world.[3] This world is based on a remarkable human achievement,[4] a modern moral order of mutual benefit and mutual respect that sees itself drawing, as far as can be seen, on purely human resources. We have discovered mutual benevolence without the need for a divine sanction, and in human history that is remarkable. 'The discovery/definition of these intra-human sources of benevolence is one of the great achievements of our civilization, and the charter of modern unbelief.'[5] Despite its secular nature, however, this benevolence is deeply indebted to the Christian tradition. The benefits of a society seeking to be benevolent should be obvious to all – it is very short-sighted simply to condemn modern secular society outright. The downside, however, of this buffered world is huge, illustrated in such problems as those Bauman has already outlined for us.

Origins of the modern self

What Taylor traces clearly, something there is no space to do here, is the way the uniquely modern buffered self arose out of particular historical circumstances deriving from the early Middle Ages, with a swift and huge boost coming from the Reformation. This was a process of a gradual disenchanting of the world. People originally made no tight distinction between natural and supernatural. Gradually there developed a distinction between them in people's thinking. Then people started to see some things as purely 'natural', separate from the transcendent; the transcendent came to be seen as 'beyond', rather than leaking out of all the things around us.[6] Gradually people lost their fear of the mysterious hidden forces in the world.[7] The Reformation took this further by drawing a firm line between the created order and the supernatural. Creation was quite separate from God – not to be reverenced but to be used and exploited for our practical needs. It was distinct from God, no longer alive with divine signs, no longer common ground inhabited by both ourselves and God, who used it to relate to us. Now the supernatural (i.e. God) had its own dimension, accessed in 'spiritual' (disembodied, interior) ways, while the physical, practical world was separate, unable to help us gain access to the spiritual. Out went all the trappings of the medieval churches and many of their liturgical practices. Now God was understood to relate to us purely within our inner, mental, selves. It was now but a small step for God quietly to fade a little and eventually drop out of our visible horizon as the deism of the Enlightenment reduced him to a distant object. God is now a notion, a specimen, if you like, that can be encompassed by our own unaided instruments of examination. Grace is not much needed – we are able to do everything ourselves. Hence the language about disenchantment of the world.

I have endeavoured to show above some ways in which this attitude pervades our worship and our manner of going about it. We can assume we are able to create an effective act of worship largely through our own resources, with God giving a gentle hand, concurring without demur.

Life in all its fullness

The buffered self has aspirations. In all our political and social debates, in our struggles to better our lot, there is a widely shared notion of what we are aspiring to.

> We all see our lives, and/or the space wherein we live our lives, as having a certain moral/spiritual shape. Somewhere, in some activity, or condition, lies a fullness, a richness; that is, in that place (activity or condition), life is fuller, richer, deeper, more worth while, more admirable, more what it should be. This is perhaps a place of power: we often experience this as deeply moving, as inspiring. Perhaps this sense of fullness is something we just catch glimpses of from afar off; we have the powerful intuition of what fullness would be, were we to be in that condition, that is, of peace or wholeness.[8]

Taylor calls this notion 'fullness'. Christ speaks to our quest for fullness when he speaks of finding peace, and finding life. He brought the message that we find life by giving it away, find our selves by giving our selves to others. For many modern people, however, the power to reach fullness is within, not outside. The person who is uniquely able to judge where it is being found is the buffered self. So religion must not only be my choice, but must speak to me, make sense in terms of my spiritual development. This development includes the quest for 'authenticity' and self-expression.

These goals are of course good ones, but the gospel has serious questions to ask about the means by which we seek them; it subverts any idea that we can seek them with the self as the main point of reference. We can be quite good at giving ourselves away in service of our neighbour, although that is patchier than in many societies: the thing we find so much more difficult is giving ourselves to God, as God comes to us in the common life of the Body of Christ and its accumulated wisdom. The buffered self can be very altruistic, very concerned, and it can touch fundamental aspects of what it is to be human, as we share our common humanity with others in humour, compassion and practical neighbourliness, and in seeking worship that will build people up and equip them. But in the long term, and in its widest reaches as one of society's building-blocks, the quest of the buffered self for 'fullness' has been cut off from the greatest and most elemental source of all. This seems often to be the case in Christian worship across the denominations. Many today can have a sense of finding fulfilment through helping others. What comes much less naturally to us today is any notion of fulfilment through enabling God to be at the centre of our lives and the object of our yearning.

Christianity, together with some other religions, throws a spanner in the works at this point: this is the notion of putting human flourishing second to the flourishing of something else.[9] This is not found in all religions. 'Pre-Axial' religion, typically the religion of primitive human beings, is largely motivated by the need for assured sources of food, good health and safety. The concern to appease deities or stay on good terms with spirits was in order to meet these material needs. 'Axial' religion by contrast can be seen in Isaiah or the Stoics, who were concerned with more than human material flourishing.[10] In Jesus it was proclaimed and lived out as sacrificial love of neighbour and a total, all-embracing love of God, even when no reward was in sight, except by the not-knowing of faith. Pre-Axial religion survives today among many ordinary believers, for whom practical, human needs are paramount. Within the total economy of a Church strong in its love of the unseen God, that can be welcomed as making its own contribution to the Christian ecology. In the secular world, however, any meaningful relation to God has gone: we now see around us both the eclipse of all goals beyond human flourishing, and the eclipse of any notion of a source of 'fullness' beyond the human horizon.[11] It is no surprise, therefore, to find in much if not most Christian worship a weak sense of God as sovereign, as *other*, and as the only source of worship. It is assumed that God does not want much in the way of direct attention compared with the attention needed by my neighbour. God of course is to be known in my neighbour, but there is a difference: the presence of God in my neighbour is mediate rather than immediate. Prayer and common worship on the other hand are capable of bringing immediate access to God.

Something more

We were equipped at our creation for such immediate access, and there is a growing and increasingly urgent sense of this. The sense that there is 'something more' presses in, and great numbers of people feel it – our age is far from settling in to a comfortable unbelief[12] and the Church is far from settling down contentedly with what it has in worship: there is a widespread sense that what we have is not enough. This spiritual thirst leads modern buffered selves on a quest for spiritual experience. All true worship has to include somewhere some element of experience that strikes us as significant, but the contemporary desire for such experience is always ambiguous, needs to be challenged and put in its place. One way of testing such experience is to probe its relation to the object of the experience. All of us sometimes (we hope) will find ourselves saying of an act of worship: 'that was great!' This can have its place, but it is a sub-ordinate place. All true religious experience is lost in the object of it. The nature of this experience is distorted if we try to see it as an entity dis-tinct from the object or agent, who is God. It is the same in human love. Our human loves always contain a selfish element, but having recognized their imperfection, we can still go on to say that real love does not notice its loving as something separate from the beloved. A 'feel-good factor' in love or in worship, however, can easily fail to rise above a simple con-cern with the experience as a separate thing from the one loved.[13] Our human love for one another will naturally find us saying of a common experience, 'that was great!', but it is subordinate to the person who for us is friend or beloved. Here lies the deep ambiguity in any quest for a 'good' act of worship. The act of worship God wants for us may be hard or difficult to take at the time. That can only happen properly in worship that comes somewhat from outside ourselves, as opposed to being a piece of our planning. Our contemporary culture disables us, however, from being able to hold this balance between the human and the divine roles in worship.

The individualistic crowd

Where buffered selves design worship for themselves, even the corporate is strongly marked by the individualistic. Taylor speaks of the peculiar nature of modern common spaces such as the park and the shopping mall. We live as isolated monads within very small groups or none at all; in the public space we rub shoulders anonymously with many, without engaging with them:

A host of urban monads hover on the boundary between solitude and communication; sometimes they flip over into common action, as with the cheering crowd at football, or a rock festival . . . [moments that] respond to a felt need of a 'lonely crowd'.[14]

Such moments can be wild and powerfully moving, as in the response to the death of Princess Diana.[15] We can tip over from fragmented community into an excess of community in rock concerts and the like: rock concerts are not religion but they sit uneasily in a secular disenchanted world, with their sense of a contact with something greater.[16]

As the balance here between the individual and the wildly corporate is so strange, not integrated, so also in worship the balance between the participation of buffered selves and the quest for corporate experience is very difficult to hold. There is something else higher than either.

Excarnation

Another element in this complicated mix is the Western assumption that the spiritual is by its nature internal and abstract, disembodied – the opposite, in fact, of the incarnation. Taylor, in tracing the historical process by which this came about speaks of Christianity going through an 'excarnation', away from enfleshed forms and towards religion in the head.[17] René Descartes (1596–1650) carried this internalizing to its logical conclusion. The colour is not in the flower, he says, but in the mind. His immensely influential thinking led to a complete disembodying of our conception of human experience.[18] This found its religious parallel on both sides of the Reformation divide in different ways, in a further separation of the spiritual life and what was done or experienced outwardly. In Protestantism, prayer was thought of as intensely going inside oneself, listening to God's voice within – something that has always been an aspect of prayer, but never hitherto in isolation or in the foreground. In Catholicism there was also the tendency to see the spiritual life in this way, with the liturgy as a formal exercise that needed to be carried out to satisfy obligations God lays on us. These assumptions still have tremendous power today, particularly in north European culture, and the attempt to rehabilitate a whole-person-in-community approach to worship, despite new and growing sympathy, involves an uphill struggle to change preconceptions; witness the constant opting for sedentary recitation (said not sung) of the daily office in churches where this is practised.

One of the main battlegrounds in this area is the tension between disembodied and holistic religion.[19] Even where a more holistic approach is
adopted, it can fail both to go far enough and to get beyond the buffered
self and its quest for a good experience. If you are uncertain what that
means, then think of two acts of worship: in one the people form a complete circle, and the vibrancy of the community thus gathered contributes
to an internal upbuilding of the participants; in the other the people use
the whole building, gather in various configurations, and take great care
to do well and beautifully a wide range of actions in a space regarded
as special, and furnished with a variety of significant objects, all uniting
with the music and other elements in an act which is done simply because
there is faith in the fruits of the doing of it, even if you might not see
much at the time. Some degree of 'excarnation', as for instance in the
Quakers, or in strict Cistercians, can bring significant fruits, but on its
own cannot give the healthy spectrum that is needed.

The ordinary

These shifts of consciousness taking place in the West have been driven
by a particular class of people who themselves were formed in a particular way. From the later Middle Ages life began to be more civilized and
polite; good manners became increasingly important to the educated
and better-off. Courtesy, restrained eating habits, cleanliness and self-
control came to be held as high ideals.[20] The upper and middle classes
became increasingly conscious of their difference in this respect from
the rest of the population. Formerly rich and poor had shared much the
same life-habits, traditions, festivals and forms of devotion, and in religious practice all participated together, but from the time of the Renaissance a divide gradually grew up: the rich wanted better, and evolved
their own ways of celebrating, worshipping and eating together. From
here it was a small step to wanting to reform ordinary people to make
them more like themselves, and so began a centuries-long campaign to
make ordinary folk like the middle-class and the rich. It produced great
benefits in areas like education and health, but terrible loss in attempts
to foist on people forms of worshipping that were alien. It is often said
of the Book of Common Prayer that, for all its treasures and beautiful
language, it lost the common people, having taken away from them
ways of worshipping that came much more naturally: lighting candles,
sprinkling water, warming to the gospel through the lens of saints' stories, worshipping with the body and the things of God's creation, and

generally living out the gospel in a way that can in a positive sense be called vulgar and vigorous. The origins of this struggle go back into the Middle Ages, but it is still in vigour in the twenty-first century. We have seen it at work under the Enlightenment: by 1800 the two levels were separated as never before by profound differences of world-view, while all the time there was a drive to raise lay folk up to the level of the rationalist elite.[21]

This process worked in two ways: as well as seeking to 'raise' ordinary people's manners and religion, it also had the effect of attracting attention to the ordinary. As early as the time of the first Franciscan friars in the twelfth century ordinary people and their way of life were brought into focus and subjected to attention perhaps for the first time. St Francis' valuing of the ordinary marked a significant turning-point in the West.[22] What Taylor calls the homecoming of the ordinary has come to centre stage in modern times, from the novels of Jane Austen to the television soap. The effect of this has been to bring about recognition of important human goods.[23] There is a double, slightly contradictory process of seeing ordinary human life to be lacking, while taking great interest in it. This should not lead us to question our efforts today to improve Christian education and commitment, but, as for instance with some attempts to turn all Christians into powerhouses of idealistic commitment, or turn them all into 'ministers', we do need to be aware of the temptation of elites to make other people like themselves to the impoverishment of the human ecology.

Presuppositions

We have suggested that the mindset and attitudes of people today, while they seem to us to be self-evident and natural, are in fact peculiar and not nearly so self-evident. Taylor refers to this kind of mindset as a 'social imaginary',[24] deeply normative images and conceptions of life and of society that make possible common practices and a widely shared sense of legitimacy.[25] Our social imaginary is an unstructured and inarticulate understanding of our whole situation: it can never be expressed in doctrines, because it is unlimited and indefinite. We can see a whole slice of our social imaginary before our eyes when we watch the television news: what it is thought necessary to tell us as news (not as obvious as might seem), what it is possible to say, what is left unsaid, the unspoken values that underpin the whole performance. (Victorian viewers would be puzzled by the mein of the announcer, the central place given to finance, the presuppositions about sex, and even contemporary viewers from other countries can be puzzled and surprised at what we would take for granted.) There is more to be recognized in the TV news than this, difficult to conjure up, and to do with the whole temper of the exercise and the way it reflects peculiarities of our society.

Closed worlds

Like the fish in a pond, we are unaware of the degree to which we live in a closed world. Taylor speaks of CWSs, 'closed world structures', ways of restricting our grasp of things which are not recognized as such.[26] He also likens the effect of this aspect of our society to 'spin' – we are unaware of the degree to which our peculiar culture puts a spin on every piece of information, every idea, every reported fact. In worship our inbuilt programming puts a spin on every element of the worship; the function of worship here, however, should be to turn the tables and put a contrary spin on our way of living. In order to do that it will need to pack a pretty powerful punch. There is only one place that punch can come from – God.

Living naively

Before modern times people believed in God in a way that could be called in a positive sense 'naive'.[27] Belief was without self-reflection, God was simply 'there'; no one noticed any ultimate distinction between religion and life. Today we can no longer believe naively in that way – we know too much about the alternatives, we have too many questions and nagging uncertainties of our own, and because of our secular culture we all to some degree are able imaginatively to stand outside our religion – the culture is too all-pervasive. There is no reason why this should not be gain rather than loss: it is a move forward to be able to wrestle with our faith enquiringly, and also to relate to other forms of belief empathetically. What is also the case, however, is that we all to some extent or other inhabit modern culture 'naively', unaware that it is possible to see things other than in this way. 'This is the truest and most reliable standpoint that there is' – that is the feel of it, and it is a naive belief, an unquestioning acceptance lacking in adequate reflection. If worship is working on the right lines it will begin to set us free from that naivety, to see it with different eyes. 'We are naively unaware of our presuppositions.'[28]

Visions that orientate

Taylor's term 'social imaginary' also refers to practical abilities. A social imaginary is 'a kind of repertory': (1) knowing what to do, and (2) being able to agree together on what is to be done.[29] In the American Revolution an old social imaginary of 'inalienable tradition' served as a platform for the genesis of the USA, eventually to fall away and be replaced by the 'will of the people'. In France (2) was lacking: there was no such stepping-stone, and that led to the chaos of a revolution that lasted over 100 years without being able to come to a resolution. In Russia (1) was completely absent, with terrible results.[30] Perhaps this could also be said of the revolution in Christian worship in the twentieth century. The repertory is there in the form of the tradition as I have outlined it, but it has not continued to be taken as a point of orientation by everybody; that is, our worship widely lacks a coherent social imaginary, a tacit knowledge of what you do, that is the subject of corporate agreement.

Vision upon vision

Each age has its own social imaginary, but particularly in more recent centuries, as each new perception arrives it joins what preceded it rather than replacing it. So the Enlightenment has lived on in many people in robust form until today, while Romanticism has done so in others. Furthermore, each new vision is as imperfect in its own way as what preceded it. Its arrival can be perceived as a moment of ascending to a higher level, but, as Taylor puts it, moments of ascent are often highly ambiguous, with important losses as well as gains. We need to be wary of mainline narratives of simple cost-free supersession – there are no unproblematic breaks, and the past is never simply left behind us.[31] If therefore we are to think of the Church as having its own social imaginary, we must remember that this will always have an ambiguity about it. What seemed a glorious revival of church life in a previous era can look rather different to us today, more like progress all rolled up with continuing failure: much-needed advance hand-in-hand with a failure to recognize all that needed to be tackled. In any age there is good and bad, and our own is no exception. We can be grateful for the undreamed-of benefits and advances of modern life, while bewailing in the same breath all its failures. We can say much the same about the Church, as we now go on to reflect on how it worships.

Seeing More than Ourselves

Worship in the twenty-first century

Christian worship varies so much in form and quality today that a general opinion on it would be difficult to hazard. Plenty of dissatisfaction is around, and plenty of undeserved self-satisfaction; it would be easy to contrast stereotypes such as those supporting the pre-Vatican II Latin mass with others singing away with music groups and projection screens. The temptation to go for easy options is as strong as ever it was, and there is a widespread failure to grasp the complex and elusive nature of the problem. While the truth is always complex, Christian worship itself does not need to tax our mental dexterity: the problem is rather with ourselves, who have difficulty recognizing the complex cultural formation we have received from our society, opening up as it has a wealth of new possibilities while in other ways seriously debilitating us.

One way of depicting the present state of worship could be this: from the 1960s the pendulum swung from romantic religious 'otherness' back in the direction of the Enlightenment; human reason and the values of society once again came to the fore, this time on a broader field than that of cold reason, and at a more popular, less elite level; people chat again in church as they did in the eighteenth century; we are not sure whether God is there, and we have much weaker respect for him or anything else. There is a belief in God as friend and supporter, and an assurance that we can be what we want to be in God's presence. Tradition counts for less, arranging worship according to our own ideas for more. Worship is close to secular culture in informality, music, dress, and in the sense of what is plausible. Sacrificial love of God for God's own sake is not for most modern people plausible, and we pick that up. There has been great advance in development of ministries, lay education and lay responsibility. Traditions of private prayer, such as they were, have collapsed. There is a continual fall in church attendance and finances. There has been exponential growth in liturgical scholarship and expertise, but a frustration at our inability to enable worship to attract people and hold them. There is bafflement as to what to do about the crisis of worship, and much resorting to strategies. Worshipping in Bauman's world is not easy. Our individualism, informality and an expectation that we should be satisfied on our own terms mean that worship is often very human-centred and shaped by contemporary society's ethos. Some see it as simply co-opted by the values and styles of the culture. We tend to have a social picture of the Church rather than a divine and supernatural one. Worship can look like a sociological event that merely reflects the group doing it. While worshipping at all is contrary to the prevailing culture, there may be little in it that is countercultural. It is not clear whether we find in contemporary worship in our local churches the exile of which Zygmunt Bauman speaks, or rather its counterpart – domestication. Worship today can be lively and upbuilding, but that on its own will not set it free from the enclosure that domestication brings. Domestication excludes what is other. Worship that takes seriously the otherness of the Christ of the Gospels would not go down very well in many of our congregations: we are tempted to box our perception of life into one single outlook, rather than juggling between nowness and God's otherness; so immune can we all become to otherness that we are tempted to reduce all reality to more of the same.[1] This comment by David Tracy invites us to look at the world in which we spend our daily lives and ask how far when we gather for worship we are simply allowing 'more of the same' to prevail. This same, is, naturally, our own work, in which humans are at the centre.

A difficult discernment

If there is a complaint that worship is too human-centred, what might this mean? There is a natural human-centredness that is right and good, coming from a sense of responsibility to our natural loves. This is as old as religion itself, familiar to anyone who reads their Bible:

> O God, I will sing to you a new song;
> I will play to you on a ten-stringed harp,
> You that give salvation to kings,
> and have delivered David your servant.
> Save me from the peril of the sword,
> and deliver me from the hand of foreign enemies,
> Whose mouth speaks wickedness,
> and whose right hand is the hand of falsehood.
> So that our sons in their youth

may be like well-nurtured plants,
and our daughters like pillars,
carved for the corners of the temple.
Our barns be filled with all manner of store;
our flocks bearing thousands,
and ten thousands in our fields;
Our cattle be heavy with young.
may there be no miscarriage or untimely birth,
no cry of distress in our streets.
Happy are the people whose blessing this is.
Happy are the people who have the Lord for their God. (Psalm
144.9–16)

Christ repeatedly put himself out to meet people's human needs, using the
notion of reward as a valid incentive for loving God: 'Great will be your reward in heaven.' Such a centring on very human hopes and needs emerges in
the survey of Lutherans in a small town in southern Brazil already referred
to in Chapter 7.[2] The research team concluded that people are fundamentally
moved by what they call 'zeal for life – one's own and that of the immediate
family'. This zeal for life is absolutely elemental for people, and includes the
need for food, a home, work and happy family life, and all that defends life,
enabling it to flourish and be improved. Religion serves and supports this:
religion receives significance to the extent that it serves this elemental notion
of life. Any element in the worship that does not serve this will be either
ignored or transformed in a way that puts it to service of zeal for life.

God helps here and there in this and that. This has been called 'coping
religion'. Christian faith and worship are there to help us cope with life.
Most of the people around Jesus could probably have responded to this
survey in the same way.

This attitude shows a clear gap between most clergy and many of the
laity. While for clergy religious practices like prayer, adoration or community can be important simply for their very selves, with many lay folk
such things are important only insofar as they relate to life: praying *for*
things, praising God for *particular* things, building community for a
practical purpose, and so on. According to the survey the people are only
able to grasp, elaborate and articulate those elements in the worship that
fit into their religious and cultural system, that serve their zeal for life,
that have to do directly with their life, and are not too abstract for them
to assimilate. The responses to the survey would of course have differed
in different locations and with different people, but anyone familiar with
parish life can see here things that count as universal.

How is it possible to respect this importance people attach to life and at the same time to worship with a sense of God's sovereign call? Many people's religion, centred on their practical needs in life, is in fact an essential ingredient for a healthy Church. This is not reluctant realism about people's limitations – it is a recognition of their vocation in life, adding the necessary element of practical earthiness to a Church prone to unearthed idealism. In Chapter 7 we looked at the way people often say contradictory things about their faith, and in fact about every aspect of their life. This inconsistency can hold realities in tension, opening up dimensions of richness closed to those who analyse, and this may help us see why Christianity needs both extrovert and introvert humanity for its health. It is a spiritual equivalent to vulgarity, without whose contribution we cannot understand life adequately. Peter Brook says of what he calls 'rough theatre':

> Every attempt to revitalize the theatre has gone back to the popular source . . . Meyerhold turned to circus and the music hall, Brecht to cabaret . . . the popular tradition is . . . the country fair . . . jolly, harmless . . . also bearbaiting, ferocious satire and grotesque caricature. This quality was present in the greatest of rough theatres, the Elizabethan one.[3]

Centring on human concerns and responsibilities and 'vulgar' normality is natural and good, a central part of our being human, and can be accompanied by a true dependence on God, sitting under God's greater wisdom. It does not follow that we are not capable of loving God. The gospel seeks to lead all of us to love God and the things of God for their very selves; but we have to be careful about comparing loves, that of God and that of neighbour and of life, for where there is love, there God is.

Unilateralism

A second kind of human-centredness is more questionable. It is the same, but with a much weaker element of dependence on God and of sitting under God's greater wisdom. It is characteristically found among people who have all they need. It is a *unilateral* attitude found in much contemporary worship, where humans are the ones in control, the ones to determine worship's nature and outcomes. We assume God is there to serve us, and that whatever God gives we are free to take or leave. We look for a shot in the arm to enable us to carry on living our lives as we like, an approach not difficult to sense in worshipping congregations made up of good and well-meaning people all over the world. In unilateral worship we will tend to feed ourselves with our own food, our eyes trained on ourselves, while true worship is bilateral, both parties, ourselves and God, regarding each other intently and in some tension, perhaps at times like two wary cats. Unilateral religion fails to distinguish between our own all-determining culture and the culture of Jesus. It sees the Church in sociological rather than supernatural terms. We assume we know enough, and what we are familiar with is sufficient – this is simply a co-opting of the gospel to our way of life.

Informality

Unilateralism should not be confused with informality, which is a different issue. Informality is to some degree characteristic of most worship today, even the more formal kind, and in some cultures whose worship is highly ritualized this informal element can be an old and longstanding part of the culture. It is a characteristic of Coptic worship: when the priest asperges the congregation with ablutions-water at the end of the eucharist, for example, it can be done in a playful way that makes everyone laugh. Holy vulgarity should not be confused with loss of a sense of God. Informality can be the spice of life of worship. Informality becomes a problem in Western worship when it arises from a climate where human concerns and habits are normative, full stop. Enjoying the civic and material freedoms we do, it is difficult for worship to be otherwise.

Balancing earthiness and holiness

Forms of popular 'coping religion' that still retain a lively sense of God and God's holiness, on the other hand, will most easily be found among people who don't have all they want, the toughness of life engendering expressions of dependence on God, balanced all the time by a healthy concern with family, work and daily needs. If life for us is a drama, there will be drama in our worship too.

The question is complex and difficult to weigh: the lengthy exchange of the peace in many congregations in prosperous Britain seems very expressive of the gospel – surely any occasion where many people wish each other peace in a corporate context should be welcomed gratefully in our world? On the other hand a much less well-off congregation in a South African township can get so carried away with their lovely singing and dancing that the four-hour service can seem to be a charismatic jamboree with a brief eucharistic interlude. We can need help to get the horizontal and vertical in balance. It is very difficult to judge, especially in contexts where a joyful, loving expression of human relating is a much-needed blessing, an element of right worship without any need to justify itself.

Mystery in worship

There are many today who are calling for a greater sense of mystery. Some are longing for the kind of worship swept away by twentieth-century reforms. There is a sound intuition here about contemporary liturgy, but the situation is infinitely complex and puzzling, and simple solutions or programmes can avoid some of the real issues. Language of 'mystery' tends to be used carelessly with a sense that God's holiness may be injected into worship as a result of human efforts to stage worship differently – this runs the risk of being as human-centred as the worship it seeks to replace. Worship intended to be other-worldly can seem to be that – a self-conscious, human-centred performance of a tradition that has become static.

The notion of *drama* may be of more help than 'mystery' as a less subjective term. The drama of the liturgy is objective, corporate and formal, but close to art in opening up awareness to wider horizons: it does this as drama, not as a quest for mysterious effects. To talk of the drama of the liturgy is to speak of roles, of suspending normal reactions, of the power of the visual, of movement, of words declaimed in a public setting, subject to form rather than formality – in fact not simply drama but a total work of art, a *Gesamtkunstwerk*[4] performed in attentive cooperation with God. If we focus on drama and art in this way it may take us further towards the goal than understandable but misplaced calls for more 'mystery' or for restoring old strata of liturgy's development that are no longer living but fossilized.

In this wider sense, rediscovering the drama of the liturgy must involve engagement with the contemporary arts. A world waits to be discovered here that is at present only meagrely evident in most of our worship. In a baptizing of the contemporary arts and attracting artists to make their contributions to worship we are likely to find an authentic way forward for all those who often justifiably feel that contemporary worship 'lacks mystery'.

Our picture of God

Part of this problem is a picture of worship as an attempt to reach out to God. Worship and prayer always begin not with our reaching out, but with God addressing us. My own private prayer is God praying in me, not me trying to pray to God. It is the Holy Spirit in our hearts crying, 'Abba, Father' (Galatians 4.6). Paul insists that 'from him . . . are all things' (Romans 11.36). Worship powered by our own efforts on the other hand will be barren – we can never save ourselves. Only the Holy Spirit can enable us to worship, by the same Spirit worshipping in us. Worship on that basis, however, needs faith: faith in the prevenient grace of God; and even that faith is God's gift, not something we can switch on.

A helpful way to look at this question is to explore the use of the arts in worship. Here are two pictures I have used with church musicians to discuss criteria by which we may select music suitable for the liturgy.

We may assume the purpose of the arts in worship is to project us into a prayerful disposition, to warm our hearts and open us up to the atmosphere of prayer. But it is possible to use the arts like a catapult – God is on the other side of a great abyss, and we seek to project ourselves over the yawning gap to him. This is problematic: we all have a picture that automatically comes into play when we think of God. We cannot operate without mental pictures and will have one of God whether we like it or not; this God-picture will always be tin-pot, inadequate. Hence the advice of Meister Eckhart to take leave of all images of God. In seeking to use the arts in prayer we risk simply projecting ourselves towards a mask of our own creating, a puny picture of God rather than the real thing.

> Each in his own imagining
> Sets up a shadow in thy seat.[5]

William Blake engraved a series of illustrations for the book of Job, where at the beginning God has the same face as Job – Job's mental picture of God is in his own image. Only at the end does Job come to see that he can never comprehend God. These engravings are a warning to us as we settle in our pews, to look and see how far the god we conceive in our minds as we pray is our own creation. The music we choose or compose for worship may partly have that god in mind. There are no formulas for resolving this dilemma: all we can do is (a) be aware of the problem, (b) rigorously test our criteria for choosing music, (c) take account of any consensus on the matter, and (d) decide, as you can only do with music, with your pores whether a piece is manipulative, sentimental, or pandering to self-orientated desires of one sort or another. What is true for church music will generally be true for liturgy as a whole: contemporary parish worship will be problematic to the degree that it is in our image, and simply does what we want to do.

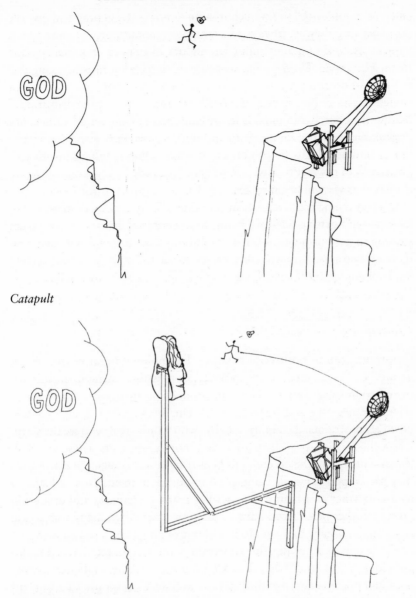

Catapult

Catapult mask

Prayer projected at God as a catapult

Our picture of ourselves

If there are problems about picturing God, the same applies to our picture of ourselves. Christianity is subversive of private notions of what is good

197

(such as 'I don't need to go to church on Sundays, I can pray walking the dog') because they are always too sanguine – about ourselves and God's view of us, and sanguine about any failure of ours to seek and live the truth. For David Tracy 'religions resist modernity by resisting sanguine versions of error . . . For Christianity . . . sin is . . . not a mere error but something more pervasive and more fatal. It is . . . systemic distortion.'[6] Within the church and outside it, we can operate from an unrealistic understanding of our own integrity and uprightness, unrealistic confidence in our individual capacity to attain to what is good, and an insufficient awareness of the fact that we are sinners. It is only by recognizing we are sinners that we will begin to get somewhere in the quest for God.

Over-sanguine estimates of our goodness, gifts and wisdom go hand-in-hand with getting what we want. Many conflicts in groups arise from striving to get our own way. If a community is to live without such conflicts and strains, this will only come about through accepting certain kinds of constraint by which we may learn to tame our own will.

Constraints

Constraints can be positive or negative. Examples of negative constraints would be illness, bereavement, poverty, oppression, unemployment, lack of self-confidence. Any of these can produce positive fruits but in themselves are negative and to be avoided. Our lives, however, also contain positive constraints: the family, a baby (who would freely choose the sleepless nights?), love, pets (they are a tie), morals, altruism. These are challenges which have the potential to bear fruit in us through the constraints they place upon us, while being good to pursue in themselves. In learning to live together as a family you sacrifice many preferences and desires: in loving another person you have to ditch or scale down many things – in fact you don't have to – you do it without thinking because you love.

A different order of positive constraint would be an odd-shaped building-plot – St Paulinus' Church in Dewsbury is strikingly tall and narrow on a fine prominence, but this was the architect's response to a difficult narrow sloping site. The same is true for some of Wren's best London churches. In the arts constraint is an essential element. Mozart's music works within tight conventional frameworks on the whole – as so often in art, the challenge spurred him on, fired him up. The artist needs a challenge that spurs in him or her a determination to rise above it. Michelangelo is supposed to have said, 'For the artist, constraint means life, freedom means death.'

Since the 1960s constraints have melted. Negative constraints are still around: illness, bereavement, unemployment, all kinds of psychological and social problems. Positive constraints tend to be in crisis: the family, love, morals, taking other people seriously; but they are the ones more able to be fruitful for us. Part of human growth lies in not always getting what we want. When I was a parish priest I evolved a way of praying the daily services in church which suited me perfectly. I devised a particular version of the daily office with music I enjoyed, and had a nice part of the church to do it in. When I joined a religious community I could no longer have what I wanted, and had to put up with ways of praying and with other people that did not suit me half so well: but it was more real, and the fruits perhaps more healthy. The words of Psalm 106 put it succinctly: 'He gave them their hearts' desire, but sent leanness into their soul' (v.15).

The notion of constraint is not entirely satisfactory – it speaks of absence rather than presence, of denying rather than embracing, and could imply a too pessimistic picture of our humanity. There is no point in pursuing constraint for its own sake – it is a requisite if certain fruits in our life are to be possible. Choosing not to enjoy some good thing is only justifiable when it is in the interest of something even better. The most fruitful constraint of all is a tradition.

Tradition

We all live within traditions whether we like it or not – an obvious example is the idiosyncratic tradition of our own language – however hard we try, we cannot escape it. David Tracy assures us that, 'There is no more a possibility of escape from a tradition than there is the possibility of an escape from history or language.'[7] The terms 'tradition' and 'culture' overlap: tradition in a way is culture traced back through time. Cultures (like ours) can lose their chronological depth and become surface-thin. Today many sense a need for tradition, but the result can be an inventing of traditions, building fantasy worlds from dead debris of real tradition: the vision of an idyllic rural England is an example. Sometimes such synthetic traditions can become dangerous, as in Serbian nationalism in the 1990s. We all, Bauman's people included, need to be steeped in a real tradition, through a continuing apprenticeship, sitting under something greater than us that we respect and trust.

Christianity depends on the wisdom provided by tradition. Even in its early years when there was not much specifically Christian tradition to speak of, it is noticeable how much attention believers gave to the Old Testament tradition out of which they had come, in a way that later ages did not need so much. Early Christian art is heavily reliant on Old Testament themes.

This drawing of life from the rock of tradition needs to be done in such a way that the Christian tradition is seen as metaculture, engaging in a mutual dialogue with all that is good in secular society. In order for there to be dialogue, however, there also has to be difference – there will be less dialogue between partners who are similar. The Church is bound to be different and to look odd. The *difference* of our worship, initially alien, will on engagement, however, spring upon the casual visitor a surprise, as they come up against something not expected, outside their experience, recognizing it to be speaking something to them to do with their own truth. Christian communities need to be strong enough in their worship and the quality of their corporate life to engender a microclimate, a climate that is singular, self-evidently of God. This is not something we can plan or aim for: it is like a work of art – it may happen if the conditions are right. The work of art emerges as the artist gives herself to a conversation in which there is both giving and receiving between artist, materials, context and tradition.

One necessary condition for the People of God, therefore, is a life framed within the 'constraints' of a tradition that is *different*: different from the ordinary run of things in contemporary society, and different from Christians themselves and their own picture of themselves. It is so different that it will never be completely encompassed: Derrida's notion of 'différance' already mentioned, a difference where comprehension is always deferred. The exploration never ends. We are incomplete without God, and our worship is incomplete the more it operates without the tradition, the 'language' of the culture of Jesus, and the more it derives purely from our modern selves.

13

Giving and Receiving

In the performing arts liturgy finds perhaps its closest parallel, and in them there is an obvious giving and receiving. The concert pianist is in receipt of a great tradition, and in the concert she receives a piece of music ready-made from the composer. All so far is received. Then she begins to perform, and the giving now begins to become two-way: starting with the givenness of the music and tradition, the pianist now gives of herself uniquely. The performance has a life of its own, but only because of the life of something else within her: the life of many things that have already been handed on. Even improvisation, as in a concerto's coda or an organ improvisation, could not exist without a great tradition. I myself could be called a lapsed organist as I don't play very often; but I am struck by the fact that, when called upon to play, if I have had time to play some of the repertoire in the preceding few days then my improvisation, poor as it is, will be more imaginative and confident – whatever life there is in it is mostly given by the repertoire. So in worship it should be no surprise to find that everything starts with what is received.

We have suggested that among many Christians today there is an emphasis on immediacy, personal expression, immediate engagement and the use of one-off creativity. Theological colleges in the Church of England have for years been exhorted by central authorities to provide opportunity for 'creative worship'. The perception is that we need to be more bold and imaginative, particularly in making the most of special occasions and times of pastoral need. Indeed, we have seen enough even in the brief historical tour provided in this book to realize that worship is always subject to change and creative innovation. In the past this has been slower and often less well-managed. In encouraging creativity those overseeing theological education are wanting people to develop their liturgical imaginations and the skills to put them to good use.

There is, however, a drawback in these exhortations from authority: an all-too-weak emphasis on solid formation in the tradition, the repertoire out of which the richest creativity can come. The liturgical expertise and awareness that are a necessary basis for such experiment are often inadequate: fruitful creativity can only happen when those involved are inhabited by a great tradition. Creative worship often runs into problems simply through lack of knowledge and experience. The paradoxical result is limited creativity or a lack of edge, through lack of familiarity with the 'repertoire' and we are then left with a repetitive falling-back on common gambits – candles, stones, projecting pictures. If liturgical creativity is to be focused and alive it needs to be businesslike about the tested sources out of which it will live. Creativity comes out of receiving, and that means we need to identify more accurately the ways in which liturgy is received rather than created here and now.

Receiving from others

Living worship always arises out of what has been received from others, in texts, music, practices, worship-spaces. We are not furthermore dealing with any old received material, but a balanced and representative corpus that continues to develop: it has to have passed the test of time and frequent use, it can come from anywhere in principle, and it has to include continuities with the whole of the past. Our receiving of it should never be mindless: all has to be subject to scrutiny, historical, psychological, spiritual, scriptural, doctrinal. That is the contribution of the liturgical scholars and other experts. We have to be sufficiently confident that this received material stands the test of reason, informed perception, and the questionings of the informed mind, while recognizing we will not appreciate all its significance. In order to tap into the tradition there has to be a confidence that comes from being steeped in it through prayer, study and a daily discipline of sitting under it, not least in the daily office. So the materials needed for creativity are not found only in the practicalities: they are also found at psychological, mental, spiritual levels in perceptions, indefinable skills, types of awareness and effortless living-out.

We are constant apprentices, therefore, never masters of worship, any more than a musician could ever finally master Beethoven. We need preparedness to learn from what we do not understand, an expectation to find more than at present we see. That is the contribution if you like of the artist and child in us, having enough faith in what we are given to be able to go with it and see what it will do. Having faith stands at the centre of a powerful scene in Shakespeare's A Winter's Tale, when Paulina assures the bystanders that a statue will come to life. 'It is requir'd you do awake your faith,' she says. Sceptical, they obey her and the statue begins to move, an unfailingly powerful moment in the theatre.[1]

In attending to what is received (that is, the received tradition), what is going on in worship is located outside the self – difficult for us in our individualistic age. The logical consequence of this may sound shocking: the central bread and butter of worship, all that is most formative of us and puts us most comprehensively in touch with God, is always received, not spontaneous. This is because the creative moment has to pass, to save us from being the prima donnas that we are, so that the liturgy can do its work of un-selfing, leading us away from looking at ourselves and acting merely out of present urges. The Levitical code in the Old Testament may seem intimidating for the likes of us, but in the tougher culture in which it arose Epstein says that its real object was 'to train the Israelite in self-control as the first step for the attainment of holiness'.[2]

Authentic worship is a combination of the immediate and the mediated – what is received from the past hand-in-hand with the inspiration of the present moment. Every received element of course had a moment of the imagination when it was first created, but that had to pass before it could attain its full effectiveness. God's method is to evolve, through us, forms which with time and use come to stand outside us. In the primitive Church people had to start from square one of course, but even for them there were things that came from outside – many Jewish practices, and the great use made in those early centuries of the Old Testament, but outstandingly of course Jesus himself. Perhaps there is always an outward movement: things of this age gradually become outsiders, speaking to us now with a different voice that stands more outside time because the immediacy is past. This foundation is necessary to any creativity because the liturgy needs to be formative of us as well as we of it.

The best

If worship is in these many ways to be compared with art, then as in the arts nothing but the best will do. It might seem obvious to say that worship should always be of the best, but we have habits, which we even sometimes justify, of offering less (see p. 103).

We can ask, 'what is the necessary minimum for a sacrament to be "valid"?' It was on this basis that the 'low mass' was invented in the Middle Ages (age-old tradition sees the solemn eucharist as the norm). This attitude could be called 'validism': it was able to conclude that by stripping liturgy down to the supposed minimum requirements it could be repeated over and over again to greater effect with God than wasting time with all that music and all those people's roles. Validism looks for what we can easily manage without undue inconvenience.

The world of art, however, can only ask: 'What is the best?' Art goes for 'Optimalism'. Christians do take a certain care over their worship: we usually expect the church building to be special, and are normally prepared to spend money (just enough) to make it so. The question rather is how far Christians rise to the level of commitment and care found in the arts. Many if not most modern artists approach their calling with a seriousness and dedication that can put Christians to shame. Paul Tillich has commented that 'it is a stinging indictment of religious art that those who take no active part in any religious worship are often more sensitive to the ultimate depths of reality'.[3] A French author has written: 'A group of actors decided to go to Church on Maundy Thursday, the day of the Last Supper. They found themselves scandalized at the way the liturgy was celebrated. It was done with great carelessness and slovenliness, while they themselves, they complained, took the greatest pains to perfect the performance even of works which were lightweight and stupid.'[4] Christians often unthinkingly offer the mediocre and halfhearted.

If parishes were to make every effort to offer the best, this does not necessarily mean spending large amounts of precious time and energy on preparations and rehearsals each week. All it needs is some initial consideration and effort in getting a 'good show' as it were on the road, and then simply letting it run. All good shows get stuck or tired, and parish communities need to maintain a level of care and alertness in their worship, in which imaginative maintenance is complemented by a special effort at imagination and creativity on the festivals and occasions that call for it. A 'good show' meanwhile is shorthand for a well-conceived liturgical action, a seriously committed, praying and serving community, in touch with the daily life around it, and all the tell-tale signs of a community in good heart and pulling together.

Worship and art

Another aspect of offering the best which has begun to receive more attention recently concerns art. The amount of public interest in the arts is so great and diverse as to be a whole facet of our society from which liturgy seems strangely cut off. It cries out for a greater place in our worship, certainly in terms of commissioning artworks for the church building and raising the standard of such work; but also arranging temporary shows and creating openings for artists, such as a parish artist-in-residence. There is in addition much to be learned for liturgical creativity from so-called conceptual art, installations, and much else in that amazingly fertile, even if often superficial, world. It is not common for secular modern art to find its way into the liturgy, but there are exceptions, and an outstanding one is the sixteenth-century church of St Peter in Cologne, which in 1987 became the 'St Peter Art-station' under the direction of Fr Friedhelm Mennekes. This church is dedicated to fostering a dialogue between Christianity and secular artists, and its success is shown in the tremendous following its activities attract. Mennekes has organized dialogues between artists and practising Christians, and the church also finances each year a young artist who lives by the church and exhibits his or her work there. In addition, there are regular exhibitions of work by artists of first rank such as Anish Kapoor, Francis Bacon or Joseph Beuys, some of which is placed in the main areas of worship, including by the altar. Some find this distracts or even hinders their ability to engage with the worship, but the vast majority of worshippers make a positive and enthusiastic response. At the Tate Gallery a few years ago a video was shown of Mennekes celebrating the Sunday mass, without an altar, in the midst of an installation of white marble pieces by the American artist James Lee Byars (Plate 11). Such practice is not possible in many places. It depends on the character of the worshipping community, but works to considerable acclaim in St Peter's Cologne.[5] It may be by such dialogue with secular artists that the standard of contemporary Christian art can be raised, and the liturgy's engagement with art develop into a tradition that has vitality.

Sitting under and sitting light

There is yet another layer to all this which we must take seriously if sacred ideals are not to become sacred cows: vulgarity is essential to sanity. People who have worked with Myers Briggs workshops have suggested that 90 per cent of clergy are 'Introvert' and 'Intuitive', 75 per cent of the population 'Extrovert' and 'Sensing' (using Jungian terminology).[6] We can see this in a clergyman going to buy a car part. Tentative about what exactly is needed, he tries to be pleasant with the assistant who looks back with stark matter-of-factness. The clergyman holds forward the broken part as if to say, 'this could be the problem, or perhaps this', adding by body movements and the way he speaks, 'what are the possible solutions to this?' and 'I'm having a bit of bad luck, aren't I?' The straight-faced, practical assistant plonks a shiny box on the counter: 'Anything else, mate?' Thrown by the severe reductiveness of this response, the blushing clergyman pays up, uncomfortable with such unadorned practicality. Pragmatism in the one and reflective intuition in the other mark two character-types in the human drama. Each of us is, among other things, somewhere on a scale between two poles, the intuitive approach of the clergyman in the car-parts department, and the down-to-earthness of the assistant.

This can be illustrated from work in a variety of congregations done by Martin Stringer, who identifies two layers to the Church.[7] On the one hand are those who study and analyse the faith and are responsible for maintaining its coherence and soundness through systematic analysis and intuitive exploration. Then there is the vast majority of believers who 'do not think in terms of systematic beliefs, and systems of theology, at all. Rather, they think almost entirely in terms of specific belief statements as and when these are needed' (they can be in contradiction with one another).[8] But they also always affirm the existence of their church's system of beliefs.

> The act of worship itself, with its actions and its words, is best understood as being a space without meaning in its linguistic sense, and that the individuals who come to worship have no need or imperative to fill that space with meaning in any but an experiential, 'significance', kind of way. Within the Christian tradition liturgy and worship is given meaning . . . but that is done by liturgists, theologians, and even sociologists, and, it would appear, the ordinary worshipper is more than happy for that to continue.[9]

We could call the two types of Christian 'Custodians' and 'Handlers'. The Custodians have among other things a specific responsibility to 'sit under' the Christ of the living tradition with clarity and purity of mind, and to encourage all Christians in that direction. The contribution of the 'Handlers' is to preserve us from illusions of consistency and keep us in touch with the world of primary colours where refined disquisition cedes to robust and invigorating contradiction. They prod the Custodians into not being too earnest about their sitting-under and their analytical explorations. We will always need the contrast between a concentrated faith and a happily scattered faith. The Handlers strongly desire to have confidence in the world of the Custodians: they depend on the Custodians and usually respect them. Sensible Custodians also delight in Handlers and are refreshed by them and so kept in touch with parts of reality that studiousness and reflection cannot reach. Lay Christians can show a tolerant tenacity of faith in the patience they show with clergy who behave less than well, while the good priest will look on life's greater sinners with sympathy and even humour. In recent centuries, however, Custodians have tried to prevent Handlers from being themselves by downplaying certain down-to-earth things of God of which ordinary Christians are the keepers, as we have already seen. Custodians want an act of worship to be meaningful, consistent and in conformity with ideals they have identified. Handlers simply get on with it, not too bothered about ideals and consistency. Either party left to their own devices are likely to lead worship astray.

Giving and receiving

Custodians and Handlers are each giving and receiving from one another. Both are receiving from God before ever they begin to give. Both our giving and our receiving, with God, with our neighbours, with the tradition, can be engaged in well or badly, and from time to time will need our conscious attention. Above all, we need to appreciate the importance of receiving, if we are going to have anything to give.

14

The Core of Worship

We have returned regularly to a notion of 'sitting under'. If there is a need for this, what is it that we are sitting under? Some might want to identify an authoritative 'thing', an absolute tradition normative down to fine details. No such understanding of tradition, however, is capable of surviving close scrutiny, in historical or doctrinal terms. If we accept the fact, then, that Christian worship has seen wide variations through time and place, it is worth enquiring how far we might distil out from such variety an essential core. Part of the quest of scholars has indeed been to refine out such a core in worship: enduring structures, practices and understandings that transcend time and place. The Second Vatican Council in its *Constitution on the Sacred Liturgy* stated confidently that 'the liturgy is made up of immutable elements, divinely instituted, and of elements subject to change'.[1] It has in practice unfortunately proven difficult, beyond certain very basic things, to identify on historical grounds much that is immutable – the quest for a 'core' turns out to be more difficult than expected. For Paul Bradshaw the assumption that there is a fundamental continuity in the Church's liturgy through the ages is mistaken: 'historical research itself does not give us grounds for concluding that there is any fundamental continuity, except in the very broadest of terms. The "deep structures" running through liturgy are very few indeed if we apply the test of universal observance to them. There are very few things that Christians have consistently done in worship at all times and in all places.'[2]

John Baldovin has also wrestled with this question: for him there is a core, but an elusive one, always existing within particular cultural forms, unable to exist without them.[3] We have already met this idea in relation to inculturation. The gospel is no free-floating cloud of abstract truths looking for local bodies to inhabit: it is always delivered to us in cultural clothes, starting with those of first-century Palestine. Baldovin, following Gordon Lathrop,[4] would say that the core is minimal and everyday, made up of basic realities of life such as bath, word and meal, lived out by us as we see best in the here and now. This view maximizes creativity.

Implicit core

It is possible, however, to turn the argument on its head. If we believe that the Holy Spirit will lead the Church into all truth, then we can see evolving Christian praxis as part of a gradual unfolding, much in the manner of Newman's insight about the development of doctrine. The actual formulation of the doctrine of the Trinity as it gradually unfolded in the fourth century is nowhere to be found in scripture, but is so obviously implied there that the eventual stating of the doctrine simply made explicit what was implicit. Jonathan Sacks observes that 'in religions of revelation discoveries are re-discoveries, a discernment of something that was always there, but not necessarily audible from where our ancestors stood. God's word is for all time, but our act of listening is of *this* time'.[5] This would lead us to say that in worship there will be some new developments that uncover eternal truths. Our method then will not be to dismiss something if it does not go back to the beginnings, but to ask whether we can justify its retention on these other grounds. In modern times for instance a new understanding has been achieved of the eucharistic prayer and the elements that make it up. It would now be difficult to reject the normative status of this recognition, even though it only goes back a couple of centuries, for it has simply made explicit what was implicit from the earliest time that clear evidence is available – the fourth century – while at the same time it works perfectly with the flow of the rite without presenting points of difficulty.[6]

It is not easy on the other hand to justify the manual acts that grew up in the institution narrative within it, not only because of their late introduction, but also for the way they create a confusion in the pattern of the eucharist which was not there before. The whole eucharistic prayer corresponds with 'he gave thanks', and while 'he took' clearly corresponds with the preparation of the gifts, the giving of communion corresponds with 'he gave it to them saying, This is my body/blood. The twelfth-century manual acts at the words of institution (as the priest picks up the bread, etc.) do nothing to make that truth more explicit, but rather confuse it.[7] We could therefore conclude that relatively recent insights about the eucharistic prayer bear a greater authority than a set of manual acts that have for much longer been a part of liturgical practice.

In this way there may be more to say about elements in the liturgical tradition that are, if not 'immutable elements, divinely instituted', at least carriers of an authority that was for long not consciously recognized – enough to make them core practices, things to be attended to a degree more than Bradshaw or Baldovin have allowed for.

Second-stage core

There is a further caveat to be applied to Bradshaw's radical diversity: such diversity was particularly characteristic of the earliest history of Christianity, the first stage as it was finding its feet: in any new corporate enterprise time can be needed for a consensus to emerge, after which there is then no going back, any more than car designers would want to return to early experiments in the invention of the automobile. Often in human invention a first exploratory stage produces inadequate results discarded in turn, but once a design has been achieved that does the job, all subsequent versions are mere variations on the established theme. It was so with coinage, with books, and seems now to be so with computers.

We would not expect the first stages of Christian worship to be fully authoritative – that comes at a second stage that marks arrival at a consensus. This definitive stage is then followed by recurring inculturation, conscious or unconscious. This is inculturation of the second-stage consensus rather than restoration of a pristine form that needs dusting off every now and again. In the trajectory followed from the second stage on its subsequent journey there will be both constancy and innovations, some permanent, some ephemeral. It does not take much effort to see both considerable constancy and continuing change of this kind in Christian worship throughout subsequent history. In this way the second stage, when the main features settle down, can be regarded as having a core status, and while not wishing to absolutize it as a reference-point, the basilica of the fourth century obviously marks such a stage.

The core of music

There may be yet more to be discovered by such comparisons: what, for instance, would be the unchanging core of music? Not simply the earliest stratum of its history or the elemental things that make it up – that would produce grunts of primitive communication and a banging of bones (the analogy is not a perfect one, as music does not look to its whole history for a sense of itself in the way Christianity does). Perhaps in music there are two cores: the basics of accumulated practice, climaxing in such complex skills as those of choirs and orchestras – the practical ability to make music as inherited, in this case, in the Western tradition; the second 'core' is something quite different, to do with the heart of music, its genius. It is something in the music that the performer could never have planned for – it simply happens, we know not how. It is the soul of real music, with a life of its own, at whatever stage in history this music may have been played. It is as if it comes from another dimension – the power and 'magic' of music latent in the score is waiting to be released from this mysterious dimension into our world. This is enabled by our human gifts, as we give ourselves to the accumulated fund of practice and wisdom. The worth of practices such as an orchestra playing a symphony is in this way assessed by a consensus on how successfully they let in that unanalysable, mysterious and deep *life* from this other dimension. It is common enough for artists to speak of the work of art creating itself in them, the work itself seeming to be the author. Novelists can feel the story writing itself as they follow its promptings, not knowing where it will lead. Any amount of such stories can be told of artists. From the Welsh poet R. S. Thomas, eccentric, inconsistent, anything but serious in appearance, a constant flow of masterpieces poured out. His daughter-in-law recounts of their first encounter: 'meeting him was so startling. It told me something about the mystery of art . . . that some people [have] an ability to create work that was not of their personality at all. For a man with such personal difficulties to write such sublime poetry . . . it was just as though something came through at times.'[8]

'It was Proust', says David Tracy, 'who insisted that art is produced by some self distinct from the self of the everyday life. Indeed, it is suggestive to think that the great artists are able to converse with both forces and questions that most of us shun, repress, or simply are unaware of.'[9] All of this can be said of that great artist, the worshipping Body of Christ, often despite the habitual behaviour and appearance of its members and despite what they think they are doing when they worship.

From another dimension

Such speculation about the 'core' of music and art might help us think about the equivalent in worship. The necessity of liturgical practices and traditions is rarely self-evident except at the most basic level (water is poured, thanks is given over bread and wine prior to sharing them, and so on, all in association with a range of meanings over which there is no complete consensus). But there is something else that is more than inherited practices: it is something definite but never finally nailed down, because our categories will always be inadequate. It will be identified not in the end by formulations (although they help) or required practices, but by a common judgement within the corporate body of Christ, consistent through time, that this 'something else' sets us more fully in the climate of

God. As with music, it is as if it comes through from another dimension – it is supernatural.

This more ethereal 'core' moreover can only be engaged with through concrete practices: the gathering of the assembly, the sacraments, the reading of the scriptures, the prayers public and private, and the ethical life. This supernatural core then reveals yet further practices as core practices, such as certain kinds of gesture (for example standing as opposed to slouching), certain kinds of music (plainsong, say, as opposed to vaudeville). This supernatural voice enables us to see the core of liturgy at more than the simple level of bath, word and meal. It is a seeing that has to go on in a very particular context: a context that cannot be described but only weighed up by all our faculties symphonically, perceived through our pores. In that context the Body of Christ can come to a consensus (for now) on the elusive but very real 'core'.

There is a necessary precondition for this: holding self-expression in tension with a turning from self (individual and corporate). That will need a careful balance between creativity and sitting-under, self-realization and self-forgetting, as we are caught up in singing with the One who is other. The core is then seen as a panoply of shifting practices, inseparable from the song that comes through them – this shifting is owed partly to cultural change, leading to changing cultural dress with the passage of time. The core is more than a short list of labels: it is the tradition in action, an action set within the Body of Christ's supernatural climate. Any mistaken attempt to spell it out too precisely is, in L.-M. Chauvet's words, 'to peel the onion in order to find the onion'.[10]

What do we 'sit under'? The 'core' of the tradition, certainly, but seen within a larger context that makes of it a conduit imparting the lifegiving vitality of God. If we ask, 'What is music?' the answer is that we discover by making it, within the context of a repertoire. The answer, therefore, to the question, 'what are we to sit under?' is: we find out by doing it, within the genetic 'language' of the tradition.

Liturgy and life

If we do find out by doing it, the next question is: what language is adequate to talking about it? First we can say that whatever we find at the core of worship is very close to what we find at the core of life. Here is one of the great issues for Christians today: the relation between liturgy and life. Elsewhere I have taken the Mystery-theology of Odo Casel as a starting point for exploring this.[11] Casel is first of all concerned with the divine presence in the liturgy. His thinking leads logically into an area which he did not develop very far, and on which he might not have been very keen: the complementary nature of the two modes of Christ's presence in worship and in secular life. This further development of his thinking, however, is too compelling not to be pursued, and it takes us further in our exploration of the core.

We start by affirming that Christ is to be known in the world, and has been since its very creation. Christ is the Mystery hidden within creation, whose hiddenness became visibility at the incarnation. He remains everywhere present but hidden, except when we come to see with the eyes of the incarnation. Anywhere that people show love to one another, there, veiled, is Christ present. Where one Aztec did something to protect the weak, or an atheistic Communist quietly worked to improve people's lot, or where a politician has sought to bring an end to war, there is a presence of Christ but veiled, not recognized or named. In the saving events of Christ the veil is then taken away – there is now a face and a name to such love: God, whom we see in Jesus of Nazareth. We now realize that the world is the work of the God of Jesus, and that we can know this God in this world. As Paul writes in Romans 1.20, 'Ever since the creation of the world his invisible nature, namely, his eternal power and deity, has been clearly perceived in the things that have been made.' For Maximus the Confessor (c. 580–662) all creation exists simply because God is constantly willing it, and that will is love. If the world only exists because it is loved by God, then that love is there at work in it and can be recognized as such by those with eyes trained to see.[12] For St Augustine, 'the Word of God . . . is present everywhere, not enclosed in any one place, nor parcelled out among all the things that exist, but everywhere whole and entire. He is not even absent from the minds of the godless, although they do not perceive him.'[13]

Presence

From Christ's presence in the world we now pass to this same presence in worship. Our tendency is to picture Jesus as a solitary Palestinian bachelor standing there doing nothing. In any form of storytelling a character only begins to become real when encountered within networks in which he or she lives and works, surrounded by relatives and associates, friends and enemies. Any picture of Christ that is going to be at least serviceable needs to be a moving picture showing him engaging with other people, and being what he is through them, during his life and ministry; but it must also do justice to the fact that Christ is a person in constant relationship within the Trinity. The picture of Christ that comes to us in worship needs to approximate to this if it is not to be a misleading picture too much of our own making, an individualistic Christ too much like us. Casel saw that our tendency to think of Christ's presence in worship as vague and shapeless is inadequate – an abstract personal nearness is not worth a great deal. Even accepted perceptions of the eucharistic presence in forms of bread and wine he criticized as oversimplified. Drawing on insights from the period of the early Christian basilicas, Casel sought to show that ultimately even the very category of 'presence' is inadequate. The Christ with whom we engage in the liturgy is the Christ of the saving events, which are the necessary light and shade of his portrait, engaging with us in a thousand ways in worship, among which the bread and wine of the kingdom are a particular focus and locus. Casel tries to wean us off our inadequate pictures of God and Christ: the only reliable picture is not the vague one in our head but the factual content of scripture as it comes alive in a worshipping assembly.

Sacred conversation

The way the saving events recorded in the scriptures are the life of our worship can be illustrated from a particular kind of painting found in different forms in Christian history, but particularly popular in the Middle Ages and Renaissance: a picture of a sacred scene – often the Virgin Mary with the child Jesus – surrounded by saints and other people from different ages. Plate 12 shows such a painting by Benozzo Gozzoli. It may seem too removed from reality: for a start it makes a nonsense of time. The scene is supposed to be in heaven, but Jesus was grown-up by the time he went back to heaven. John the Baptist is portrayed as a grown man, but he was the same age as Jesus. The other saints here come from different periods altogether.

In these paintings all the saving events are visibly or implicitly present. This painting speaks of the incarnation, but struggles of other ages and other times are present in characters gathered around. There is a sense in this painting that all is done. Christ *has* died on the cross and is risen – the peace of the scene speaks of that. The saints are so at home that they don't all need to look at the Virgin and child. There is no fear of being discourteous. In these paintings the whole saving story is complete and has come to a standstill – it just sings. The saving events coalesce into an a-temporal peace.

In Christian worship the story of our salvation similarly sings. It is no isolated Palestinian that we meet in Jesus, but the Christ of the saving events, inseparable from all the other characters in the drama. These illustrations from Renaissance art may help us see why Odo Casel was anxious to get us away from oversimple pictures of Christ and his presence in the liturgy: if we have any sense of encountering the Lord in worship, the picture that most adequately illustrates that experience is not my own picture of Christ, nor any picture of an impossibly isolated Jesus – that presence, that encounter, that experience, is an encounter with the saving events in whose fabric Jesus is the key player.

Liturgy and the world

Now we come to the question, 'How do the two experiences of Christ (in worship and in life) relate?' First of all, liturgy has power to transform our sight, so that having encountered Christ in it we go out ready and prepared to recognize him in the world. As tracker dogs smell the clothing of a criminal in order to track him down, so we gain a whiff of Christ in worship in order that we may go out and find him in life. This is not automatic: it can come with that gradual conversion of the person we call holiness, but this deliberate quest to see Christ in life can also be consciously pursued as a result of teaching – that is, through simply being told to look. The result is individuals growing in readiness to see Christ in everything. More and more we look on life and people and events with the eyes of the Church at worship. Certain things then will grow in us: courtesy, openness, readiness to listen, a valuing of the good in others, and not least, peace.

That is at the level of individual virtue, but there is more: corporate virtue involves corporate action issuing from a community seeing with corporate eyes. One result will be a corporate passion for social justice. It is often said in South Africa that only a small proportion of Christians engaged in the struggle against apartheid. Most went to their churches week by week without getting involved. In South Africa searing injustice was (and still often is) on everyone's doorstep, while in most developed countries of the West injustice on that scale is remote from experience. If it is possible to overlook such things in a country like South Africa (and that is not true of all people there by any means), then in a country like Britain the challenge to look on our global society with prophetic Christian eyes is an even more tough assignment: this message about the liturgy needs all the more to be brought home to Christians at every level when we are talking about worship. If we are not seeing the needy and oppressed, if we edit them out, then there are things we are not understanding about what worship is.

Ethics

Since the 1960s we have recognized a need for the Church to be more engaged with the needs of people all over the world, especially their needs for justice, freedom from oppression and exploitation, for secure provision of basic needs of life, and freedom from war and violence. There has been great emphasis among the churches on this *immediate* ethical call. A second dimension, just as important, has been neglected: the *long-term* ethical call. This call links ethics with worship. It requires a strong awareness of the state of contemporary society and particularly those problems which promise trouble in the future. An example would be family life, the ability of the family to form young people in civic and human values, its widespread failure to do this, and the resulting disorientation, amorality and destructiveness of some youngsters today, such as the feral youth who run loose in cities causing havoc and suffering. Even the law of the land in the United Kingdom recognizes the role of religion in forming ethically motivated people.[14] One of the strongest motivations for Christian believers to pray seriously and within the tradition can come simply from taking stock of the serious problems to be found in our society. If we need motivation for throwing all our efforts into creating a vibrant, dedicated and praying Church, we need only keep society's problems before our eyes. For society to change, it needs a vibrant and thriving Church in its midst. Our call is not to build a better world now by our own efforts (although that helps), but also to do it by the back-room task of building a praying Church that derives its strength from confidence in God. This is the prudence of the wise investor; it is the seed in a field that grows quietly by itself to become abundantly fruitful. A Church that takes prayer and worship seriously will come to command people's attention and attract them, and so will contribute to the building of a more caring society that will attend with greater commitment to the problems of society and world. A Church mediocre in prayer will never hope to do that. The poet Philip Larkin has spoken of a church building as 'a serious house upon serious earth':

> A serious house on serious earth it is,
> In whose blent air all our compulsions meet,
> Are recognized, and robed as destinies.

And that much never can be obsolete,
Since someone will forever be surprising
A hunger in himself to be more serious,
And gravitating with it to this ground,
Which, he once heard, was proper to grow wise in . . . [15]

The destructive moral vacuum in our society has need of serious people standing on graced terrain, quietly working for the long-term future. As well as the *immediate* ethical call to roll up our sleeves for service of our neighbour, there is the *long-term* ethical call to become a Church that, in the midst of a disorientated society will be a people passionately given to prayer, a people 'proper to grow wise' among, a task that has a longer trajectory.

A Church at the service of society

While it is essential for Christians to work alongside all those working for a good society, and even though we need to seek all ways to make our contribution to the good running of society (seen, for example, in a priest who becomes a town councillor), nevertheless, treatment of symptoms has to be accompanied by treatment of cause. Without the gospel of Christ there are limits to the building of a good society because only the gospel, and life in the Body of Christ, are adequate means and an adequate end. We can be tempted to think that Christian practical service of others is sufficient, but ultimately we are always brought up against society's need not just of the good, which is always hampered by human limitation, but for more – for the life and energy that only God can bring. The best contribution we can make to society's long-term good, then, is communion in the Body of Christ. Working for that may slow down some of our efforts for short-term goals, but pay off in the long run. A monitory example comes from the Netherlands, where in the 1980s there was a huge process in the main Christian denominations called the Conciliar Process, focused on peace, justice and the environment. There was a tendency to reduce time available for worship, prayer and theological study, the urgency being thought to be so great. Ten years on, the whole process was gone.

Eyes in both directions

Worship is capable of turning us into people who see, and who then train their sight on daily life. The resulting knowledge of God present in the world then turns us back to our worship, to seek God more closely there.

That may lead us to criticism of aspects of the Church and its worship. Each dimension, Church and world, in this way illuminates the other. Each subverts the false in the other: liturgy subverts aspects of life that cannot stand up to the encounter with it (such as enmity); life subverts aspects of liturgy that cannot stand up to the encounter with it (such as bad church art). We have already seen this at work in inculturation (see p. 84). Whenever there is an encounter between our secular way of life and the culture of the Church, both come under judgement, and both gain an opportunity to learn and move on.

The opposing poles of sacred and profane are deeply rooted in us. They reflect a correct instinct that there is a difference between sacred and secular, but we can fail to appreciate that this is a difference between two things closely bound together. Because we conceive of this difference in a simplistic form it can be hard for people to make sense of language about Christ present in everything. We can have an innate sense of holiness transmitted through the physical world, but usually in beautiful things of life such as sunsets, gardens or babies, not the broken glass on a housing estate, the drawn face of the sex worker on a street corner or an argument in the family. Before modern times people had often been more able to see Christ in everything, but perhaps in ways no longer easy for us.

Contemporary bridges

To return to Casel, the Christ we see is Christ in the drama of the saving events, which present a pattern always visible in the daily events of life. The story as recounted in scripture mirrors life at every point. We are drawn to recognize Christ in the world's stories, great and small. The events recounted in scripture are a matrix recognizable in all the ordinary events of life. There is, however, often a plausibility gap between the scriptural stories Christians tell and most people's gut experience. For this reason each generation has in the past created its own bridges between daily life and the saving events. David Brown has shown how through history believers have retold Christ's story in terms of the contemporary. The Western composite figure of Mary Magdalene was an early example, close to us in her life and character, while close to Jesus in the story. Through the centuries stories of the saints have tended to march with the changes in culture. As Christianity emerged from times when there was deep suspicion of sex and marriage for instance, stories of married saints start appearing in the hagiographies. Brown suggests that in more recent times the novel has performed this bridging function.

'It is astonishing how resilient Christian reflection through literature has proved to be. Some have explored the darker side of Christianity in its doctrines of fall and sin [such as William Golding] . . . others the whole question of psychological growth in self-perception and religious perceptivity [such as Susan Howatch] . . . [one major contrast with older stories of sanctity is that] many a contemporary novelist encourages us to detect saintliness despite the presence of continuing faults' (for example Graham Greene).[16] 'The life of Jesus has in effect moved from being a set of specific examples for close copying to the status of being an analogous case that requires imaginative re-identification under very different circumstances, and for that our greater debt is now to the imaginative work of novelists or their equivalent on stage or in film.'[17] In the visual arts Brown cites the example of 'an alternative Chartres in broken plates and glass built next to its more famous rival'.[18] One can imagine the observer looking from the medieval cathedral to its reincarnation in the detritus of a run-down suburb and then back again, and seeing both the cathedral and all such detritus in a new light from then on.

How can we bring about such a new way of relating Church and world, and thereby continue to gain access to the life of the saving events? Discourse about the Christ known in the liturgy and the Christ known in ordinary life needs to become common currency first of all. That discourse then needs to be backed up by its exploration in the arts. That can set the scene, but the main work is yet to be done: evolving ways for this belief to engage with our actual experience and become real for us. This will need to emerge from the grass roots, but does not have much of a chance if the scene is not first set. Too often the local church does not set the scene very well. As Brown puts it, 'there is too much of a mismatch between what the church takes to be significant and the actual experience of the wider population'.[19] People are looking for stories to make sense of their story, but they choose their own, they pick and mix. Football is many people's grand narrative. When photos appeared in the newspapers of David Beckham with a broken finger bone, people could be seen putting a damaged or troublesome finger on the photo to help make it better – we have to work even at that level.

Recognizing Christ within the Church

If we need to find ways of creating bridges between the Church and the world, there is also a need for bridges within the Church. The church building may be seen as holy and the sacred actions as holy, but it is difficult for a congregation to look on each other as holy. 'People can be aware of the mystery of what takes place at the altar, but not of the mystery of the assembly itself.'[20] Parish communities often trip themselves up, hinder and wound each other through this inability. What is often found in a church council or other form of decision-making in the parish is a play of unprocessed dynamics from the secular world: rivalry, competition, wanting my own way, inability to put myself in the other person's shoes, unawareness of the greatness of the whole corporate undertaking, unwillingness to learn new things, and similar manifestations of sin. Where Christians are straining to see Christ in one another, there they discover in themselves the virtues of mutual submission, listening, setting the other before oneself, and even love, conscious of sitting under something infinitely greater than themselves that has supernatural power to draw from us things we do not realize are in us. 'Love one another with fraternal affection; outdo one another in showing honour. Never flag in zeal' (Romans 12.10f).

Lingering effects

What may we hope to take home from worship? Good theatre treats its audience as adults – it assumes they are open to being challenged and made to work hard – it is not enough to aim at sending an audience home feeling good. Peter Brook asks what remains after the performance:

> I know of one acid test in the theatre. It is literally an acid test. When a performance is over, what remains? Fun can be forgotten, but powerful emotion also disappears and good arguments lose their thread. When emotion and argument are harnessed to a wish from the audience to see more clearly into itself – then something in the mind burns. The event scorches on to the memory an outline, a taste, a trace, a smell – a picture. It is the play's central image that remains, its silhouette, and if the elements are highly blended this silhouette will be its meaning, this shape will be the essence of what it has to say. When years later I think of a striking theatrical experience I find a kernel engraved on my memory: two lamps under a tree, an old woman dragging a cart, a sergeant dancing, three people on a sofa in hell – or occasionally a trace deeper than any imagery. I haven't a hope of remembering the meanings precisely, but from the kernel I can reconstruct a set of meanings. Then a purpose will have been served. A few hours could amend my thinking for life. This is almost but not quite impossible to achieve.

. . . the question comes back to the spectator. Does he want any change in his circumstances? Does he want anything different in himself, his life, his society? If he doesn't, then he doesn't need the theatre to be an aid, a magnifying glass, a searchlight or a place of confrontation – on the other hand, he may need one or all of these things. In this case, he not only needs the theatre, he needs everything he can get there. He desperately needs that trace that scorches, he desperately needs it to stay.[21]

In Christian worship we are looking for nothing other than our transformation, even if what we consciously take home is a single trace somewhere inside us. For that, we need worship where those participating, however thin their gifts, have given the whole of themselves, they 'not only [need the liturgy, they need] everything [they] can get there'.

Yitzhak Hen in a monograph on Merovingian Gaul in the sixth to eighth centuries says that,

According to Aristotle the *catharsis*, that is the relief that comes from releasing piety and terror, was the main purpose of the tragedy, and was extremely important to its audience . . . A similar cathartic effect . . . and thus an acknowledgment of the cathartic qualities of the mass, is essential in an analysis of its relation to society and culture. Pity for the suffering Christ and terror of the Last Judgement, subjects which arose several times during the mass, must have given relief to these feelings. Thus the people came to celebrate the mass because it was the major religious rite, a social event and a dramatic enactment, which also offered a psychological relief for the soul.[22]

That makes me think of many times participating in the Orthodox liturgy in Romania when a great slowness and stillness descends on music, words and all participants from the eucharistic prayer through to communion. That has always seemed a cathartic moment. The alert peace that the liturgy can induce may be partly physiological and psychological, but there is more, just as there is a difference here between the theatre and the Church. While for Brook the 'trace' is something in the essence of what the play has to offer, in worship we can never say what that essence is, apart from its being Christ, and acknowledging that every act of worship, if we will have it, is one step further in the process of our transfiguration. As we have been saying, worship is not about seeking such experience, but there are moments when it is given.

The living heart of the Christian way

Gordon Lathrop's 'core' of such primal realities as word, bath and meal
are interchangeable between worship and life, and found in both. This
interchangeability should be one of the tests of core features of worship.
What I have called 'implicit core' and 'second-stage core' need to pass
the same test, as, for instance we have shown in the connections between
basilica liturgy and the theatre. But that is not all: the core of all true
worship will also be different, other, and this becomes particularly clear
when comparing the heart of worship with what I have called the 'ethereal core' of music. The ultimate core of the apple is Christ himself, not
only the Christ of the story and of abstract perception, but the embodied Christ of the Church's worship. Even if we seem to gain no experience in an act of worship, somewhere deep inside our many layers we
shall be taking home a trace that will quietly contribute to our gradual
transformation.

If 'the liturgy is made up of immutable elements, divinely instituted,
and of elements subject to change', then the task of identifying the 'immutable elements' would seem as complex as the vision that greeted André Mocquereau when he first looked on the medieval manuscripts he
had photographed (see p. 156): a body of data that refused to be pinned
down, but had to be looked on in its ensemble, from which the mind
could gain a sense and a feel for a tradition that was truly alive and, as it
were, pulsating before our eyes.

15

A Complex Shaping

I once had the experience of being shown around a foreign city by someone I had only met once before, several years previously. His enthusiasm knew no bounds as the information poured out. The whole day, including a meal in a restaurant, was spent like that. Through all of it there was, extraordinarily it seemed to me, no personal engagement – no space for my views, no interest in how I was, or even what sort of a person I was; no possibility for me on my part to engage with the other. When we came to farewells, it was as if nothing had happened all day – I was left feeling like a cipher.

In the last few chapters we have been examining the relationship between two parties: God and ourselves. My experience in the foreign city would have been different had there been a place in it for the art of human relating. Our experience of Christian worship too will be very different where there is a place in it for the art of conversation with a God in whom we actually show an interest.

How do I go about sitting under?

The catholic tradition will always be a matter for some disagreement and debate, like anything that is alive and constantly developing. Although it is constant and reasonably consistent with itself, it flourishes where its followers interpret it with the creative elan of the artist. It is at the feet of this tradition, which is the present state of play of the 'culture of Jesus', that we need to sit attentively, as two people attend to one another. I have called this 'sitting under'. How are we to go about it?

There is a need to be 'formed'. We are not dealing with something straightforward that can be filleted, labelled and set out in instruction manuals: we are faced with an obliqueness that comes to us from the Gospels, where Christ repeatedly refuses to spell out what he is trying to draw out of people. The formation that he sought to impart is passed on by his disciples in three key ways, two practices and an attitude: praying in the Word, sharing in the koinonia, and seeing the unity of all.

Praying in the Word is not any kind of personal prayer, but a specific tradition, the Church's tradition of daily prayer, centring on offering the scriptures and becoming steeped in them. Often known as the 'daily office' or 'the hours of prayer' or similar names, it links our sitting under the Word with time and with discipline, in the context of the whole people on earth and in heaven, from whom prayer constantly rises. If we want to find the secret, then the first thing we must do, whoever we are, and whatever our role in the People of God, is to take up the daily prayer of the Church and be formed by it.[1]

Sharing in the koinonia starts with regular participation in the eucharist, which sets forth what fellowship in Christ is about. The eucharist is our 'audience with heaven' (a phrase found on an eighth-century Christian stone in China), the place par excellence where Christ's secret is caught not taught. If the eucharist makes manifest the Church, then it follows that the koinonia is further discovered outside the eucharist by other ways of sharing with the people of God, especially in seeking experienced teachers and studying the texts of the tradition.

Seeing the unity of all works in two particular ways: first by our being aware of the Church as the 'mystical body . . . of all faithful people'.[2] Living aware of our company with countless others in the Church, and wanting to be at one with them, will dispose us towards the desire to 'sit under' Christ's 'culture'. Second, awareness of our unity with all humanity will hold together our love of the body of Christ and the drive to love and serve our neighbours and our world.

If anyone is wanting to know how to set about that attentive disposition we have been exploring, these three ways will get them started.

Liturgical formation

In the early twentieth century Romano Guardini wrote a little book pleading for liturgical formation for Christians.[3] Since then little has happened in the particular area that has been interesting us. Lay people and clergy have learned to use skills in the common offering of worship, but for many clergy the formation they receive in their training is inadequate, and most layfolk continue to do things in church without understanding much about why they do them. There is a new interest in liturgical formation, but it seems to skip over the heart of the matter: an awareness

of God's centrality, informed by growth in a feel for the life-giving nature of the tradition, a sense of the Church, the Body which Christ loved
and for which he died (Ephesians 5.25, 29–33) – a sense of being set
within something infinitely larger than our small horizons. A guided and
informed imagining-beyond-our-box must be fundamental in any liturgical formation. With this as the foundation, all people, ordained and lay
today, need to be articulate in basics of liturgical history – something
usually lapped up when provided – and to be wise in the business of being
praying human beings in community.

Praying communities

In order to help with this there is a need for small communities of prayer
– they do not need to be monastic or even resident communities. There
are different ways of creating places where the climate of God is found
and attracts people. It has to be approached like a work of art where
various elements are needed. First there is place – such communities of
prayer need to have a home, a place that resonates with what they are
about, resonates with contemporary culture, makes people feel at home,
at peace, attentive and focused, with a sense that this is holy ground.

Second it needs community, not necessarily residential, not necessarily
permanent, but a community that has entered into some commitment
to each other and to the praxis, and are able to meet to pray every day,
the backbone of their prayer being some form of the daily office of the
Church performed imaginatively. Such communities of prayer will not
survive without a degree of obedience: not so much to superiors as mutual obedience.

There is at present an unexpected flowering of such groups: an example would be '24–7 Prayer', which has grown from small beginnings
to become a network of mainly young people dispersed in various countries who establish places where they come together to pray several times
a day, adopting some of the characteristics of the monastic tradition.[4]
One is hospitality, including shared meals, and keeping open a place of
prayer that draws people in. Ministry among the poor and needy is a
priority and tends to bring them in as well. An example would be a run-
down area where young people gathered to drink and be rowdy in the
park. Louts, Goths and drug takers were drawn in by the hospitality, but
gravitated to the chapel and the worship that went on in it, and became
hooked by it. The groups in 24–7 Prayer take a variety of forms, and
are usually separate from the structures of the churches but in dialogue

with them. Anyone who cares to investigate will find many groups of this kind within the Church and on its edges. Andy Freeman, who helped found 24–7 Prayer, speaks of the powerful attraction of the Church's tradition and not least monasticism for many young people, and of their discovering an enthusiasm for a structured Christian life. The signs are that the renewed Church of the future will become alive again in its own traditions at least partly through the explorations of such groups on the fringes of the conventional church.

Social capital

There is a connection here between capacity for worship and capacity for civic life. Jonathan Sacks has eloquently spoken of 'social capital', which he understands as the level of trust in a society.[5] He imagines a stranger being introduced to the productivity of the financial and other institutions in the City of London. The visitor then turns to the many churches and asks, 'What do houses of worship create and distribute?' What they produce is something significantly different from wealth and power: non-contractual relationships that are based on covenant rather than contract, 'contracts are about the self, while covenants are about the larger groupings in and through which we develop our identity'.[6] The family is one example. 'A group in which getting along together was achieved only by the threat of violence on the one hand, or by paying for services rendered and received on the other, would not be a *family*.'[7] Friendship is another example. Covenants

> express 'the idea that people can freely create communities and polities, peoples and publics, and civil society itself, through such morally grounded and sustained compacts' (D. Elazar). Covenantal relationships – where we develop the grammar and syntax of reciprocity, where we help others and they help us without calculations of relative advantage – are where trust is born, and without them there would be no selves and no contracts . . . A world systematically bereft of fidelity or loyalty would be one in which neither states nor markets would ever get under way.[8]

For Francis Fukuyama 'If the institutions of democracy and capitalism are to work properly, they must coexist with certain premodern cultural habits that ensure their proper functioning.'[9] Sacks clarifies that 'Markets depend on virtues not produced by the market, just as states depend on virtues not created by the state. Where are they created? In families, communities, friendships, congregations, voluntary associations and fellowships of various kinds.' Alexis De Tocqueville for example observed that the American habit of forming associations and joining churches worked to protect freedom through encouraging the exercise of citizenship.[10]

Marcel Barnard and Cas Wepener have conducted interesting research into the contribution of the liturgy to building 'social capital' in the new South Africa. Social capital is understood by them as those gifts and abilities in people that can contribute to civic life and the building-up of society.[11] In the opinion of Barnard and Wepener Christian worship is a unique contributor to social capital. An example would be the singers of the Cape Town Opera who came from church choirs. Christian liturgy gave them the capacity to develop practical skills in leadership and public performance, gather in purposeful assembly, and gain personal confidence through a sense of belonging in relationships of trust. Participation in worship in South Africa has had the capacity (not universal or automatic) to develop in people a whole range of qualities needed for civic life, the liturgy itself being in fact a foretaste of the life of the divine city, the City of God.

Worship as matter for public discourse

The formation that Christians need will by its very nature tend to their becoming fuller human beings, equipping them for life in society. Once again we find this parallelism, provoking us to ask whether Christian formation should only be internal to the Church, or whether it should not also be directed outwards towards society. We tend to think of worship as a pursuit going on behind closed doors, but wherever the Church has been free the relationship between liturgy and life starts a dialogue not only for the benefit of Christians – it is such for contemporary society as well. Liturgy has many aspects that are capable of discussion in the public arena and so far we do not seem to have tumbled to this fact. In recent years there has been growing interest in the notion of 'public theology', theological discussion conducted in terms which outsiders can understand and engage with. Edward Foley has drawn attention to the applicability of this to worship.[12] There are many aspects of worship that can be discussed rationally with outsiders and in the public arena on a basis of shared understandings and presuppositions; several such aspects spring immediately to mind:

1 Worship engages with a widespread contemporary quest for life's meaning and for spiritual realities.

2 It embodies certain characteristics of healthy community where all are welcome, all equal, high and low brought together cheek-by-jowl.

3 Such transcending of secular status replaces the worldly order with one of its own, marked by roles that operate not by status but on a basis of common ownership. This engages with many outside who are looking for meaning, for community and for an understanding of self which they sense has to do with community.

4 Christian worship is universal: not only is it open to all, but it encourages an awareness of all, in its consciousness of the worldwide Church, and so encourages international solidarity and responsibility.

5 Worship is capable of strengthening people's ethical motivation.

6 The capacity of the Christian worshipping community to build up 'social capital' is demonstrable.

7 When in a healthy state worship helps human beings to live with their whole person and to express themselves with the whole of their humanity.

8 Christianity bases its worship on verifiable historical fact in the life of Christ and the history of his followers.

9 Worship, by its narrative nature, strengthens people's awareness of the importance of story in human living.

10 Christian liturgy makes a major contribution to society in its use of the arts, not least literature, music, architecture, the visual arts and theatre.

11 In cultures with a longstanding Christian tradition worship has a historical role to fulfil of putting people in touch with the foundations of the local culture and its history.

12 Christian worship is a metaculture in action, completing secular cultures in areas they are incapable of handling without its help, such as providing significant rituals and significant places for corporate lament after a tragedy.

God

In all of the above areas and probably others liturgy is capable of being part of public discourse in a secular society. Our list, however, runs a risk: believers made conscious of this quasi-manifesto could come to see it as setting a sufficient horizon, a human-centred agenda easily exchangeable with other utilitarian schemes. There is, however, another goal greater still than all of them, the divine mystery, who is beyond capturing in interchangeable languages, and without whom the Church has no credible voice. We have the additional challenge of enabling the divine mystery too to be part of public discourse, while avoiding caricatures associated in the popular mind with the English word 'God' (which after all is a cultural artefact: 'Bóg' in Polish, 'Dumnezeu' in Romanian, and so on through all languages). That may need a transitional period when we try to refer to God with other terms.

Liturgy has a distinct advantage over simple theorizing or God-talk here, for it aligns with the world of performance, enabling us to work by analogy. In a concert, over and above the practical elements that make it up, there is something ineffable that happens for people or it does not, and it is on the basis of this that hearers will judge the concert. The ability to discern this ineffable has to be learned, as it has to be with all the arts. It is part of public discourse about music, and offers a model for public discourse about God. Crudely put, as a critic may talk about a concert, so may Christians talk about worship, sometimes particular acts of worship, but more usually the long-term fruits of it. If one can for a moment be prosaic about the ineffable, this ineffable reality supplies the energy that enables the Church to function, and so in any exercise of 'public theology' in relation to the liturgy we must be very careful to make sure that God in Trinity is part of the public debate in this kind of way (even though we cannot hope to do the matter justice), and is also the life at the heart of our own understanding and proclamation.

Where to say it

If liturgy is capable of being a matter of public discourse (and therefore a form of outward-looking formation), then in the present secularizing climate it is time we began to see it as such. According to Foley, congregations need to become more aware of their worship as a public act, and to be articulate about the ways this is so. This suggests a new and unsuspected facet of liturgical formation and of mission. If the churches were to present their worship in the public arena as a model for the ideal society, that would certainly open them up to stiff criticism, and some healthy and interesting debate. Where could such debate go on? Possible areas would include:

- Defending the broadcasting of worship on radio and TV, but also providing adequate criteria and standards for it.
- Making challenges to political parties.
- Debate over religions' charitable status.

- Common cause with other faiths, especially Islam.
- The churches' own apologetics and self-presentation. In particular, the churches need to say publicly that only religion and its practice can build social capital that in the long run actually works; perhaps that should be one of our banner headlines.
- In the media and 'marketing' the faith (see for example the TV series *Priest Idol* on use of marketing methods to bring people to Christ). Once again we are challenged to make a place for the vulgar.
- Raising the matter among Christian believers, so that the liturgy may be better appreciated and delighted in, and that in our daily lives we may be articulate about the social benefits of worship.

The last point may well be the main one. I think of the vitality of the British TV programme *Songs of Praise*, and how the witness of *individuals* that it regularly features could become instead a testimony to the *corporate* contribution of Christianity to the common good of society. The programme would benefit from some corporate testimonies.

Complexity

We are complex – far more than we are prepared to believe or have patience with. When learning to play the piano we learn to push down keys and gain the muscular agility to have control over very complex forms of finger-movement. We learn to read musical notation, transforming signs into notes. Hours of practice gradually meld these activities to a unity. Even then, all you are is a music-making machine. Other faculties now come into play to create real music, and, as any pianist knows, you no longer have complete control over what is happening. Increasingly there come moments when you learn to fly as it were, to leave thinking and planning behind and let the music live. Somehow it happens. Our thinking is too slow and laborious to be of great help at such a moment. Every pianist will know the experience of playing a very complex piece without thinking about it, but starting to stumble once she concentrates on the playing of the notes. One can have the same experience in touch-typing or even learning to drive a car. A complexity of simultaneous actions needs to happen instinctively, deftly enabled by capacities beyond our ken. The footballer who instinctively kicks the ball to the right place without knowing how he did it, the secretary tossing a crumpled page deftly into a distant bin while feeling that her arm rather than her brain achieved it, the juggler, the acrobat, the mother walking confidently in contrast to her toddler who is trying to train his instincts, muscles and whole being but stumbling uncertainly. We benefit all the time from these mysterious skills, while at the same time we have an innate tendency to reduce ourselves to something far more simple. Our constant inclination is to reduction: reduction of others to ciphers, of ourselves to less than we are – life is less hard work that way. This leads into a cyclic process where resulting woes bring us up once more against the mystery and complexity of ourselves. Parents who bring up children badly can pay the price later on: a more complex relationship with them than they would have wished for. Governments that choose aggression before conciliation may reap a whirlwind. Reduction, oversimplification, are our constant tendency. Reduction of ourselves, reduction of the other. They go together, for any understanding of what is within us is only possible when hand-in-hand with understanding of what is outside us.

This book has sought to explore this question in relation to Christian worship. Worship requires an unselfconscious instinctive operation in which many complex elements are mysteriously melded together. We never achieve the right balance, and there are always some vital elements pushed onto the back burner. In medieval Europe an unthinking following of the nose in Christian worship made it stray from its proper course simply through impoverishment of the thinking faculty, combined with lack of adequate information about the past. In modern reforms the thinking faculty has come to the fore at the expense of others: we can plan an act of worship in the same way the theatre producer plans an opera. We decide what we want and the kind of effect to aim for. We repeatedly see ourselves and our contemporary culture as the reference-point, without taking sufficient account of the hard work required in responding to a spiritual reality that is *other* than ourselves. These problems are nothing new in the history of liturgy. Our worship will never be right until we are perfect, and in the meantime we have to work hard to be aware of the complexity of ourselves, never mind the complexity of the Divine. Easy quick fixes are no good, be they happy-clappy rave-ups, old-fashioned solemn masses, or any other placing of all our bets on straightforward answers to deal with our discomfort and the unyielding complexity of life and truth.

Analysis of any reality naturally tends to reduce it to less than it is, but if we carefully bear that danger in mind, analysis can help take us forward. Part of the project of this book therefore has been a quest to identify some of the realities needing to be taken seriously when we engage in worship, first by identifying them, and then by forgetting them as we 'swoop' in an instinctive activity which we need to work hard at discovering.

The early Christian basilica has earned a name for itself because of the way, within the terms of its own culture, it encapsulated many principles of worship that seem to be fundamental. The basilica itself and its surrounding culture have gone, never to be recovered, but many principles live on and continue to prove their worth in different times. Among them some are particularly needed in the demanding situation of today: were we to devise a succinct aide-memoire for Christians to paste on their bedroom walls, perhaps it might look something like this:

God, the fountain and origin of all worship;
Obedience leading to authentic freedom:
Sitting-under attentively, expectant listening for truth, through
Gifts of God that enable transformation, especially:
    the **Community** and culture of Christ's Body the Church,
    the **Scriptures** proclaiming God's saving deeds,
    the **Tradition,** tested by corporate reason and use, and lived in worship.
Holy things, places and actions as part of incarnation's language for us with God.
Symphonic apprehending as the way to God's truth, whose simplicity is always complex;
Swimming of body, faculties and the arts together in the liturgical setting, the
Arena of the people's action with God in a corporate
Drama with manifold
Roles.
Formation necessary today after a disabling loss of gifts:
Kinesic Communion at a time of 'untaught bodies';
a **Sense of the Church** in a society of autonomous individuals and groups;
Liturgy and Life in dialogue, idealistic principles arm-in-arm with earthiness.
Ethical consequences in
Reverence for neighbour and for creation and the struggle for justice;
the **Inner life** and the centrality of prayer, worshipping and living with desire
to draw all to Christ by sharing God's
Mission;
Becoming selves singly and jointly given to
God who is
All in all.

And so . . .

Christian worship is God's activity in us. Human beings always find it difficult to be open to God worshipping in us, we naturally shun this divine activity or seek to avoid or repress it. For this history shows two main reasons: human sin and the culture of societies.

Sin needs the continual quest for conversion, so that we might submit ourselves one to another and to God's wisdom coming to us in the Christian tradition and the culture of the Church. This quest for conversion never ends.

Cultural blockages formed in each of us by our society need the same process at the corporate level. It is a process that requires faith, obedience and the giving-away of self. This paradoxically opens the way to that radical freedom for which human beings were made – a freedom indistinguishable from love.

Notes

1 Introduction

1 See especially Bradshaw, *Search for the Origins*.

2 Dix, *Shape of the Liturgy*. Current views on Dix's legacy are usefully summarized in the 2005 edition of this book by Continuum Press, in the Introduction by Simon Jones, pp. x–xxviii.

3 The text of this prayer is available in numerous publications, such as Cuming and Bradshaw, *Prayers of the Eucharist*, pp. 34f.

4 Taft, 'How Liturgies Grow', p. 355; also in Taft, *Beyond East and West*, pp. 167f.

5 Turner, *From Ritual to Theatre*, p. 89.

2 From House to Hall

1 The oldest parts of the *Didache*, a kind of handbook for travelling apostles, are thought to be first century. Scholars cannot agree whether these prayers in chapters 9 and 10 are intended as eucharistic prayers or not. The text is available on http://www.earlychristianwritings.com/didache.html.

2 See Wright, *Jesus and the Victory of God*, p. 276.

3 See Bradshaw, *Search for the Origins*.

4 See Douglas, *Natural Symbols*, pp. 61ff.

5 See Turner, *The Pattern of Christian Truth*; discussed in Ford and Stamps, *Essentials*, pp. 81ff.

6 Burtchaell, *From Synagogue to Church*, p. 227.

7 Burtchaell, *Synagogue*, p. 339.

8 White, *Social Origins,* Vol. 1, p. 44.

9 See n. 1 this chapter.

10 White, *Social*, p. 138, n. 123.

11 See Petts, *Christianity in Roman Britain*.

12 It was not a simple adoption of this architectural form: recent scholarship has wanted to point out the significant differences between the secular basilica and these new churches – see Crippa, *La Basilica*, p. vii.

13 See for example Kähler, *Frühe Kirche*, p. 100.

14 On the so-called 'open façade' see Casti, 'S. Pietro in Vincoli', in *Le Chiese Paleocristiane*, p. 67.

15 See Zizioulas, *Being as Communion*, p. 60. The key word here is 'communion' (*kiononia*).

16 See Anon., *Roles in the Liturgical Assembly*, p. 224.

17 See Arranz, *Functions*, p. 37.

18 See Braniște, *Liturgical Assembly*, pp. 73ff.

19 See Cattaneo, *Ministeri*, pp. 175–9.

20 Ap. Con. 8.1.20, quoted in Braniște, *Liturgical Assembly*, p. 97.

21 See Alzati, *Ambrosianum Mysterium*, Vol. 2, p. 43.

22 Eccl. Hist. 10.4 (translation by Wilkinson, *From Synagogue to Church*, p. 191).

23 See Langlotz, 'Basilika'.

24 Wilkinson, *Synagogue*, p. 193.

25 Wilkinson, *Synagogue*, pp. 198–200.

26 Lara, 'Versus Populum', p. 217.

27 Mainstone, *Hagia Sophia*, pp. 229f.

28 Lara, 'Versus Populum', p. 218.

29 Wagner, 'Le Lieu', pp. 37, 39.

30 Koch, *Early Christian Art*, p. 48.

31 Methodius, *Banquet of the Ten Virgins*, 5.8, see http://www.newadvent. org/fathers/0623.htm.

32 Eusebius, *Ecclesiastical History* 2.4.2, see http://www.newadvent.org/ fathers/2501.htm.

33 Ambrose, *Letters* Bk 1, Letter 5.3f; quoted in Crippa, *La Basilica*, p. 51.

34 Letter XXXII, quoted in Crippa, *La Basilica*, pp. 118ff.

35 See Piva, *La Cattedrale Doppia*.

36 Miles, *Image as Insight*, p. 45.

37 Letter 190.5, 19; see Crippa, *La Basilica*, pp. 127f.

38 Miles, *Image as Insight*, p. 50; quote from Eusebius, *Ecclesiastical History* 10.4.65.

39 Budde, *Improvisation*.

40 Budde, *Improvisation*, p. 138.

41 Herwegen, *The Art-Principle*, pp. 17f., 41.

3 Drama

1 Brook, *Empty Space*, p. 11.

2 Balthasar, *Theo-Drama*, see for example p. 249. (See also Irvine, 'Celebrating the Eucharist'.)

3 Balthasar, *Theo-Drama*, p. 76.

4 Balthasar, *Theo-Drama*, p. 112.

5 Williams, *Lost Icons*, pp. 135f.

6 See Stosur, 'Liturgy and (Post) Modernity'.

7 Balthasar, *Theo-Drama*, p. 78.

8 Balthasar, *Theo-Drama*, p. 19.

9 Balthasar, *Theo-Drama*, p. 17.

10 See Brook, *Empty Space*, p. 69.

11 See note 6 this chapter.

12 Balthasar, *Theo-Drama*, pp. 70f.

13 Brook, *Empty Space*, p. 25.

14 Balthasar, *Theo-Drama*, p. 307.

15 Brook, *Empty Space*, p. 28.

16 See Baldovin, *Urban Character*.

17 Origen, *De Oratione* 31.2, 4, 5 and 7, pp. 324f.

18 Kähler, *Die Frühe Kirche*, pp. 16–27; G. Koch, conversely, in *Early Christian Architecture*, p. 20, suggests that a Christian interpretation of this is uncertain. For further information and extensive bibliography on both sides of the argument see Giordano and Kahn, *Testimonianze ebraiche a Pompei*, pp. 31–5, and Catalano, *Case abitanti e culti di Ercolano*, pp. 180ff. An alternative theory on the violent removal of the cross is suggested by remarkable records of a trial found in a nearby room. The householder's wife had taken to court one of her slave-girls, challenging her entitlement to the possessions of her deceased mother, who had an apparently Hebrew or Christian name. Giordano and Kahn speculate whether in a fit of anger the householder's wife destroyed this recalcitrant slave's place of worship. The trial was still in course at the time the volcanic eruption engulfed them all.

19 Book review in *Praxis News of Worship*, issue 16, Winter 2007, p. 6.

20 Text in: http://www.bombaxo.com/didascalia.html.

21 Cyril of Jerusalem, *Mystagogical Catecheses*, 5.3 (trans. author), see http://www.newadvent.org/fathers/3101.htm.

22 Zizioulas, *Being as Communion*, p. 82, n. 53.

4 A Strange Warping

1 See Kelly, *Exultet*.

2 See Bishop, 'The Genius of the Roman Rite', in Bishop, *Liturgica Historica*, pp. 1–18.

3 Klauser, *A Short History*, p. 40.

4 Ratcliff, *Expositio*.

5 See Hen, *Culture and Religion*; Porter, *Gallican Rite*; Ehrensperger, *Die Westlichen, Gallikanischen Liturgien*.

6 Hen, *Culture*, p. 67.

7 Hen, *Culture*, p. 70.

8 Augustine *Sermons* 252.4, see http://www.newadvent.org/fathers/1603.htm.

9 For the Latin text see Andrieu, *Les Ordines*, Vol. 2, pp. 65–127. The only easily available English translation is unreliable and out of date, in Atchley, *Ordo Romanus Primus*; Romano, *Ritual and Society* gives a modern translation, mostly excellent but strange in some of its choices, on pp. 422–39. For background information and summaries of the content: Vogel, *Medieval Liturgy*; Jungmann, *Mass of the Roman Rite*, Vol. 1, pp. 67ff.

10 Later Frankish interpretations refer to his turning east here and at other points, something that would not work in the randomly orientated Roman churches as it would in French ones which all faced east. See Vogel, *Versus ad Orientem*, pp. 447–69. Romano's theory (see previous note) that the Pope would face east even if the building's orientation meant he would be at an angle to everybody is unconvincing: the single reference to this in verse 51 is most easily interpreted as a quasi-superfluous clarification that, once at the seat, he turns around.

11 See Jungmann, *Mass of the Roman Rite*, Vol. 2, pp. 321ff.

12 See n. 10 this chapter.

13 See Baldovin, 'Accepit Panem', pp. 123–39. Any abolition of the taking up of the bread and cup at Christ's words will be long in the doing, so deeply has the notion of a 'moment of consecration' become embedded in eucharistic piety. Although gesture helps articulate the prayer for the worshippers, this cannot mean that any old gesture will do.

14 See Doig, *Liturgy and Architecture*, pp. 50f.

15 See Jungmann, *Christian Prayer*, pp. 60–3.

16 From the *Missale Gothicum*, apologia following the collect after the *Benedicite* in the eucharist; quoted in DACL Vol. 1, Pt. 2, col. 2592.

17 Confession at Morning and Evening Prayer in the Book of Common Prayer 1662.

18 Jungmann, *Christian Prayer*, quoting Godel, 'Liturgisches Beten', p. 389.

19 German: '*Umbruch*'.

20 'At no point in two thousand years of church history has there been so great a disruption as this – in religious thought or in the corresponding directions followed – as in the five centuries between the end of the patristic era and the beginning of scholasticism ... [within the possibilities defined by dogma] changes of emphasis and of appearance quietly took place, the extent of whose effects is obvious in the stamp they have put upon the liturgy right up to our own day.' (Jungmann, *Die Abwehr*, p. 3, cited in Angenendt, *Liturgik und Historik*, p. 96, trans. author.)

21 Nineham, *Christianity Mediaeval and Modern*, pp. 45, 51.

22 Nineham, *Christianity*, p. 32.

23 Angenendt, *Religiosität und Theologie*, pp. 3–33.

24 See Angenendt, *Religiosität*, pp. 25f.

25 Jungmann, *Mass of the Roman Rite*, Vol. 1, p. 82.

26 Nineham, *Christianity*, p. 53.

27 See Girard, *Things Hidden*, p. 175 and Ch. 3.

28 Cyril of Jerusalem, *Mystagogical Catecheses*, 4.8.

29 Using documents of differing age and provenance – see Vogel on the Sacramentaries in *Medieval Liturgy*, Ch. III.

30 Lafont, 'The Eucharist', pp. 301f.

31 Klauser, *Short History*, p. 81.

32 Netzer, *L'Introduction de la Messe*, p. 41.

33 Pott, *La Réforme*, p. 43.

34 The following account draws on Reynolds, 'Image and Text'; and C. Heitz, *Eucharistie, Synaxe et Espace*.

35 Reynolds, 'Image and Text', p. 69ff.

36 Heitz, *Eucharistie, Synaxe et Espace*, p. 612.

37 Reynolds, 'Image and Text', p. 72. See: http://hss.ulb.uni-bonn.de/diss_online/phil_fak/2001/will_madeleine/will-abstract-franz.htm. (image at Appx.19). These *cancelli*, once in St-Pierre-aux-Nonnais, are now in the Musée La Cour d'Or.

38 See http://www.stgallplan.org.

39 Heitz, *Eucharistie, Synaxe et Espace*, p. 614.

40 See Chélini: *L'Aube*, esp. pp. 288ff; Nickl, *Der Anteil*.

41 See Duffy, *Stripping of the Altars*.

42 The kissing of a small object bearing a holy picture or the crucifixion ('Pax-board or Pax-brede') came to replace the sharing of the peace among the people. The clergy at the altar, however, continued to share the peace.

43 See a list of characteristics of Patristic liturgy over against medieval compiled by Joseph Jungmann (my own list of the medieval characteristics to correspond is shown in brackets):

PATRISTIC	MEDIEVAL
Community worship	(a sense of community originating outside the worship)
Loud amens	(none)
Close relation with the altar	(distant)
Repeated greeting and response	(little or no dialogue)
Address and consent	(none)
Prayers in the plural; the community character of the texts	(individualistic prayer)
Paschal	(Christmas and the cross)
Only the Father is addressed	(also Christ, the Holy Spirit, the Saints)
Art presents salvation-history	(art is historical and illustrative)
Objective	(subjective)
(J. Jungmann, *Liturgisches Erbe*, pp. 4ff.)	

5 God and Culture

1 From Gallagher, *Clashing Symbols*, p. 22.

2 For introductory reading: Chupungco, *Cultural Adaptation*; Tovey, *Inculturation*; Pecklers, *Liturgy in a Postmodern World*, Chapter 5 by P. C. Phan.

3 See Thomas A. Kane, *The Dancing Church*, Paulist Press video 0-8091-8099-5.

4 See Bibliography.

5 In addition to the books in n. 2, see Cronin, *Wise Man*; Gabrielson, book review; Minamaki, *Chinese Rites Controversy*; Mungello, *Chinese Rites Controversy*.

6 T. E. Hulme, quoted in Nineham, *Christianity Medieval and Modern*, p. 29.

7 I am grateful to Stephen Wakelam for this observation.

8 Clark, *Civilization*, pp. 29, 31.

9 The text is cited in the Church of England's *Common Worship: Daily Prayer* (Church House Publishing, 2005), Canticle 82, p. 639, without a reference.

6 The Cross and the Font

1 Wilkinson, *Egeria's Travels*. Since going to publication, Woolfenden, *Processional Appendix* has come to my attention, an important article examining more closely some of the data.

2 See Guiver, *Company of Voices*, Ch. 11.

3 Pudichery, *Ramsa*, p. 168, n. 9; Winkler, 'Das Offizium', p. 311.

4 de Bhaldraithe, *High Crosses*.

5 The texts can be found in Uspensky, *Evening Worship,* pp. 51f.

6 Winkler, 'Über die Kathedralvesper', p. 95.

7 See Guiver, *Company of Voices,* Ch. 12.

8 Fischer, *Bernhardi,* p. 4. Variations in the texts for the procession to the font are prescribed for the following feasts: Vigil of the Nativity p. 9, St John p. 15, St Silvester p. 16, vigil of the Epiphany and the following Sunday pp. 18ff, Epiphany to Septuagesima p. 22, Paschal Vigil pp. 63ff, Easter week (the visit to the cross is omitted) pp. 88ff, Sunday after Ascension p. 104, daily in the week of Pentecost pp. 109ff, John the Baptist p. 139.

9 See Baumstark, *Comparative Liturgy,* pp. 41f; Brooks-Leonard, *Easter Vespers;* Cuva, *I Vespri Pasquali;* Fischer, *Formen;* Van Dijk, 'Medieval Easter Vespers'; Jounel, 'Les Vêpres'; E. de Bhaldraithe, *A Local Irish Project;* Waddell, in 'Some Appended Notes' gives a racy and readable account of the service.

10 See Andrieu, *Les Ordines,* especially *Ordos* XIV and XXVII (in Vol. 3).

11 'per diversa altaria diversorum locorum, saepissime tamen ad crucem et ad fontes'; *De Ordine Antiphonarii,* LII, in PL, CV 1295. See Bailey, *The Processions,* p. 107.

12 Baumstark, *Comparative Liturgy,* pp. 41f.

13 Waddell, 'Some Appended Notes', p. 93.

14 Waddell, 'Some Appended Notes', pp. 90f.

15 See Gy, 'L'Influence'.

16 See Alzati, *Ambrosianum,* Vol. 2, p. 27.

17 See Guiver, *Company of Voices,* pp. 149f., 260, n. 3.

18 Bhaldraithe, *High Crosses,* pp. 1, 6.

19 Personal communication.

20 See Vogel, *Medieval Liturgy,* Ch. V.

21 See Cuva, *I Vespri Pasquali,* p. 112, and Fischer, 'Formen', pp. 89f. NB also liturgical books of religious orders, such as the Premonstratensian breviary.

22 *General Instruction on the Liturgy of the Hours,* n. 213.

7 Swimming

1 Brooks-Leonard, *Easter Vespers,* p. 451.

2 Buhler, *Schéma.*

3 Summary in Felde, *Report,* pp. 38–41.

4 See Guiver, *Company of Voices,* p. 73.

5 Wegman, *Christian Worship,* p. 349.

6 See Guiver, *Company of Voices,* pp. 137–41.

7 Kuhn, *Structure of Scientific Revolutions.*

8 See Häußling, 'Liturgiereform', p. 25.

9 Total quotation is from Driver, *Magic of Ritual,* pp. 83f.

10 Mauss, *Sociology:* 'Techniques of the Body' (1935), p. 108.

11 Asad, 'Remarks', p. 47.

12 Mauss, *Sociology,* p. 122.

13 Asad, 'Remarks', p. 48.

14 Coakley, *Religion and the Body,* p. 9.

15 Quoted in Driver, *Magic of Ritual,* p. 86.

16 Zizioulas, *Being as Communion*. See for example on p. 60: 'When it is understood in its correct and primitive sense ... the eucharist is first of all an assembly (synaxis), a community, a network of relations in which man "subsists" in a manner different from the biological as a member of a body which transcends every exclusiveness of a biological or social kind.'

8 The Enlightenment

1 Taylor, *Sources of the Self*, p. 218. See also Jedin, *History*, Vol. VI, p. xi.

2 Chadwick, *The Popes*, pp. 3f.

3 Chadwick, *The Popes*, pp. 67f.

4 McManners, *Church and Society*, Vol. 1, pp. 434f.

5 McManners, *Church and Society*, Vol. 1, p. 435.

6 McManners, *Church and Society*, Vol. 2, pp. 106f.

7 McManners, *Church and Society*, Vol. 2, p. 96.

8 McManners, *Church and Society*, Vol. 2, p. 97.

9 Brovelli, 'Per uno Studio', p. 548; quote from M. Fréchard (author's translation from French).

10 See for example Brooks-Leonard, *Another Look at Neo-Gallican Reform*, p. 479.

11 F. Brovelli, 'Per uno Studio', pp. 292–406.

12 Fontaine, 'Présentation', pp. 113f.

13 See Johnson and Ward, *Missale*.

14 Jounel, 'Les Missels', pp. 95f.

15 *Alternative Service Book 1980*, pp. 1092f.

16 McManners, *Church and Society*, Vol. 2, p. 40.

17 Brémond, *Histoire*, Vol. 10, p. 87.

18 Brémond, *Histoire*, Vol. 10, pp. 60f.

19 Chevalier, *Poésie liturgique*, p. xix; cited in Brémond, *Histoire*, Vol. 10, p. 62.

20 From *Hymni Sacri et Novi*, J–B Santeul, Paris 1698 (cited in Brémond, *Histoire*, Vol. 10, illustration opp. p.104).

21 See *English Hymnal* 125 (tune: Rex Gloriose) and 51 (tune: Lucis Creator).

22 McManners, *Church and Society*, Vol. 2, p. 46.

23 McManners, *Church and Society*, Vol. 2, p. 46.

24 McManners, *Church and Society*, Vol. 2, p. 45.

25 See Guiver, *Company of Voices*, pp. 126–37.

26 Bouyer. *Life and Liturgy*, pp. 53f.

27 McManners, *Church and Society*, Vol. 2, p. 56.

28 See, for example, Brovelli, 'Per uno Studio', pp. 541ff. One has to comb through the material very closely to find anything at all. Possible influence can be found, for instance, in an exhortation in the 1744 Coutances marriage rite, but only at the level of preference for phrases innocent in themselves (see Brooks-Leonard, 'Another Look', pp. 480–2). The whole matter awaits adequate research.

29 Sullivan, 'Letters from a Nuncio', pp. 149–57; for the texts: Sullivan, 'Recently Discovered Roman Documents'.

30 Brooks-Leonard, 'Another Look', p. 479.

31 Franklin, *Nineteenth-century churches*. (An earlier version is to be found in: R. W. Franklin, 'Guéranger: a view on the centenary of his death', *Worship* 49 (1975), pp. 318–28; 'Guéranger and pastoral liturgy', *Worship* 50 (1976), pp. 146–62; 'Guéranger and variety in unity', *Worship* 51 (1977), pp. 378–99; 'The nineteenth-century liturgical movement', *Worship* 53 (1979), pp. 12–39; 'Humanism and transcendence in the nineteenth-century liturgical movement', *Worship* 59 (1985), pp. 342–53.

32 See Swidler, *Aufklärung Catholicism*; Trapp, *Vorgeschichte*.

33 Heinz, 'Die gottesdienstliche Feier', p. 206.

34 See note 25 this chapter.

35 Swidler, *Aufklärung Catholicism*, p. 31.

36 Swidler, *Aufklärung Catholicism*, p. 28.

37 Heinz, 'Die gottesdienstliche Feier', pp. 198f.

38 Swidler, *Aufklärung Catholicism*, p. 31.

39 Swidler, *Aufklärung Catholicism*, p. 75, n. 29. In the following I depend closely on Swidler.

40 Swidler, *Aufklärung Catholicism*, p. 39.

41 Swidler, *Aufklärung Catholicism*, p. 39.

42 Swidler, *Aufklärung Catholicism*, p. 39.

43 Swidler, *Aufklärung Catholicism*, p. 11.

44 See Guiver, *Company of Voices*, pp. 132–7.

45 Swidler, *Aufklärung Catholicism*, p. 50.

46 Swidler, *Aufklärung Catholicism*, pp. 51f.

47 Swidler, *Aufklärung Catholicism*, p. 52.

48 Swidler, *Aufklärung Catholicism*, p. 61.

49 Paraphrase from Heinz, 'Das Gottesdienstliche Leben', pp. 257–61.

50 Vacant, *Dictionnaire*: 'Pistoie'.

51 See Crichton, *Worship in a Hidden Church*, Ch. 6.

52 See Grisbrooke, *Anglican Liturgies*.

53 Rowan Williams, *Lost Icons*, p. 163.

54 Rowan Williams, *Lost Icons*, p. 164.

55 These comments come from a public lecture by Edoardo Boncinelli at Sarzana, Italy on 30 August 2008, abridged in the *Corriere della Sera* of the same date, p. 43.

9 The Movements of 1833

1 Newsome, *Parting of Friends*, pp. 5f.

2 Chadwick, *Victorian Church*, Vol. 1, p. 47.

3 See Dalby, *Anglican Missals*.

4 See Gray, *Earth and Altar*.

5 Sir Walter Scott, 'Lay of the Last Minstrel', Canto 2. There is a small body of literature on the connection between Tractarianism and Romanticism. See Nockles, *The Oxford Movement in Context*, p. 197, n. 78.

6 Rousseau, in Franklin, *Nineteenth-Century Churches*, p. 46.

7 See Doll, *After the Primitive Christians*.

8 Doll, *After the Primitive Christians*, pp. 28, 38f.

9 See Gray, *Earth and Altar*, p. 159.

10 See the previous chapter, p. 117.

11 Franklin, *Nineteenth-Century*, p. 361.

12 Franklin, *Nineteenth-Century*, p. 389.

13 Franklin, *Nineteenth-Century*, p. 362.

14 Franklin, *Nineteenth-Century*, p. 389.

15 Franklin, *Nineteenth-Century*, p. 392; see Franklin, p. 406 for more on this.

16 Franklin, *Nineteenth-Century*, p. 382f.

17 Franklin, *Nineteenth-Century*, p. 425.

18 Franklin, *Nineteenth-Century*, p. 450.

19 Guéranger, *Institutions Liturgiques*, Vol. 2, pp. 249ff. His other very famous work was *The Christian Year* (English edn Burnes Oates 1908).

20 Franklin, *Nineteenth-Century*, p. 428ff.

21 Franklin, *Nineteenth-Century*, p. 436.

22 Franklin, *Nineteenth-Century*, p. 445.

23 Franklin, *Nineteenth-Century*, p. 67.

24 Franklin, *Nineteenth-Century*, p. 68.

25 Franklin, *Nineteenth-Century*, p. 478.

26 Franklin, *Nineteenth-Century*, p. 48.

27 Brémond, *Histoire littéraire*, Vol. X, p. 72, n. 1.

28 Franklin, *Nineteenth-Century*, p. 84.

29 Franklin, *Nineteenth-Century*, p. 126f.

30 Franklin, *Nineteenth-Century*, p. 167.

31 See Bibliography.

32 Franklin, *Nineteenth-Century*, p. 206.

33 Franklin, *Nineteenth-Century*, p. 258.

34 Franklin, *Nineteenth-Century*, p. 17.

35 Jungmann, 'Liturgische Erneuerung', pp. 9f.

36 Franklin, *Nineteenth-Century*, p. 75.

37 Franklin, *Nineteenth-Century*, p. 424.

38 Franklin, *Nineteenth-Century*, p. 474.

39 Franklin, *Nineteenth-Century*, p. 8.

40 Franklin, *Nineteenth-Century*, p. 7.

41 Lydia Goehr in Krausz, *Interpretation of Music*, p. 183.

42 Möhler, review of J. Milner, 'Ziel und Ende religiöser Kontroversen', ThQ 1838, p. 339, quoted in Franklin, *Nineteenth-Century*, pp. 167f.

43 The story is told in Bergeron, *Decadent Enchantments*.

44 Mayer, *Liturgie, Romantik und Restauration*.

45 Jungmann, *The Mass of the Roman Rite*, Vol. 1, pp. 157f.

10 Another World

1 Especially Bauman, *Liquid Modernity*, and *Liquid Love*.

2 Bauman, *Liquid Modernity*, p. 153.

3 See Bauman, *Liquid Modernity*, p.208; includes reference to an essay by C. Brooks-Rose, 'Exsul', no ref.

4 Bauman, *Liquid Modernity*, pp. 208f.

5 Bauman, *Liquid Modernity*, p. 206.

6 *The Tablet*, 7 May 2005, p. 6.
7 Quoted in Bauman, *Liquid Modernity*, p. 209.
8 *The Tablet*, 21 May 2005, pp. 10f.
9 MacIntyre, *After Virtue*, p. 245.

11 Naively Presupposing

1 All page numbers in this chapter refer to Taylor, *A Secular Age*.
2 pp. 37f.
3 p. 239.
4 p. 255.
5 p. 257.
6 p. 143.
7 p. 74.
8 p. 5.
9 p. 17.
10 pp. 151ff.
11 p. 19.
12 p. 727.
13 See p. 730.
14 p. 715.
15 p. 516.
16 p. 482.
17 p. 554.
18 p. 284.
19 p. 767.
20 pp. 137ff.
21 p. 110.
22 p. 94.
23 p. 628.
24 pp. 159ff.
25 p. 171.
26 p. 551.
27 p. 18ff.
28 p. 30.
29 p. 200.
30 pp. 198ff.
31 p. 772.

12 Seeing More than Ourselves

1 Tracy, *Plurality and Ambiguity*, p. 15.
2 See Ch. 7, n. 3.
3 Brook, *The Empty Space*, pp. 76f.
4 See p. 32f.
5 Gerard Manley Hopkins, 'Nondum' *Poems*, pp. 32–4.
6 Tracy, *Plurality and Ambiguity*, p. 74.
7 Tracy, *Plurality and Ambiguity*, p. 16.

13 Giving and Receiving

1 Shakespeare, *A Winter's Tale*, Act 5, Sc. 3; I am grateful to Ian Burton for this insight.

2 I. Epstein, quoted in Douglas, *Purity and Danger*, p. 44.

3 Begbie speaking of Tillich in *Voicing Creation's Praise*, p. 30.

4 Lavergne, *Art Sacré et Modernité*, p. 165.

5 See Mennekes, *Künstlerisches Sehen*; and also Mennekes: 'Liturgy as question'.

6 For an introduction to the Myers Briggs personality type indicator see http://www.myersbriggs.org.

7 Stringer, *On the Perception of Worship*.

8 Stringer, *Perception*, p. 179.

9 Stringer, *Perception*, p. 218.

14 The Core of Worship

1 *Constitution on the Sacred Liturgy*, 3.21.

2 Bradshaw, 'Difficulties in doing Liturgical Theology' (quoted in Johnson, 'Can we avoid Relativism', p. 142).

3 Baldovin, 'The Changing World of Liturgy', p. 3.

4 See Lathrop, *Holy Things*.

5 Sacks, *Dignity of Difference*, p. 19.

6 See Bradshaw, *Eucharistic Origins*, esp. Ch. 7.

7 See Baldovin, 'Accepit Panem'; see also Ch. 4, n. 13.

8 Rogers, *The Man Who went into the West*, p. 26.

9 Quoted in Tracy, *Plurality and Ambiguity*, p. 20.

10 Chauvet, *Du Symbolique*, p. 51.

11 Guiver, *Pursuing the Mystery*.

12 See Zizioulas, *Being as Communion*, p. 96f: 'So truth is located simultaneously at the heart of history, at the ground of creation, and at the end of history', p. 97.

13 Augustine, *Letters*, no reference.

14 See the *Charities Act 2006* and accompanying literature, particularly:

3.7 To be charitable a religious purpose must tend directly or indirectly to the moral and spiritual improvement of the public. The moral and spiritually improving impact of the religious purpose must be capable of being demonstrated. The benefits may be of many types.

3.8 This might be shown in the consequential effect that the beliefs and practices promoted by the particular teachings, codes and doctrines have on the followers and others (encouraging them to act as more responsible members of society). Religious organizations will generally promote volunteering time and/or money to help others in society, respect for property and people and the world, abhorrence of violence, honesty, and the shaping of collective values in moral ways. They may promote trust, reciprocity, civil engagement and community cohesion, providing a bridge or link between people in communities diverse in terms of age, gender, class, ethnicity or language.

Analysis of the Law underpinning Public Benefit and the Advancement of Religion section 3, accessible on: http://www.charity-commission.gov.uk/Library/publicbenefit.

15 'Church Going', in Larkin, *Collected Poems*, pp. 97f.

16 Brown, *Discipleship and Imagination*, p. 98.

17 Brown, *Discipleship*, p. 99.

18 Brown, *God and Enchantment of Place*, p. 386.

19 Brown, *God*, p. 2.

20 Davis quoted in McPartlan, 'Liturgy', p. 163.

21 Brook, *Empty Space*, pp. 152f.

22 Hen, *Culture and Religion*, pp. 80f.

15 A Complex Shaping

1 See Guiver, *Company of Voices*; Guiver, *Everyday God*.

2 From the second post-communion prayer in the Book of Common Prayer of 1662.

3 Guardini, *Liturgische Bildung*.

4 See www.24-7 Prayer.com; and Freeman, *Punk Monk*.

5 Sacks, *The Dignity of Difference*, p. 148.

6 Sacks, *Dignity*, pp. 148ff.

7 Sacks, *Dignity*, p. 149.

8 Sacks, *Dignity*, p.151.

9 Fukuyama, *Trust*, p. 11, quoted in Sacks, *Dignity*, p. 151.

10 Sacks, *Dignity*, pp.151f.

11 Marcel Barnard and Cas Wepener, *Religious Ritual, Social Capital and Poverty in South Africa*, Presentation given at *Societas Liturgica* Congress, Palermo, August 2007.

12 Foley, 'Engaging in the Liturgy of the World'.

Bibliography

Alzati, C., *Ambrosianum Mysterium: The Church of Milan and its Liturgical Tradition*, 2 vols (trans. G. Guiver), Alcuin/GROW Joint Liturgical Studies 44 (1999) and 47–48 (2000).

Andrieu, M., *Les Ordines Romani du haut Moyen Âge*, Spicilegium Sacrum Lovaniense 11, 23, 24, 28, 29 (5 vols), Louvain, 1957–61.

Angenendt, A., *Liturgik und Historik*, Herder, 2001.

Angenendt, A., *Religiosität und Theologie: Ein Spannungsreiches Verhältnis im Mittelalter*, in *Liturgie im Mittelalter*, LIT Verlag Münster, 2005.

Anon., *Roles in the Liturgical Assembly: The 23rd Liturgical Conference Saint Serge*, English trans M. J. O'Connell, Pueblo, 1981.

Arranz, M., *The Functions of the Christian Assembly in the Testament of Our Lord*, in Anon., *Roles*.

Asad, T., 'Remarks on the Anthropology of the Body', in Sarah Coakley (ed.), *Religion and the Body*, Cambridge University Press, 1997, pp. 42–52.

Atchley, C., *Ordo Romanus Primus*, London, 1905.

Bailey, T., *The Processions of Sarum and the Western Church*, Toronto, 1971.

Baldovin, J. F., 'Accepit Panem: The Gestures of the Priest at the Institution Narrative of the Eucharist', in N. Mitchell et al, *Rule of Prayer, Rule of Faith; Essays in Honour of Aidan Kavanagh*, Liturgical Press, 1996.

Baldovin, J. F., 'The Changing World of Liturgy', *Anglican Theological Review*, Winter 2000, available at http://findarticles.com/p/articles/mi_qa3818/is_200001.

Baldovin, J. F., *The Urban Character of Christian Worship*, Rome 1987 (OCA 228).

Balthasar, H. Urs von, *Theo-Drama: Theological Dramatic Theory. Prolegomena* Vol. I, trans. G. Harrison, Ignatius Press, 1993.

Bauman, Z., *Liquid Love*, Polity Press, 2003.

Bauman, Z., *Liquid Modernity*, Polity Press, 2000.

Baumstark, A., *Comparative Liturgy*, Mowbray, 1958.

Begbie, J., *Voicing Creation's Praise*, Continuum/T&T Clark, 1991.

Bergeron, K., *Decadent Enchantments: The Revival of Gregorian Chant at Solesmes*, University of California Press, 1998.

Bhaldraithe, E. de, 'A Local Irish Project for Paschal Vespers', *Liturgy* (Gethsemani Abbey) 12.2 (May 1978), pp. 25–52.

Bhaldraithe, E. de, *The High Crosses of Moone and Castledermot*, Bolton Abbey, Moone, n.d.

Bishop, E., *Liturgica Historica*, Oxford, 1918.

Bouyer, L., *Life and Liturgy*, Sheed & Ward, 1956.

Bradshaw, P. F., *Search for the Origins of Christian Worship*, SPCK, 2nd edn, 2002.

Bradshaw, P. F., *Eucharistic Origins*, Alcuin Club collections 80, SPCK, 2004.

Bradshaw, P. F., 'Difficulties in Doing Liturgical Theology', *Pacifica* 11 (June 1998), pp. 184–5.

Branişte, E., *The Liturgical Assembly and Its Functions in the Apostolic Constitutions*, in Anon., *Roles*.

Brémond, H., *Histoire littéraire du sentiment religieux en France depuis la fin des guerres de religion jusqu'à nos jours*, 11 vols, Paris, 1932.

Brook, P., *The Empty Space*, Penguin, 1972.

Brooks-Leonard, J., 'Another Look at Neo-Gallican Reform: a Comparison of Marriage Rites in Coutances', *Ephimerides Liturgicae* 98.5–6 (1984), pp. 458–85.

Brooks-Leonard, J., *Easter Vespers in Early Medieval Rome*, thesis, Notre Dame University, 1988.

Brovelli, F., 'Per uno Studio dei Messali Francesi del XVIII secolo', *Ephimerides Liturgicae* 96 (1982), pp. 279–406, and 97 (1983), pp. 482–549.

Brown, D., *Discipleship and Imagination: Christian Tradition and Truth*, Oxford University Press, 2000.

Brown, D., *God and Enchantment of Place*, Oxford University Press, 2004.

Budde, A., 'Improvisation im Eucharistiegebet: Zur Technik freien betens in der Alten Kirche', *Jahrbuch für Antike und Christentum* 44 (2001), pp. 128–41.

Buhler, F. M., *Schéma de l'Évolution du Baptême et des Installations Baptismales*, C.R.I.E., Boîte Postale 1422, F–68071 Mulhouse, n.d.

Burtchaell, J. T., *From Synagogue to Church: Public Services and Offices in the Earliest Christian Communities*, Cambridge University Press, 1992.

Cabrol, F. (ed.), *Dictionnaire d' Archéologie Chrétienne et de Liturgie*, Paris, 1910.

Casti, G. B., *Le Chiese Paleocristiane di Roma*, Roma Archeologica, Itinerario 16–17, ed. A. Milella, Rome, 1999.

Catalano, Virgilio, *Case, abitanti e culti di Ercolano*, Naples, 1963, and Bardi, 2002.

Cattaneo, E. (ed.), *I Ministeri nella Chiesa Antica*, Milan, 1997.

Chadwick, O., *The Victorian Church*, 2 vols, Oxford University Press, 1970.

Chadwick, O., *The Popes and European Revolution*, Oxford University Press, 1981.

Chauvet, L.-M., *Du Symbolique au Symbole*, du Cerf, 1979.

Chélini, J., *L'Aube du Moyen Âge*, Paris, 1991.

Chevalier, U., *Poésie liturgique des Églises de France aux XVIIe et XVIIIe siècles*, Paris, 1912.

Chupungco, A. J., *Cultural Adaptation of the Liturgy*, Paulist Press, 1982.

Church of England, *Alternative Service Book 1980*, Clowes/SPCK/CUP, 1980.

Clark, Sir Kenneth, *Civilization*, John Murray, 1969.

Coakley, S., *Religion and the Body*, Cambridge University Press, 2000.

Crichton, J. D., *Worship in a Hidden Church*, Columba Press, 1988.

Crippa, L. (ed.), *La Basilica Cristiana nei Testi dei Padri dal II al IV Secolo*, Libreria Editrice Vaticana/Cad & Wellness, 2003.

Cronin, V., *The Wise Man from the West*, Rupert Hart-Davis, 1955.

Cuming, G. J. and Bradshaw, P. F., *Prayers of the Eucharist Early and Reformed*, Pueblo, 1987.

Cuva, A., *I Vespri Pasquali della Liturgia Romana*, 35 (1973), pp. 101–18.

Dalby, M., *Anglican Missals and their Canons*, Alcuin/GROW Liturgical Study 41, 1998.

Dix, G., *The Shape of the Liturgy*, Dacre Press, 1947.

Doig, A., *Liturgy and Architecture: From Early Church to the Middle Ages*, Ashgate, 2008.

Doll, P., *After the Primitive Christians: The Eighteenth-Century Anglican Eucharist in its Architectural Setting*, Alcuin Club/GROW Joint Liturgical Study 37, 1997.

Donovan, V., *Christianity Rediscovered*, SCM, 1978.

Douglas, M., *Natural Symbols*, Cressett Press, 1970.

Douglas, M., *Purity and Danger*, Penguin, 1966.

Driver, T., *The Magic of Ritual*, Harper San Francisco, 1991.

Duffy, E., *Stripping of the Altars*, Yale University Press, 1992.

Ehrensperger, A., *Die Westlichen, Gallikanischen Liturgien*, in www.liturgiekommission.ch/Orientierung/III_B_08.

Felde, M. P. D., *Report of Regional Research*, in S. A. Stauffer (ed.), *Christian Worship: Unity in Cultural Diversity*, LWF Studies 1, Lutheran World Federation, Geneva 1996. Full text in *Worship and Culture in Vale da Pitanga*, Instituto Ecumênico de Pós-Graduação, Escola Superior de Teologia, São Leopoldo, RS–Brazil, 1995 (Co-ordinator Nelson Kirst).

Fischer, B., 'Formen gemeinschaftlicher Tauferinnerung im Abendland', *Liturgisches Jahrbuch* 9 (1959), pp. 87–94.

Fischer, L., (ed), *Bernhardi ... Ordo Officiorum Ecclesiae Lateranensis*, München and Freising, 1916.

Foley, E. C., 'Engaging in the Liturgy of the World: Worship as Public Theology', *Studia Liturgica* 38 (2008), pp. 31–52.

Fontaine, G., 'Présentation des Missels Diocésains Français du 17e au 19e Siècle', *La Maison Dieu* 141 (1980), pp. 97–166.

Ford, D. and Stamps, D., *Essentials of Christian Community*, T&T Clark, 1996.

Franklin, R. W., *Nineteenth-Century Churches: The History of the New Catholicism in Württemberg, England and France*, Garland, 1987.

Freeman, A., *Punk Monk*, Survivor Press, 2007.

Fukuyama, F., *Trust*, Hamish Hamilton, 1995.

Gabrielson, C., Book review on Chinese rites controversy in *Worship* 59, 1985, pp. 546ff.

Gallagher, M., *Clashing Symbols: An Introduction to Faith and Culture*, Darton, Longman and Todd, 1997.

Giordano, C. and Kahn, I., *Testimonianze ebraiche a Pompei, Ercolano, Stabia e nelle città della Campania Felix*, Bardi, 2001.

Girard, R., *Things Hidden Since the Foundation of the World*, trans. S. Bann and M. Metteer, Athlone Press, 1987.

Godel, W., 'Liturgisches Beten im frühen Mittelalter', ZKTh 85 (1963), pp. 261ff.

Gray, D., *Earth and Altar*, Alcuin Club, 1986.

Grisbrooke, J. J., *Anglican Liturgies of the Seventeenth and Eighteenth Centuries*, SPCK, 1958.

Guardini, R., *Liturgische Bildung*, Rothenfels-Deutsches Quickbornhaus, 1923.

Guéranger, P., *Institutions Liturgiques*, 4 vols, Paris, 1880.

Guiver, G., *Company of Voices*, SPCK, 1988; Canterbury Press, 2001.

Guiver, G., *Everyday God*, Triangle 1994.

Guiver, G., *Pursuing the Mystery*, SPCK, 1996.

Gy, P.-M., 'L'Influence des Chanoines de Lucques sur la Liturgie du Latran', *Revue des Sciences Religieuses* 58 (1984), pp. 31–41.

Häußling, A., 'Liturgiereform', *Archiv für Liturgiewissenschaft* 31(1989), pp. 1–32.

Heinz, A., 'Das Gottesdienstliche Leben', in M. Persch and B. Schneider, *Geschichte des Bistums Trier*, Vol. 4, Paulinus Verlag, 2000.

Heinz, A., 'Die gottesdienstliche Feier des Sonntags aus der Sicht des Pastoraltheologen Peter C. (1745–1816)', in *Trierer Theologische Zeitschrift* 93.3 (July 1984), pp. 1193–211.

Heitz, C., *Eucharistie, Synaxe et Espace Liturgique*, in *Segni e Riti nella Chiesa Altomedievale Occidentale*, Centro Italiano di Studi sull'Alto Medioevo, Spoleto, Issue XXXIII, Vol. 2 (1987), pp. 609ff.

Hen, Y., *Culture and Religion in Merovingian Gaul A.D. 481–751*, Brill, 1995.

Herwegen, I., *The Art-Principle of the Liturgy*, Liturgical Press, 1931 (*Das Kunstprinzip in der Liturgie*, Paderborn, 1920).

Hopkins, G. M., *The Poems of Gerard Manley Hopkins*, 4th edn ed. W. H. Gardnes and N. H. Mackenzie, OUP 1970.

Irvine, C., 'Celebrating the Eucharist: A Rite Performance', *Theology* 97, No. 778 (July 1994), pp. 256–64.

Jedin, H. (ed.), *History of the Church*, 10 vols, Burns & Oates, 1981.

Johnson, M., 'Can we avoid Relativism in Worship?', *Worship* 74.2 (March 2000), p. 142.

Johnson, C. and Ward, A. (eds), *Missale Parisiense, Anno 1738 Publici Iuris Factum*, Bibliotheca 'Ephimerides Liturgicae' Subsidia, Supplementa 1, CLV Rome 1993.

Jounel, P., 'Les Vêpres de Pâques', *La Maison Dieu* 49 (1957), pp. 96–111.

Jounel, P., 'Les Missels Diocésains Français du 18ᵉ Siècle', *La Maison Dieu* 141 (1980), pp. 91–6.

Jungmann J., *Christian Prayer Through the Centuries*, SPCK, 2007.

Jungmann, J., *Die Abwehr des germanischen Arianismus und der Umbruch der religiösen Kultur im frühen Mittelalter* (no publisher cited), 1947.

Jungmann, J., ' Liturgische Erneuerung zwischen Barock und Gegenwart', *Liturgisches Jahrbuch* 53 (1962), pp. 1–15.

Jungmann, J., *Liturgisches Erbe und Gegenwart,* Innsbruck 1960 (English trans., *Pastoral Liturgy,* Challoner, 1962).
Jungmann, J., *The Mass of the Roman Rite,* 2 vols, Benziger Bros., 1950.

Kähler, H., *Die Frühe Kirche: Kult und Kultraum,* Frankfurt 1952 and 1972.
Kelly, T. F., *The Exultet in Southern Italy,* Oxford University Press, 1996.
Klauser, T., *A Short History of the Western Liturgy,* Oxford University Press, 1969.
Koch, G., *Early Christian Art and Architecture,* SCM, 1996.
Krausz, M. (ed.), *The Interpretation of Music,* Clarendon, 1993.
Kuhn, T. S., *The Structure of Scientific Revolutions,* Chicago University Press, 1996.

Lafont, G., 'The Eucharist in Monastic Life', in *Cistercian Studies* XIX, No. 4 (1984).
Langlotz, E., 'Basilika', in T. Klauser (ed.), *Reallexikon für Antike und Christentum,* Stuttgart 1950, Vol. 1, col. 1225ff.
Lara, J., 'Versus Populum Revisited', in *Worship* 68.3 (1994), pp. 210–19.
Larkin, Philip, *Collected Poems,* A. Thwaite (ed.), Marvell/Faber, 1988.
Lathrop, G., *Holy Things: A Liturgical Theology,* Fortress, 1993.
Lavergne, S. de, *Art Sacré et Modernité,* Namur, 1992.

MacIntyre, A., *After Virtue,* Duckworth, 1981.
Mainstone, R. J., *Hagia Sophia: Architecture, Structure and Liturgy of Justinian's Great Church,* Thames & Hudson, 1988.
Mauss, M., *Sociology and Psychology: Essays,* trans. B. Brewster, Routledge & Kegan Paul, 1979.
Mayer, A. L., 'Liturgie, Romantik and Restoration', in *Jahrbuch für Liturgiewissenschaft* 10 (1930) pp. 77–141.
McManners, J., *Church and Society in 18th-century France,* 2 vols, Oxford University Press, 1998.
McPartlan, P., 'Liturgy, Church and Society', *Studia Liturgica* 34.2 (2004), pp. 147–64.
Mennekes, F., *Künstlerisches Sehen und Spiritualität,* Dusseldorf, 1995.
Mennekes, F., 'Liturgy as Question: James Lee Byars' *The White Mass*', in *The Month,* July 1999, pp. 266–70.
Miles, M., *Image as Insight: Visual Understanding in Western Christianity and Secular Culture,* Boston, 1985.
Minamaki, G., *The Chinese Rites Controversy from its beginnings to Modern Times,* Loyola University Press, 1985.
Möhler, J. A., *Symbolism, or Exposition of the Doctrinal Differences Between Catholics and Protestants as Evidenced by Their Symbolical Writings,* trans. J. B. Robertson, Gibbings, 1906.
Mungello, D. E. (ed.), *The Chinese Rites Controversy: Its History and Meaning,* Monumenta Serica Monograph Series XXXIII, Steyler Press, 1994.

Netzer, H., *L'Introduction de la Messe Romaine en France sous les Carolingiens,* Paris, 1910.
Newsome, D., *The Parting of Friends,* Murray, 1966.

Nickl, G., *Der Anteil des Volkes an der Meßliturgie im Frankreiche von Chlodwig bis auf Karl den Großen*, Innsbruck, 1930.
Nineham, D., *Christianity Mediaeval and Modern: A Study in Religious Change*, SCM, 1993.
Nockles, P. B., *The Oxford Movement in Context*, Cambridge University Press, 1996.

Origin, *De Oratione* (trans. J. E. Oulton and H. Chadwick), Library of Christian Classics, 1954.

Pecklers, K., *Liturgy in a Postmodern World*, Continuum, 2000.
Petts, D., *Christianity in Roman Britain*, Tempus, 2003.
Piva, P., *La Cattedrale Doppia: Una Tipologia Architettonica e Liturgica del Medioevo*, Bologna, 1990.
Porter, W. S., *The Gallican Rite*, SPCK, 1958.
Pott, T., *La Réforme Liturgique Byzantine: Étude du Phénomène de l'Évolution non-spontanée de la Liturgie Byzantine*, CLV Edizioni Liturgiche, 2000.
Pudichery, S., *Ramsa: An Analysis and Interpretation of the Chaldean Vespers*, Dharmaram College, 1972.

Ratcliff, E. C. (ed.), *Expositio antiquae liturgiae gallicanae*, Henry Bradshaw Society, 1971.
Reynolds, R. E., 'Image and Text: A Carolingian Illustration of Modifications in the Early Roman Eucharistic Ordines', in *Viator* 14 (1983), pp. 59–75.
Rogers, B., *The Man Who Went into the West*, Aurum, 2006.
Romano, J. F., *Ritual and Society in Early Medieval Rome*, dissertation, Harvard University, 2007 (available from www.umi.com).

Sacks, J., *The Dignity of Difference*, Continuum, 2002.
Stosur, D., 'Liturgy and (Post) Modernity: A Narrative Response to Guardini's Challenge', in *Worship* 77 (2003), pp. 22–41.
Stringer, M., *On the Perception of Worship*, University of Birmingham Press, 1999.
Sullivan, J., 'Letters from a Nuncio: Reports to Rome about the Paris Breviary of 1736 According to Some Recently Discovered Codices', *Manuscripta* XXII, November 1978.
Sullivan, J., 'Recently Discovered Roman Documents on the Breviary of Paris 1736', *Ephimerides Liturgicae* 92 (1978), pp. 481–93.
Swidler, L., *Aufklärung Catholicism 1780–1850*, Missouri, 1978.

Taft, R., *Beyond East and West*, Pastoral Press, 1984.
Taft, R., 'How Liturgies Grow: The Evolution of the Byzantine Divine Liturgy', *Orientalia Christiana Periodica*, 43 (1977).
Taylor, C., *A Secular Age*, Belknap Press/Harvard University Press, 2007.
Taylor, C., *Sources of the Self*, Cambridge University Press, 1989.
Tovey, P., *Inculturation of Christian Worship*, Ashgate, 2004.
Tracy, D., *Plurality and Ambiguity*, SCM, 1988.
Trapp, W., *Vorgeschichte und Ursprung der Liturgischen Bewegung, vorwiegend in Hinsicht auf das deutsche Sprachgebiet*, Regensburg, 1940/1979.

Turner, H. E. W., *The Pattern of Christian Truth: A Study in the Relations Between Orthodoxy and Heresy in the Early Church*, Mowbray, 1954.
Turner, V., *From Ritual to Theatre*, PAJ Publications, 1982.

Uspensky, N., *Evening Worship in the Orthodox Church*, St Vladimir's Seminary Press, 1985.

Vacant, A. (ed.), *Dictionnaire de Théologie Catholique*, Paris, 1903.
Van Dijk, S. J. P., 'The Medieval Easter Vespers of the Roman Clergy', *Sacris Erudirii* (Brugge) 19 (1969–70), pp. 261–363.
Vogel, C., *Versus ad Orientem: L'orientation dans les Ordines Romani du haut Moyen Age*, Studi Medievali, Spoleto, 3rd Series, I.2, 1960.
Vogel, C., *Medieval Liturgy: An Introduction to the Sources*, rev. and trans. W. G. Storey and N. K. Rasmussen, with the assistance of J. K. Brooks-Leonard, The Pastoral Press, 1986.

Waddell, C., 'Some Appended Notes about Paschal Vespers in Ordo Romanus XXVII', *Liturgy* (Gethsemani Abbey) 12.2 (May 1978), pp. 53–96.
Wagner, J., 'Le Lieu de la Célébration Eucharistique dans Quelques Églises Anciennes d'Orient', *La Maison Dieu* 70 (1962), pp. 32ff.
Wegman, H., *Christian Worship in East and West*, Pueblo, 1990.
White, J. M., *The Social Origins of Christian Architecture: Building God's House in the Roman World–Architectural Adaptation Among Pagans, Jews and Christians*, 2 vols, Trinity Press, 1997.
Wilkinson, J., *Egeria's Travels*, SPCK, 1971.
Wilkinson, J., *From Synagogue to Church: The Traditional Design: Its Beginning, Its Definition, Its End*, Routledge, 2000.
Williams, R., *Lost Icons*, T&T Clark, 2000.
Winkler, G., 'Das Offizium am Ende des 4.Jahrhunderts und das heutige chaldäische Offizium, ihre stukturellen Zusammenhänge', *Ostkirchlichen Studien* 19 (1970), pp. 289–311.
Winkler, G., 'Über die Kathedralvesper in der verschiedenen Riten des Ostens und Westens', *Archiv für Liturgiewissenschaft* 16 (1974), pp. 53–102.
Woolfenden, G., 'The Processional Appendix to Vespers: Where and Why?' in *Worship* 82.4 (July 2008), pp. 339–57.
Wright, N.T., *Jesus and the Victory of God*, SPCK, 1996.

Zizioulas, J., *Being as Communion: Studies in Personhood and the Church*, Darton, Longman and Todd, 1985.

Acknowledgements of Sources of Plates

Where a plate is not listed below, it is the author's own image or is in the public domain.

3(a)–3(c) Fourth-century lamp in the form of a basilica, found in Algeria. F. Cabrol, ed., *Dictionnaire d'Archéologie Chrétienne et de Liturgie*, Paris, 1910, vol. II.2, col. 582f.

4 Cross-shape in wall plaster in Herculaneum. Catalano, *Case, abitanti e culti* (in Bibliography) plates LXI.4, LXII and LXIII.

5(b) Mozarabic. G. Prado, *Manual de Liturgia Hispano-Visigótica o Mozárabe,* Madrid, 1927, p. 165.

5(c) Drogo Sacramentary, Metz, ninth century. F. Cabrol, ed., *Dictionnaire d'Archéologie Chrétienne et de Liturgie*, Paris, 1910, vol. XI.1, col. 865.

5(d) Saint Basil celebrates the divine liturgy. A miniature from 1429. Liturgical scroll n. 708, Patmos, Monastery of St John the Theologian.

5(g) Pontifical Mass, Mainz, tenth century. *Ornamenta Ecclesiae: Kunst und Künstler der Romanik,* Catalogue for an exhibition by the Schnütgen Museum in the Josef-Haubrich Gallery, Cologne, 1985, vol. 1, p. 389.

5(h) St Mark celebrating the eucharist: Antependium, St Eufemia, Grado, Italy, 1372. *Spazio e Rito*, Papers of the 23rd Conference of Liturgy Teachers, CLV Rome, 1996, p. 99.

7 Ivory cover of the Drogo Sacramentary, Metz, ninth century. Copy of a nineteenth-century lithograph in Otto Nussbaum, *Der Standort des Liturgen am christlichen Altar vor dem Jahre 1000, Eine archäologische und liturgiegeschichtliche Untersuchung,* Bonn, Hanstein, 1965.

9 An eighteenth-century picture of an ancient basilica. C. De Vert, *Explication simple, littérale et historique des cérémonies de l'Église,* Paris, 1706–13.

10 Two pages from F. G. Lee, *Directorium Anglicanum,* London, 1865.

11 Fr Friedhelm Mennekes celebrating the White Mass in St Peter's, Cologne. *The Month*, July 1999.

12 Benozzo Gozzoli (*c.*1421–97), *The Virgin and Child Enthroned among Angels and Saints*, National Gallery, London.

Index